Sin
in the
Sixties

Sin
in the
Sixties

Catholics and Confession, 1955–1975

Maria C. Morrow

The Catholic University of America Press
Washington, D.C.

Copyright © 2016
The Catholic University of America Press
All rights reserved

Cataloging-in-Publication Data available from the Library of Congress
ISBN 978-0-8132-3632-2

Dedicated with love to Jeffrey L. Morrow

❖

With gratitude to St. Joseph the Worker

❖

Pray for us, O great St. Joseph,
and by thy love for Jesus and Mary,
and by their love for thee,
obtain for us the supreme happiness of living and dying
in the love of Jesus and Mary.

Contents

List of Illustrations   ix

Preface   xi

Acknowledgments   xv

Introduction   1

1 Sin and Penance: Interwoven History of Interwoven Concepts   12

2 From Actual and Personal to Relative and General: The Change in Lay Catholics' Conception of Sin   43

3 From Responsibility to Freedom: Changes in the Conception of Sin among Theologians   79

4 Penance in a New Land: Developments in Nonsacramental Penitential Practice   117

5 To Eat Meat or Not?: *Paenitemini*, the NCCB's Pastoral Statement, and the Decline of Penance   160

6 Thinking outside the Box: The Decline of Sacramental Confession   191

Bibliography   245

Index   259

Illustrations

All illustrations reproduced courtesy of the American Catholic History Research Center and University Archives of The Catholic University of America.

- **4-1** "The Time Rich in Grace," P. Karch, illustrator   129
- **4-2** "Advent Action"   136
- **6-1** "Sacraments: Penance," Lloyd Ostendorf, illustrator   200

Preface

A Friday evening at Lakefront Brewery in Milwaukee, Wisconsin, finds the parking lot packed, with cars lining the road as well. Visitors to the brewery on a Friday evening have to wait in a lengthy line to get a spot inside. The reason for the crowd is the brewery's popular Friday fish fry. Indeed, the Friday fish fry continues to be ubiquitous in the city of Milwaukee, such that a web search for Friday fish fries in that city returns numerous sites, all geared toward helping readers make the very important decision of where to eat their fish (and drink their beer) on a Friday evening.

This weekly Friday fish feast, widespread throughout Milwaukee, is actually a relic of Milwaukee's Catholic culture from the first half of the twentieth century, when Catholics were obligated to abstain from meat on all Fridays of the year. While the penitential obligation of meat abstinence has long been forgotten, the social and commercial aspect of the Friday fish fry continues year-round in Milwaukee. For most of the United States, however, the year-round Friday meat abstinence, coupled with the popularity of eating fish on Friday, has all but disappeared. The season of Lent each year provides but a glimpse of the former practice, with fast-food deals on fish sandwiches, supermarket discounts on fish, and the occasional parish fish fry bringing together the local Catholic community. Outside of Lent, few Catholics know of the obligation of making a Friday sacrifice.

During the time period examined in this book, enormous changes occurred for American Catholics. From the replacement of the Tridentine Latin Mass that had been normative since the Council of Trent, through the Second Vatican Council and its implementations in the midst of an American Catholicism undergoing dramatic demographical changes as well as witnessing social and political conflicts ranging from racism to the Vietnam War—these were vital years in the history of the modern church. Among the upheavals of that time period experienced by American Catholics, one is often left behind—namely, the alterations in longstanding penitential practices, such as Friday meat abstinence.

While the Friday fish fry has become for Milwaukee something of its own commercial niche among breweries, pubs, and restaurants, it was only half a century ago that meatless Fridays were obligatory for all Catholics in the United States. This Friday abstinence was meant to be penitential in nature, a sacrifice that would atone for sins committed by the person. It was a practice that set Catholics apart from their compatriots. Though most Christians, including Catholics, attended church on Sundays, Catholics were the only group of Christians that did something unique on Fridays. The fact of this could even lead to unkind nicknames for Catholics, such as "minnow-munchers" or the simpler "fish eaters." Friday meat abstinence was a definite marker of Catholic identity. Writing in 2004, almost four decades after the change, the great Catholic sociologist Fr. Andrew Greeley remarked that among the implementations of Vatican II, dropping the Friday meat abstinence "may have been the most unnecessary and most devastating."[1]

The story in these pages is that of sin and penance during the mid-twentieth century. While it includes the more frequently discussed topic of the decline of the sacrament of penance, it considers the sacrament

---

1. Andrew M. Greeley, *The Catholic Revolution: New Wine, Old Wineskins, and the Second Vatican Council* (Berkeley: University of California Press, 2004), 54.

Preface

alongside other penitential practices, which were also at their height in the 1950s. This provides added context, as does considering the change in the conception of sin at both the popular and academic levels. Sin had been regarded as something concrete, understood in terms of the individual Catholic's personal actual sin, defined as any willful thought, word, deed, or omission contrary to God's law expressed by the church; this personal, actual sin was identified in order to be confessed in the sacrament of penance.[2] As the 1960s progressed, personal actual sin was less easily identified as the conventional list of sins defined by the church came under fire and more abstract notions such as sinful structures and sin understood socially rather than individually grew in popularity, laying the groundwork for the decline in both the sacrament of penance and nonsacramental penitential practices.

The curiosity of this contemporary situation—the packed Lakefront Brewery Friday fish fry, filled throughout the year with Catholics and non-Catholics alike but lacking in penitential sentiment—provides one motivation to consider anew the changes within the 1960s. The concept of sin and penance is but one particular lens through which to view Catholicism in the United States during this dynamic and crucial time period. Its contribution is to add depth to the usual accounts of the time period, which often forget the rigorous penitential practices in place for most of American Catholic history: not only the Friday meat abstinence, but Lenten fasting, vigil fasts, Advent, and Ember Days all added to the penitential character of Catholicism. Though it has been only half a century since these practices all but disappeared, most have been forgotten and remain unknown, particularly to the post–Vatican II generations.

Given this, the history narrated here has general appeal for those Catholics interested in the question of how we got here. For older folk, it may be a reminder of past rigors, of the weaknesses and failings of a penitential system tending toward legalism, and of the post–Vatican II attempt to revitalize the church through the maturity and responsibility of the laity. For those born after Vatican II, this narrative provides a bit of missing history, a crucial part of Catholic tradition that diminished as

---

2. The commonly understood definition of actual sin was found in the *Baltimore Catechism*, lesson 6, no. 64, http://www.catholicity.com/baltimore-catechism/lesson06.html; accessed on March 11, 2015.

American Catholics pushed forward in the 1960s, hoping to improve the church and the United States. The account here is useful for historians of the church in America, and it also provides helpful background for those in the field of Catholic moral theology, which has seen a change in focus from sin- and confession-based morality to a plethora of approaches to ethical issues.

Acknowledgments

A professor of mine drilled into my head that "there's history, and then there's history." There are the events that took place in time, and then there is the narrative of those events, which always bears some amount of interpretation and, although truthful in various ways, cannot ever do justice to the history itself. One task of a historian is to attempt to tell the historical narrative in a way that remains faithful to the events. These acknowledgments likewise try to give an accurate account of the great number of people who helped me in the writing of this book. Much like historical narratives, however, these acknowledgments are limited, as there are too many people to mention.

I am grateful for several faculty at the University of Dayton whose comments on this project were helpful: Sandra Yocum, William Portier, Jana Bennett, and Kelly Johnson. Thanks also go to Bill Mattison, Pat Carey, Fr. Steven Avella, and John Cavadini for conversations about my work. The thorough comments (and proofreading!) of two gracious reviewers assisted me greatly to improve the manuscript, and I am thankful for them, as well as for Aldene Fredenburg, Theresa Walker, and Trevor Lipscombe, who guided me through the publishing process smoothly.

The writing of this book would not have been possible without the generous funding I received from the University of Dayton. The New Wine, New Wineskins organization of young Catholic moral theologians assisted me in thinking more carefully about this topic—especially Melanie Barrett, whose conference presentation on Thomas Aquinas and nonsacramental penance first caught my interest. The feedback of attendees at a regional meeting of the American Catholic Historical Association was also helpful to me, particularly as regards what became chapters 2 and 3 of the book.

This book touches on the topic of spiritual direction and the role played by priests during a tumultuous time in American Catholic history. I am grateful for the support and helpful insights of several priests during the years of my research, writing, and revising: Fr. Jim Schimelpfening, SM, Fr. Pablo Gadenz, Fr. Bob Connor, and especially Fr. Jim Spera, whose excellent knowledge of theology, liturgy, and the time period were of enormous assistance in working out the details and overarching arguments of this work.

Because I undertook the writing of this manuscript basically at the same time that I undertook raising a family, I could not have done it without the assistance of many friends who helped me to write by caring for and entertaining my kids. Nikki Coffey Tousley, Mary Lou and Rob Guizzo, Sue Sack, Anna Nuñez, Anna Palmarozzo, and Suzanne Covine deserve special mention. My parents, Robert and Kathryn Feilmeyer, sometimes purposely and other times accidentally, came for a visit right when I had deadlines to meet and needed some extra work time. Many thanks to them, as well as to other members of my family: Jeremy and Tricia Feilmeyer, Ann and Kyle Ledbetter, John Mark Feilmeyer, and also my supportive in-laws, Cheryl Banks and Daphne and Jay Morrow.

I always said, as I was writing, that my goal was to "keep the number of my chapters ahead of my children." It may seem odd to mention the children here, as they distracted me and slowed me down in the writing of this book; I may even be confusing the telling of my own historical narrative to extend my thanks to them in the acknowledgments. But while they proved to me the impossibility of work-family balance in my situation, they also proved the joy of having both work and family, whatever the imbalance at any particular moment. Thank you, Maia Bernice, Eva Marcella, Patrick Benjamin, Robert Sebastian, and John Gabriel Rocco.

Last, where the historical narrative surely falls short: I cannot do justice to the significance of Jeffrey Morrow's support. He is an excellent husband, father, scholar, and friend, and I could not have done it without him. It is to Jeff that this book is dedicated, with gratitude also to St. Joseph the Worker.

Sin
in the
Sixties

Introduction

In recent years there have been initiatives for the revival of the sacrament of penance among American Catholics. Each year, especially during Lent, different dioceses of the United States of America make efforts to promote the reception of the sacrament among the faithful. The Archdiocese of Washington, D.C., for example, turned to billboards and advertisements on the sides of buses to encourage use of the sacrament of confession.[1] In the Archdiocese of Newark, every church was open for the hearing of confessions on Wednesday evenings during the season of Lent. Other dioceses have tried similar approaches to rekindle a sacrament that has definitely faded since the end of the Second Vatican Council. Such efforts indicate both the overall disuse of the sacrament and the church's continuing conviction of its importance in the lives of the faithful. Furthermore, both the unpopularity and the continued value of the sacrament of penance have been the subjects of much popular Catholic writing in the last few decades.[2]

---

1. Michelle Boorstein, "A Call to Confession, for It Is Fading," *Washington Post*, February 22, 2007.

2. Examples of popular Catholic works on this topic include the following: Christopher

This book seeks to contribute to the discussion surrounding the sacrament of penance by placing it in a broader context. While the sacrament of confession often receives substantial attention, there are related topics that are often neglected in the conversations regarding the initial decline of the sacrament; these are important in thinking about the sacrament in the future, as well. It is beneficial to examine two areas in particular. Hence, this project first emphasizes the early understanding as to the importance of sin and the recognition of one's personal, actual sin, suggesting that this idea changed during the time period at hand. Second, this book seeks to consider the sacrament of penance at its height as one among many penitential practices regularly observed by the faithful during this time period. This book therefore considers penance more broadly conceived than just the sacrament and examines the faithful's use of penance in direct relation to their understanding of sin, in particular with regard to the faithful's inclination to identify their own personal and actual sins through an examination of conscience and as it would be confessed in the sacrament of penance.

In his masterful essay "In the Court of Conscience: American Catholics and Confession, 1900–1975," historian James O'Toole presents a detailed and valuable historical account explaining the popularity of the sacrament of penance in the United States and suggesting explanations for its rapid collapse in the years following Vatican II.[3] O'Toole indicates that the popularity of the sacrament was in part due to regular clerical encouragement. By the Civil War, "promotion of frequent confession was having its effect, especially in the cities, where the Catholic population clustered."[4] Efforts were made to regularize the sacrament of confession, particularly with the Plenary Councils of Baltimore in both 1852

Walsh, *The Untapped Power of the Sacrament of Penance: A Priest's View* (Cincinnati, Ohio: St. Anthony Messenger Press, 2005); Paul Jerome Keller, *101 Questions on the Sacraments of Healing: Penance and Anointing of the Sick* (Mahwah, N.J.: Paulist Press, 2010); Frank O'Loughlin, *The Future of the Sacrament of Penance* (Mahwah, N.J.: Paulist Press, 2009); Paul Farren, *Freedom and Forgiveness: A Fresh Look at the Sacrament of Reconciliation* (Dublin: Columba Press, 2014); Scott Hahn, *Lord Have Mercy: The Healing Power of Confession* (New York: Doubleday, 2003); and Vinny Flynn, *7 Secrets of Confession* (Stockbridge, Mass.: MercySong, 2013).

3. James M. O'Toole, "In the Court of Conscience: American Catholics and Confession, 1900–1975," in *Habits of Devotion: Catholic Religious Practice in Twentieth Century America*, ed. James M. O'Toole (Ithaca: Cornell University Press, 2004), 131–86.

4. Ibid., 133.

and 1866, when the American hierarchy set a requirement for conspicuous confessional boxes in all newly constructed churches.[5] Though there were regional, ethnic, and gender differences in regard to the faithful's commitment to the sacrament of penance, in general the sacrament of penance was considered crucial to the practice of Catholicism and remained popular until the late 1960s or early 1970s.

Of the contributing factors for the decline in the popularity of the sacrament, O'Toole suggests numerous possibilities: dissatisfactions with the sacrament; the advent of vigil masses overlapping with usual confession times; liturgical changes, such as reciting the *Confiteor* in English, that made sin and forgiveness more obvious; psychologizing of the sacrament; disagreement with *Humanae vitae*; a shifting relationship to the Eucharist; and a change in the conception of sin and morality.[6] But while each of these seems beneficial for understanding the collapse of the sacrament, it is noteworthy that O'Toole makes little reference to the overall penitential culture of Catholicism in the United States. Though he indicates various practices related to the practice of the sacrament of confession, such as parish missions and the First Friday novena, O'Toole fails to mention the multifaceted penitential culture operating among American Catholics. In the Catholic subculture of the United States, penance was not simply understood as identical to the sacrament of penance, nor were trips to the confessional the faithful Catholic's only regular instances of penance.

Though the sacrament was crucial and even paradigmatic for the practice of penance, there were many other penitential practices that were a regular part of Catholic life. They were such a part of being a Catholic that they were often taken for granted; indeed, many of these appeared to be performed by the faithful out of unreflective habit. The Friday meat abstinence in particular identified Catholics as distinct from their Protestant compatriots; everyone seemed to know that Catholics did not eat meat on Fridays. The daily fasting of Lent was also an extended annual reminder of the need to do penance, to make reparation for sins. Other occasions, such as the Ember Days and Vigil Fasts, regularly brought fasting and abstinence from meat to the Catholic calendar. And

5. Ibid., 133.
6. Ibid., 171–81.

in addition to these obligatory penitential practices, there was also the understanding that bearing the ills of life—sickness, poverty, misfortune—could be embraced as voluntary penance.

One of the assets of these penitential practices was that they were communal. Though daily fasting and even abstinence from meat once a week could be difficult, this was a challenge taken up by a community and lived out in a community. The obligatory nature of these practices—defined first and foremost in canon law—assured social support for them (everyone was doing them), often further instituted in the structure of parish fish fries or Catholic school lunches that followed church regulations. Penance was the rule, and aberration from the rule, when willful, was not simply an exception, but rather was depicted in terms of mortal sin. The social support for living these penances was crucial for their perpetuation in the religious pluralism of the United States.

The concurrent collapses of the sacrament of penance and other penitential practices might be taken as a coincidence in the historical narrative. This book suggests, however, that it is beneficial to view them together and, furthermore, to understand them as intrinsically connected. Without the social support for the penitential culture that had been fostered among American Catholics, it is not surprising that the appeal of the sacrament of penance would wane. And it makes sense that without the regular identification and confession of one's personal, actual sin in the sacrament of penance, nonsacramental penitential practices diminished in meaning and practice when they were no longer obligatory. Both the sacrament of penance and the other nonsacramental penitential practices depended upon a conviction in the reality of sin, especially as one's personal, actual sin and the belief that it was possible and necessary to make satisfaction for that sin.

Significantly, both the sacrament of penance and nonsacramental penitential practices were subjected to a similar critique. They were regarded as routine and unreflective, a matter of habit rather than a result of strong interior conviction. Many people perceived these penitential acts as superficial and hence inadequate for addressing the real need for penance. Moreover, the sacrament of penance and other penitential practices were criticized for being narrow and overly focused on the individual's sin and personal salvation rather than identifying and concretely addressing larger social problems. Some contemporary theologians criticized the faithful for seeming obsessed with sins such as missing Mass on Sunday or eating meat on Friday, and these theologians likewise faulted the church for being overly concerned about sexual sins such as contraception. They noted that the faithful often neglected acting against major social sins such as racism and the rights of farm workers; many failed to question or change their attitudes in regard to such pressing social issues. The sincerity of penitents was hence often questioned in discussions among Catholics, particularly as the theological emphases came to favor the language of conversion rather than contrition. A person might appear committed to penitential practices, including the sacrament of penance, while living a hypocritical life that failed to seek reconciliation with God, the church, and the world by attention to important social concerns.

Such perceived problems, and the reality of these problems in regard to the practice of penance, led to proposals for renewing penance. Those who advocated for changes to penance often were guided by and relied upon the popular theological language of the time period in advocating for change. There was an emphasis on freedom—particularly expressed as choice—in addition to an emphasis on responsibility, which was seen as related to the newfound maturity of the laity. The National Conference of Catholic Bishops' 1966 "Pastoral Statement on Penance and Abstinence," which altered penitential regulations in the United States, perhaps best indicates this conviction that penance would become more meaningful if freely chosen rather than accepted in obedience as an obligation. So also, many priests emphasized that the faithful should not come to the sacrament of confession out of a sense of obligation, duty, and habit, but rather an interior desire for conversion. The new rite for the sacrament of penance aimed at making the sacrament more meaningful and less routine, but by the time it was implemented, the sacrament had already declined significantly in popularity.

One sticking point for the revitalization of penance was the fact that the conventional list of sins had changed. Eating meat on Friday had long been described as a mortal sin; now it was not any kind of sin—not even venial! Had the church been wrong for all those years? If so, in what other teachings had the church been mistaken? In a sense, the church had undermined its own authority by changing. The quick turnabout on Friday meat abstinence and inadequate explanation for the alteration caused confusion and contributed to the false hope that the church would also alter its teaching against artificial birth control. Rather than ending the debate, the 1968 release of *Humanae vitae* occasioned a shift in argument, involving the nature of church authority and the value of dissent as a precursor for the development of church teachings.

The long lists of sins, divided as mortal and venial, were not compelling to the younger generation of Catholics raised amidst American religious pluralism; these younger Catholics believed in the importance of questioning authority and a correlative notion of freedom of conscience on determining what constituted sin. They sought other answers, such as those found in popular psychology and counseling, rather than the sacrament of penance, to address their problems. Hence, though a general sense of sin remained, it was not primarily understood in terms of one's personal, actual sin that called for satisfaction in the sacrament of penance and other penitential practices.

The changes to penance made in an effort to renew effective penance largely undermined the practices of penance as a whole. For example, the newfound emphasis on communal sacramental penance services communicated the important theological point that sin and reconciliation involve the entire body of Christ, rather than simply the individual and Jesus. And yet these communal services, though initially popular, did not revitalize penance, in part because they made it more time-consuming and impractical than the two-minute trip to the confessional on a Saturday afternoon. Likewise, the diminishment in days of obligatory penance and a greater freedom of choice in regard to choosing one's own penances—for instance, on Fridays throughout the year, or on all the days of Lent—also undermined penitential practice. The aim was to make penance more effective, or meaningful, with an improved interior disposition of contrition, but the reduction of obligatory penance, which coincided with the dissolution of the Catholic subculture, did not ultimately increase penitential practice. The valuable critiques as to an unreflective routine of sacramental and nonsacramental penance were answered by an emphasis on freedom and responsibility. But these concepts had little structural or social support that could sustain penance in any substantial way, as had the communal penitential practices required by church law or the constant exhortations to the sacrament of penance.

Chapter 1 provides the historical background prior to the 1950s. It provides narrative on the concepts of sin and penance and particularly the development of penance that took place in the church's history. One particular point of emphasis is that the conviction in the existence of sin—and, in particular, the individual's identification of his or her own sin—has long been connected with the notion of making satisfaction for that sin by penance. While the sacrament of penance seems to have begun initially as a response to the sin of apostasy, and then of murder and adultery, as well, other nonsacramental penitential practices were accepted and expected for all. Thus, although the private, repeatable sacrament of penance seems to have been a later development, the practice of nonsacramental penance by the faithful predates the practice of regular use of the sacrament of penance, and these nonsacramental penances continued to exist alongside the sacrament. This was certainly the case in the United States in the 1950s, where penitential practices like the Friday meat abstinence and Lenten fasting were as much a part of the fabric of Catholic life as was the sacrament of penance.

Chapter 2 considers the notion of sin among the faithful from 1955 to 1975, with particular attention to the cultural circumstances of the laity during this time period. The examination of many of the primary sources from the time period reveals a change in how sin was considered by the faithful. While sin had primarily been understood in terms of one's own personal, actual sin, it soon became a much more elusive concept. The chapter proposes several possible explanations for this change, including the diminishment of Catholic subculture, the rise in popularity of psychology and sociology, the perplexity regarding church teaching on contraception, and the esteem for the notion of freedom in contrast to respect for authority. The conviction as to one's personal, actual sin had been a foundational aspect of American Catholicism, but this conviction was increasingly modified to the point where there was a general sense of sin and being a sinner, but without the knowledge and identification of one's personal, actual sins and the corresponding desire to make satisfaction for those sins in the sacrament of penance.

Concurrent with this change in the popular notion of sin was a modification in professional theologians' discussions surrounding sin. Chapter 3 explores these alterations by examining several of the most important authors of the time period. On the one hand are Fr. John C. Ford and Fr. Gerald Kelly, two American Jesuits who have been described as the last of the neo-scholastic moralists. On the other hand, Fr. Bernard Häring, a Redemptorist priest, provides an interesting contrast to Ford and Kelly. Though German, Häring had a far-reaching influence on moral theology in the United States, publishing numerous books—some for popular audiences and others for professional theologians—in English, lecturing at various American universities, and training some of the most significant moral theologians of the following generation, such as Fr. Charles E. Curran of the infamous "Curran Affair."[7] For Ford and Kelly, the confessional remained the primary locus for thinking about sin; determining culpability was hence of the utmost importance. Authority—especially papal authority—was crucial for these authors in thinking about moral issues, and they argued that a person's freedom was advanced by obedience to the obligations delineated by the church. Häring, having lived through World War II and witnessed its atrocities, did not exalt obedience to authority or obligations, but rather favored the concepts of freedom and responsibility and sought to diminish the obsession with legalism in order to get beyond minimalistic morality associated with rules in favor of "the law of love," reaching beyond the matters normally brought to the sacrament of penance.

Häring's popularity and the collapse of Ford and Kelly's style of moral theology indicate the change in the notion of sin for professional theologians. In accord with the changes at the popular level, sin became less defined in terms of an individual's personal, actual sin to be addressed in the confessional but rather moved to larger, often more elusive categories, such as social sin. Moreover, what constituted one's personal, actual sin was no longer judged against the conventional lists of sins, regularly divided into mortal and venial; rather, the mature Christian conscience was regarded by many theologians as capable of determining whether an act were a sin or not, even though it might contradict church teaching.

7. For an extensive discussion on this topic, see Mark S. Massa, SJ, chap. 4, "The Charles Curran Affair, " in *The American Catholic Revolution: How the Sixties Changed the Church Forever* (New York: Oxford, 2010).

Introduction

Chapter 4 begins the narrative concerning the practice of penance in American Catholicism at this time period. Given the dearth of description on this topic in scholarly literature, it provides a detailed account of the many nonsacramental penitential practices and their development in the United States. While in many ways these practices are merely the universal practice of the transnational church, in other ways local customs provided for certain modifications, whether due to the particular American context (scarcity of certain foods) or to critical events (times of war). Among the many universal penitential practices of the church, Friday meat abstinence and Lenten fasting stand out as two crucial penitential practices that remained as Catholic identifiers into the 1960s. The importance of offering up one's suffering as penance complemented and reinforced the penitential culture of American Catholicism, as did numerous devotions, in addition to the sacrament of penance. These penitential practices, however, also could be criticized and observed as being too routine and unreflective to be of much value as genuine penance. Habits such as Friday meat abstinence were firmly entrenched in Catholic culture, and their obligatory observation secured social practice and hence communal support. While this social and communal aspect of penance assisted in Catholic identity and might ease the difficulty of penance, it could also foster routine focused on exterior acts rather than interior contrition when it came to penance as a response for sin.

Such a concern was not unlike Bernard Häring's claims as discussed in chapter 3. Legalism seemed to engender minimalism when it came to these penitential practices. Chapter 5 hence opens with Pope Paul VI's conviction at the close of Vatican II that the renewal of penance was tantamount for the future of the church. With his 1966 apostolic constitution, *Paenitemini*, therefore, the pope invited local episcopal conferences to consider how they might make changes to penitential practices in their jurisdictions such that penance would be revitalized. In the United States, the National Conference of Catholic Bishops responded to this clarion call with their "Pastoral Statement on Penance and Abstinence."

This brief document ushered in dramatic, far-reaching changes to penitential practice among Catholics in the United States. It greatly diminished the obligatory penitential days and seasons and, relying on theological emphases akin to that of Häring, exalted freedom of choice as one key to making penance in the United States more effective. Voluntarily selected and practiced penance, combined with the renewal of the Eucharistic liturgy, was regarded as the best way to revitalize the often routine and unreflective penance in the United States. While the intent of the bishops was admirable, the timing of the letter—when Catholic subculture was declining and a strong Catholic identity among religious pluralism was diminishing—meant that the renewal of penance was not assured by these changes. Rather, the lack of communal support made it more challenging to adhere to penitential practices that had once been so habitual as to seem unreflectively routine.

It is within this context that chapter 6 moves to examine the decline of the sacrament of penance. The reduced popularity of the sacrament during this time period is certainly noteworthy, though it can be argued that the coinciding diminishment of the nonsacramental penitential practices is certainly more dramatic. Chapter 6 observes the similarity in criticism given to penance of both sacramental and nonsacramental forms. Like the Friday meat abstinence, the sacrament of penance was often described as too routine and unreflective, lacking in a sufficient interior disposition of contrition. Akin to the nonsacramental penitential practices, the sacrament of penance seemed to foster a legalism and minimalism, focusing on ritual rules rather than larger issues and social sins such as racism. As with the nonsacramental penitential practices, Catholics looked to renew the sacrament of penance by addressing some of these problematic tendencies.

Some priests proposed a reduction in frequency for reception of the sacrament. Relying on psychological counseling trends, they suggested a change in venue from the darkened box of the confessional. In order to communicate the important social element of reconciliation, communal penance services were heralded as emphasizing the communal aspect over the focus upon individual sin. Often the removal of the sacramental nature of the sacrament of penance was prescribed as a cure for scrupulosity and a mechanistic understanding of the sacrament. Spiritual direction without absolution and absolution without verbal confession were both proposed as good options for fighting the perceived problems of the sacrament. As with the alterations made to the nonsacramental penitential practices, however, the actual modifications to the sacramental rite and practice were not followed by a renewed commitment to the practice of the sacrament but rather coincided with its steady decline.

This book hence considers the diminishment in the popularity of the sacrament of penance as occurring in relation to the changes in the concept of sin for both the faithful and the professional theologians among them. Most significantly, the book observes the noteworthy coincident decline in nonsacramental penitential practices. The project hence seeks to provide a broader context for considering the sacrament of penance in the United States, while also offering a unique historical window to view American Catholicism in the 1960s.

1 Sin and Penance

Interwoven History of Interwoven Concepts

In recent times, the word "penance" has fallen into disuse. Perhaps the primary identification of this word would be with the sacrament of penance. And yet, even that sacrament is no longer identified as much with penance as with reconciliation. Despite the present unfamiliarity with the broader category of penance in the popular understanding of the faithful, the concept of penance has been a crucial counterpart to the notion of sin, as recorded in the Old Testament, since before the advent of Christianity. The conviction that people commit sin has remained throughout all of Christianity, and the practice of penance in various forms has been the way of acknowledging sin and seeking to atone for it. "Penance" has not always been identified solely with the sacrament of penance; rather, penance was a feature of the church even before the sacrament of penance became obligatory and even popular. Penances such as prayer, fasting, and almsgiving—the traditional triad—were promoted and often required. Abstinence from meat or dairy or other foods associated with celebration or indulgence was also common in both the Eastern and Western Church.

This chapter historicizes penance in both its sacramental and non-sacramental instances and describes penance in relation to sin. Non-sacramental penance clearly predates Christianity, and the sacrament of penance has undergone historical development while maintaining a sort of unity in relation to the conviction that one must atone for sin. This narrative is helpful as a reminder of the important role played by penance throughout Christian history, especially since its prominence has lessened in the lives of American Catholics since Vatican II.[1] The necessity of the sacrament of penance and other penitential practices as a response to sin has been contested since the Protestant Reformation, particularly given reformers' objections to the problematic indulgence system. The brief account in this chapter simply aims at illustrating two points. First, the awareness of sin and presence of corresponding penitential practices originated prior to Christianity. Second, penitential practices in the Christian era, including the sacrament of penance, continued to change and develop through the years as the church responded to the church's needs and its failures. Christians, and Jews before them, have recognized their sins and striven to atone for them.

Because of the conviction of the need for penance, the church has often made penitential practices obligatory, as when in 1215 at Lateran IV the church decided that the faithful must seek the sacrament of penance at least annually. And yet, while the institutionalization of penance generally leads to greater participation in penitential practices by mandating penance, there is always the possibility that the very requirement of penance might lead its practice to become an unreflective routine. It could happen that the faithful would fail to cultivate a true sense of interior sorrow, which accompanies acts such as fasting or abstaining from meat, for sins. On the other hand, penitential obligations required of all the faithful bring with them social support; penance is something done

---

1. Many other countries also experienced a decline in the popularity of the sacrament of confession. In Spain there have been attempts to revive the sacrament; see Patrick O'Banion, *The Sacrament of Penance and Religious Life in Golden Age Spain* (University Park, Pa.: Pennsylvania State University Press, 2012), 178. It would be interesting to compare the data from other countries and to compare common factors contributing to the decline, such as those discussed in chapter 4 of this book.

as a church. Without such regulations, even those who believe themselves truly sorry for their sins may find it difficult to persevere in penance.

The chapter concludes with an explanation as to the benefit of this historical background. In the United States, the decline of penitential practices may be linked to the changing notion of sin and a corresponding lessening of the conviction as to the need for penance. Both of these changes have been tied to cultural and societal changes among U.S. Catholics. Some will argue that the established practices of penance during this time period failed to retain popular practice in part because they had failed in cultivating contrition among the faithful while dwelling too much on the legal aspect of the regulations. Others will choose to highlight the idea that ending a specific obligation diminished the social aspect of penance, making it difficult for the faithful to continue with penance. Without a Catholic culture permeated with penitential practices, the awareness of personal, actual sin also declined.

This chapter will provide a brief summary of the admittedly enormous history of sin and penance throughout Christianity, with roots in the Jewish tradition and hence the scripture that constitutes the Old Testament. The language of sin as a debt, in particular, was used by Jesus and the authors of the New Testament when they sought to describe sin. Like the Jewish people who had numerous atonement rituals, the early church sought a way to restore its members who had been ostracized due to major sins. This public, canonical penance eventually gave way to the practice of private confession, which began in the monasteries of Ireland in the sixth century. One of the two most significant events in the history of the development of the sacrament of penance was Lateran IV's 1215 mandate requiring annual reception of the sacrament of confession preceding annual reception of the Eucharist at Easter. The second crucial event occurred when Martin Luther called into question the value and divine sanction of the sacrament of penance while particularly challenging the often problematic penitential practices that had come to accompany the sacrament, such as the selling of indulgences. The purpose of the summary that follows is to establish the longstanding tradition of acknowledging sin and addressing it through penitential practices, both in the sacrament of penance and in nonsacramental penances such as fasting, almsgiving, and prayer.

Sin and Penance

Sin and Penance in the Old Testament

The theme of sin and reconciliation is pervasive throughout the Old Testament, where the people of God are constantly failing to do God's will, being forgiven by God, and beginning again, only to fail again. In his book *Sin: A History*, the biblical scholar Gary Anderson describes how sin, the rebellion against God's laws, was represented in scripture.[2] He observes that in the earlier scriptures, sin (in Hebrew, 'äwōn) was regarded as a weight or a burden to be borne or as a stain on one's person. Hence Leviticus describes the tradition of the Day of Atonement wherein the people's sins were transferred to an animal that would bear away the sins of the people, taking them out of the people's midst and out of God's sight into some unknown wilderness.[3] Anderson emphasizes that sin was not an abstraction; rather, "the physical material of the sin that has rested on the shoulder of every Israelite must be carted away into oblivion."[4]

Beginning in the fifth to second centuries B.C.E., sin was described in biblical books such as Isaiah and Daniel as a "debt" owed to God. Anderson argues that this was due to the influence of Aramaic, which had an impact on the dialect of Hebrew during this time. The term denoting the debt that one owed a lender (in Aramaic, hôbâ) was the standard term used for sin. Aramaic translations of the biblical text used "assume

---

2. Gary A. Anderson, who received his Ph.D. at Harvard in 1985, is an expert on the reception of the Bible in early Judaism and Christianity. Anderson, *Sin: A History* (New Haven: Yale University Press, 2009), provides an exceptional account of change in the metaphors used for sin and how this language affected how Jews and Christians regarded sin and its effects, as well as how sins could be forgiven. It is the most recent and thorough exploration of this topic and hence provides good historical background for developments in regard to sin and penance.

3. Anderson, *Sin*, 6; see also Anderson, "Redeem Your Sins by the Giving of Alms: Sin, Debt, and the 'Treasury of Merit' in Early Jewish and Christian Tradition," *Letter and Spirit* 3 (2007): 39–40; Anderson, "From Israel's Burden to Israel's Debt: Towards a Theology of Sin in Biblical and Early Second Temple Sources," in *Reworking the Bible: Apocryphal and Related Texts at Qumran*, ed. Esther G. Chazon, Devorah Dimant, and Ruth Clements (Leiden: Brill, 2005), 8; Jacob Milgrom, *Leviticus: A Book of Ritual and Ethics* (Minneapolis: Augsburg Fortress, 2004), 16, 133, 158, 166, 171–72, and 267; Baruch J. Schwartz, "The Bearing of Sin in Priestly Literature," in *Pomegranates and Golden Bells: Studies in Biblical, Jewish, and Near Eastern Rituals, Laws, and Literature in Honor of Jacob Milgrom*, ed. David P. Wright, David Noel Freedman, and Avi Hurvitz (Winona Lake, Ind.: Eisenbrauns, 1995), 7, 9–15, 17–18, and 20–21; Milgrom, "The Paradox of the Red Cow (Num. XIX)," *Vetus Testamentum* 31 (1981): 62–72; and Julian Morgenstern, "The Book of the Covenant, Part III: The Ḥuqqim," *Hebrew Union College Annual* 8–9 (1931–32): 16–22.

4. Anderson, *Sin*, 6, and Anderson, "From Israel's Burden," 8; see also Schwartz, "Bearing of Sin," 10, 18, and 21.

a debt" in place of "bear the weight of a sin." Hence, sin did not have the same precise meaning in Genesis as in Daniel or Matthew.[5] In this later imagery for sin, it was understood that every time a person or nation sinned, he incurred a debt to God. The New Testament does not primarily use the earlier metaphors of stain or a weighted burden for sin as in many parts of the Old Testament, nor do the contemporary Jewish texts.[6] Rather, the New Testament employs the language of sin as debt; by the time of Jesus, sin as debt was the common Hebrew and Aramaic idiom in Palestine. The exact word used in commercial contexts for debt was also used in religious contexts as the word for sin, implying that to sin was to owe.

Along with the metaphor of sin as debt came another counterpart from the commercial world: "Physical punishments ... came to be thought of as a means of paying for one's crime."[7] This debt-slavery had a long legal precedent in the ancient Near East, and hence 2 Isaiah interpreted the Babylonian captivity as a debt-slavery, given to Israel that she might raise the currency to pay off the debt she owed from her sin. This system recognized that consequences follow upon human sins, and the tangible form of evil created in the world by sin must be accounted for and then compensated.[8] In the case of debt, there was a need for satisfaction; in

---

5. Anderson, *Sin*, 6, 16, 27; Anderson, "Redeem Your Sins," 39–41, 43–44, 56; Brant Pitre, "The Lord's Prayer and the New Exodus," *Letter and Spirit* 2 (2006): 87; Anderson, "From Israel's Burden," 3, 5–13, 7n10, 10n14, 15, 17–18, 20–22, 24–25, 27–28, and 30; Michael E. Stone, *Adam's Contract with Satan: The Legend of the Cheirograph of Adam* (Bloomington: Indiana University Press, 2002), 8, 37, 96, 104, 144–45; Anderson, *The Genesis of Perfection: Adam and Eve in Jewish and Christian Imagination* (Louisville: Westminster John Knox Press, 2001), 158–61; and Raymond E. Brown, SS, "The Pater Noster as an Eschatological Prayer," *Theological Studies* 22, no. 2 (1961): 200–201.

6. Anderson, *Sin*, 7; Anderson, "Redeem Your Sins," 39–41; and Anderson, "From Israel's Burden," 5–13, 17–18, and 20–30.

7. Anderson, *Sin*, 8, and Anderson, "From Israel's Burden," 26–29.

8. Martien A. Halvorson-Taylor, *Enduring Exile: The Metaphorization of Exile in the Hebrew Bible* (Leiden: Brill, 2011), 7, 30, 40, 107, 109–27, 149, and 198; Anderson, *Sin*, 54; John Sietze Bergsma, *The Jubilee from Leviticus to Qumran: A History of Interpretation* (Leiden: Brill, 2007), 2, 22–23, 28–29, 35, 37, 191–92, 203, and 206–7; Anderson, "Redeem Your Sins," 43–44; Pitre, "Lord's Prayer," 88; Anderson, "From Israel's Burden," 12, 15–17, 19–20, and 20n34; Milgrom, *Leviticus 23–27* (New Haven: Yale University Press, 2000), 2212–41; Joseph Blenkinsopp, *Isaiah 40–55* (New Haven: Yale University Press, 2000), 180; Jeremiah Unterman, "The Social-Legal Origin for the Image of God as Redeemer גואל of Israel," in Wright, Freedman, and Hurvitz, *Pomegranates and Golden Bells*, 401–3; Gregory C. Chirichigno, *Debt-Slavery in Israel and the Ancient Near East* (Sheffield: Journal for the Study of the Old Testament Press, 1993); Klaus Baltzer,

---

Sin and Penance

the case of sin, there was a need for penance. Physical suffering was one form of penitential satisfaction, and it was matched by God's saving act of redemption. Sometimes the physical suffering was self-inflicted—for instance, the Ninevites donning sackcloth and ashes—and at other times it was not—for instance, the exile of the Hebrew people—but both kinds could be understood and embraced as penitential. Thus as interpreted by Isaiah and Ezra, God released the Hebrew people from their Babylonian bondage in slavery through the Persian emperor Cyrus; the debt of sin owed to God was satisfied by their efforts.[9] Moreover, this act of penance was in the best interest of the people, allowing them an opportunity to return to God, to recommit themselves to living holy lives, and to make some reparation for their injustice against God. Penance was not about God needing payment for God's sake, but about the people needing to do penance for their sake, in order to renew their love for and dependence upon God.

Notably, the interior sentiment of penance—to borrow a later word, we might say "contrition" —was not emphasized as the sole or even primary response to sin in the relevant passages of the Old Testament, perhaps because these were cases of communal sin. Rather, the people indicated their sorrow for sin through exterior acts. Leviticus 26:43–45, for example, portrayed the people as making up for all the Sabbath years they failed to observe by letting the land lie fallow for each year that they had ignored the Sabbath prescription.[10] The sorrow for sin was thus embodied, expressed in action that concretely attempted to atone for the sins committed—a repayment of the debt owed to God. The suffering that Israel endured as a result of dishonoring the years of Sabbath rest was not merely a one-for-one punishment, but also allowed for a

---

"Liberation from Debt Slavery after the Exile in Second Isaiah and Nehemiah," in *Ancient Israelite Religion: Essays in Honor of Frank Moore Cross*, ed. Patrick D. Miller Jr., Paul D. Hanson, and S. Dean McBride (Philadelphia: Fortress Press, 1987), 477–84; and Carroll Stuhlmueller, *Creative Redemption in Deutero-Isaiah* (Rome: Biblical Institute Press, 1970), 99–131.

9. Anderson, *Sin*, 46; Anderson, "Redeem Your Sins," 44; and Anderson, "From Israel's Burden," 29.

10. Anathea E. Portier-Young, *Apocalypse Against Empire: Theologies of Resistance in Early Judaism* (Grand Rapids, Mich.: Eerdmans, 2011), 269–71; David M. Carr, *The Formation of the Hebrew Bible: A New Reconstruction* (Oxford: Oxford University Press, 2011), 302; Anderson, *Sin*, 65; Bergsma, *Jubilee*, 208, 229, and 303; and Michael Fishbane, *Biblical Interpretation in Ancient Israel* (Oxford: Clarendon Press, 1985), 481.

physical healing of the land and a spiritual healing for the people who had returned to God to honor his law. The penance of letting the land lie fallow to make up for the years that were missed was therefore "a process of restoration."[11] Hence this satisfaction was not simply a penalty, but an opportunity for mercy and forgiveness and for the land to renew itself. Rather than embittering or isolating, penance healed the damage caused by sin and drew the people back to God.

In sum, several important themes regarding sin and penance occur in the Old Testament, laying the foundation for the Christian understandings of sin and penance. First, sin was regarded as something very real. The language of sin as a stain, burden, or debt leads Anderson to describe sin as having a particular quality that he names as "thingness." The counterpart to such a real and tangible notion of sin was real and tangible penance to atone for the sins committed against God. Physical suffering was one way of paying off the debt owed to God through sin; most often the physical suffering was described as something experienced socially—that is, by the whole people of Israel. In other circumstances, however, the suffering due to sin was accorded to the individual who committed the sin, such as in the case of David committing adultery with Bathsheba. Penance was hence both social and individual, both communal and personal. Moreover, the sorrow for sin was always embodied in penance. Simply feeling sorrow for sin was insufficient; action was required to make amends for offenses. Last, the difficulty of penance as described in the Old Testament—for example, in enforced exiles—served to bring the people back to God, renewing their dependence upon God. Penances were not simply about a strict accounting so as to pay back God for offenses regarded as debt; rather, they were meant to work conversion and a renewal of belief in the people's dependence upon God, as well as their trust in his mercy and hence an increase in faith.

Sin and Penance in the New Testament and Early Church

These themes of sin and penance—in particular, the language of sin as debt—were continued in the New Testament. In the Gospel of Matthew,

11. Anderson, *Sin*, 66.

for instance, Jesus instructed his disciples to pray, "Remit (*aphiemi*) us our debts (*opheilema*) as we remit those who hold debts against us" (Mt 6:12).[12] This word choice reflects the Aramaic, applying words that in Greek had commercial but not religious usage; these Greek words would have seemed unusual unless the person knew the original Semitic quotation. The words reflect the image of God imagined as a gracious creditor who releases the bonds of debt for those individuals and peoples who ask for forgiveness. The death of Jesus on the cross added depth to this understanding of God's love and generosity. God is just, but God is also generous, as Anderson explains: "In forgiving a debt, the creditor is in a sense making a gift of it—and God is always free to make a gift."[13] The Lord's Prayer as contained in Matthew attests not only to the realization of the reality of sin but also to trust in God's willingness to forgive, as well as the Christian's desire to imitate this model of forgiveness, embodied in Jesus' own ministry.

Repentance is a recurring theme in the Gospels. The Gospel of Mark, for example, begins with John the Baptist and Jesus calling for repentance (Mk 1:4, 1:15). The Gospel of Luke also advises, "Be on your guard! If your brother sins, rebuke him; and if he repents, forgive him."[14] The acknowledgment of sin and desire to repent of it is seen as an important part of the Gospel message. Likewise, the first-century document the *Didache* bolsters the Gospel themes when it similarly says, "reprove one another, not in anger, but in peace, as you have it in the Gospel. But to anyone that acts amiss against another, let no one speak, nor let him hear anything from you until he repents. But your prayers and alms and all your deeds so do, as you have it in the Gospel of our Lord."[15]

The early Christian document called *The Shepherd of Hermas* provides another illustration of early Christian thinking on the topics of sin and penance.[16] This text is a noncanonical, though influential writing from the apostolic age, ca. 100–60, and it specifically addresses the problem

12. Ibid., 31. This is Anderson's translation.
13. Ibid., 108; see also Brown, "Pater Noster," 200–201.
14. Luke 17:3.
15. *Didache*, chap. 15; http://www.earlychristianwritings.com/text/didache-roberts.html; accessed on January 27, 2013.
16. While not canonical, this text was widely used by early Christians and was even considered to be canonical by Irenaeus. It was also controversial, with some, like Tertullian, highly critical of the text.

of sin after baptism. The ultimate message seems to be that repentance followed by God's forgiveness is possible, even when it is a response to post-baptismal sin. In one part, a woman appears to the writer as a figure of the church who explains that Hermas has become like the non-Christians and has failed in admonishing his sons and wife. It is important that he do so that they might repent and be forgiven of their sins: "Then they will be forgiven their sins, which they have heretofore committed, and so will the sins of all the saints who have sinned even to this day, if they will repent with all their hearts, and remove all doubts out of their hearts."[17] Hermas is constantly depicted as kneeling, praying, and confessing his sins, and the woman who appears to him encourages this repentance and the reformation of his life. This text hence provides a picture of the sin of a Christian that is redeemable through acknowledgment of sin, repentance, and a life of virtuous works.[18]

The Gospels, *Didache*, and *Shepherd of Hermas* indicate that the early church recognized the ongoing problem of sin, even after baptism, and sought penitential ways to address it within the community of believers.[19] Regular penitential practices such as the acknowledging of one's sins, prayer, and almsgiving occurred as ways for making reparation for sins among early Christians. Early Christians furthermore recognized that sin caused a rupture in the church. In particular, early Christians struggled with how to reincorporate Christians who had apostatized under the pressure of persecuting regimes.

---

17. *Shepherd of Hermas*, Vision 2:13.

18. Ibid., Vision 3:90–91. For a more thorough discussion of the *Shepherd of Hermas*, see Cornelia B. Horn, "Penitence in Early Christianity in Its Historical and Theological Setting: Trajectories from Eastern and Western Sources," in *Repentance in Christian Theology*, ed. Mark J. Boda and Gordon T. Smith (Collegeville, Minn.: Liturgical Press, 2006), 154–58; Carolyn Osiek, *Shepherd of Hermas: A Commentary* (Minneapolis: Fortress Press, 1999), especially 173–95; Joseph A. Favazza, *The Order of Penitents: Historical Roots and Pastoral Future* (Collegeville, Minn.: Liturgical Press, 1988), 96–108; and Karl Rahner, *Theological Investigations*, vol. 15, *Penance in the Early Church* (New York: Crossroad, 1982), 125–51.

19. The fourth–seventh-century text known as *The Life of Adam and Eve*, popular among both Jews and Christians during the medieval period, also has a penitential theme, wherein Adam and Eve seek to do penance for their sin by standing up to their neck in water: the Jordan for Adam and the Tigris for Eve; see http://wesley.nnu.edu/sermons-essays-books/noncanonical-literature/noncanonical-literature-ot-pseudepigrapha/the-books-of-adam-and-eve/. On the *Life of Adam and Eve*, see especially Brian Murdoch, *The Apocryphal Adam and Eve in Medieval Europe: Vernacular Translations and Adaptations of the Vita Adae et Evae* (Oxford: Oxford University Press, 2009).

Sin and Penance

First the Novatianists in the third century and then the Donatists in the fourth and fifth centuries thought that those Christians who had succumbed to the persecutions of Decius and Diocletian, respectively, should not be readmitted to the church. Such a post-baptismal sin of denying Christ was viewed simply as unforgiveable; those who apostatized were clearly not Christians and hence could not share in the Christian assembly. Non-schismatic Christians, on the other hand, responded to the apostates by asking them to undergo public penance in order to be readmitted to communion in the church.[20] This public penance was fitting given the public nature of the sin of apostasy, which was a sin against the community with the potential to destabilize the community through scandal, as it provided a poor example for others in the church. The witness of sorrowful repentance in the performance of public penance, meanwhile, helped to make reparation for the harm caused by public denial of the faith while providing a structure for reincorporation into the church in a way that demonstrated both the individual's penitence and God's forgiveness represented by the church body.

It was this public penance that came to be recognized as sacramental penance. In addition to the sin of apostasy, the sins of murder and adultery were also regarded as requiring public penance.[21] Like apostasy, murder and adultery were sins that would likely be publicly known and cause rupture within the church. The sacrament of penance at this time was observed only once in a person's life, as it was understood to bear similarity to the forgiveness of sins in baptism, which was also celebrated only once. Like in the aforementioned case of penance as a response to the sin of apostasy, the canonical sacrament of penance involved the public confession of sins and performance of penance. By the beginning of the third century, public penance had a consistent process, involving a period of penance and exclusion from communion, followed by formal absolution and restoration, with the last part normally bestowed by a

20. Dale T. Irvin and Scott W. Sunquist, *History of the World Christian Movement*, vol. 1, *Earliest Christianity to 1453* (Maryknoll, N.Y.: Orbis, 2001), 139 on Novatianists, 171 on Donatists. For this controversy, over the readmission of Christians who had apostatized during times of persecution and the role of penance, see also Robert Louis Wilken, *The First Thousand Years: A Global History of Christianity* (New Haven: Yale University Press, 2012), 68–71.

21. John A. Gallagher, *Time Past, Time Future: An Historical Study of Catholic Moral Theology* (1990; repr. Eugene, Ore.: Wipf and Stock, 2003), 6.

bishop.[22] This entire process was called *exomologesis*, which is the Greek word for confession. Historian J. N. D. Kelly notes:

> There is plenty of evidence that sinners were encouraged to open their hearts privately to a priest, but nothing to show that this led up to anything more than ghostly counsel. Indeed, for the lesser sins which even good Christians daily commit and can scarcely avoid, no ecclesiastical censure seems to have been thought necessary; individuals were expected to deal with them themselves by prayer, almsgiving and mutual forgiveness. Public penance was for graver sins; it was, as far as we know, universal, and was an extremely solemn affair, capable of being undergone only once in a lifetime.[23]

Kelly suggests that in practice the sins of apostasy, murder, and adultery were initially considered as irremissible. Hence the most noteworthy advance in the conception of penance during these early centuries in fact came when those who committed these sins could be readmitted to communion through *exomologesis*.[24] The practice of public penance, though intense and difficult for the penitents, was nonetheless an improvement over permanent exclusion from the Eucharist and the church, such as that enforced by the Novatianists.

Documents of the fourth and fifth centuries contain numerous references to the church's practice of remitting sins after baptism.[25] Augustine's writings indicate a sense of penance at this time, for example. Augustine divided penance into three categories: (1) penance preceding baptism; (2) daily remission of venial sins through prayer and fasting; and (3) the formal penitential discipline for grave and mortal sins. Augustine considered penance as occurring in two situations: before and after baptism. Belief in the forgiveness of sins was the underlying foundation for both of these.[26] We might say that the second and third categories of penance—namely, the daily remission of venial sins through prayer (the Lord's Prayer especially) and fasting and the formal penitential discipline for grave and mortal sins—attest to the importance of

---

22. John Norman Davidson Kelly, *Early Christian Doctrines* (1960; repr. San Francisco: Harper and Row, 1978), 217.
23. Ibid., 217.   24. Ibid., 217–18.
25. Ibid., 436.
26. Allan D. Fitzgerald, OSA, "Penance," in *Augustine through the Ages: An Encyclopedia*, ed. Allan D. Fitzgerald (Grand Rapids, Mich.: Eerdmans, 1999), 641.

Sin and Penance

both nonsacramental penance and sacramental penance for the life of the church. Though a sacramental process was viewed as necessary to respond to grievous sins such as apostasy, murder, and adultery, importance was also accorded to the many nonsacramental penances practiced by the church.

Moreover, daily penance and formal penance were related in the sense that they both aimed at the reform of the sinner. Augustine's view of the punishment of penance was that it ought to heal the fault and make the person better. The forgiveness of sins was seen as a task of the whole community and not just the bishop; the willingness to invite someone to repentance was seen as an act of mercy, and it was hoped that such correction and the embrace of daily penance would prevent the need for formal penance.[27] Furthermore, not every serious sin would be a matter for public penance because much depended on the sinner's strength and ability to accept penance profitably.[28] The person's salvation and reconciliation with the church were the foremost objectives; public penance was not vengeful but rather was seen by Augustine as instrumental for increasing the desire for healing and restoring the Christian to the life of faith with the church.[29] Daily penance, such as the recitation of the Lord's Prayer, was in continuity with this public penance. The Christian's constant forgiveness of others' sins assured God's forgiveness of their sins, and Augustine regarded this forgiveness of sins as the perfection sought in the earthly life rather than the acquiring of virtue.[30]

There is no strong evidence of repeatable private penance at this time, although it is possible that bishops sometimes chose to deal privately with sinners. It is unlikely that such encounters between bishop and penitent culminated in sacramental absolution with the formal forgiveness of sins as later practiced in the church.[31] The severity, non-repeatable nature, and publicity of the sacrament of penance practiced as formal canonical penance at this time led many to defer it until their deathbed and must ultimately have contributed to its lack of popularity

---

27. Ibid. 642.
28. Ibid., 642.
29. Ibid., 643.
30. Augustine, *City of God*, trans. Henry Bettenson (New York: Penguin, 1972), book 19, ch. 27:892.
31. Kelly, *Early Christian Doctrines*, 438–39.

and eventual decline.³² Augustine's writings, however, attest to the importance of nonsacramental penitential acts that were prescriptive for the remission of venial sins. Though the public sacrament described previously was reserved for those who committed grave and mortal sins, these many other penitential practices—such as prayer, fasting, and almsgiving—did remit sin and hence were recommended to be a constant part of the Christian's life.³³ Though not all Christians would go through the process of *exomologesis* or canonical penance, all Christians were expected to partake of penitential practices as the obvious counterpart to the sins they committed.

The Advent of Private Penance

While nonsacramental penitential practices continued after the time of Augustine, the sixth century brought a new approach to penance from Irish monks. These monks composed texts known as penitentials, which included specific definitions of sin that were correlated with specific penances.³⁴ Although these penitentials began in Ireland among those religious who were seeking spiritual perfection, they were soon transported by Irish missionaries to the Continent, with the purpose of guiding those who administered the sacrament of penance. The older practice of public penance had declined throughout Europe in favor of this private, auricular, repeatable confession administered by a priest rather than a bishop. John Gallagher notes that the Celtic penitentials were the product of a monastic conception of Christianity in the context of primitive Celtic culture.³⁵ While the monks transferred some of the expectations of religious life to the laity, they also were aware of the particular issues pertinent to that situation, such as tribal battles. The topics covered in the Celtic penitentials, then, were not simply limited to the concerns of monastics but rather extended to include the struggles of Celtic

---

32. Ibid., 439; see also Thomas Tentler, *Sin and Confession on the Eve of the Reformation* (Princeton: Princeton University Press, 1977), 4–6.

33. Kelly does not present Augustine's position on the daily penance as causing a transformation—i.e., inhibiting bad behavior or preventing sin and vice—but it would make sense that the daily remission of sin would also work positively toward transformation of the sinner.

34. Gallagher, *Time Past*, 7.

35. Ibid., 8.

cultures. The penitentials took on social, political, and legal functions as well as religious. Certain sins were also regarded as crimes that caused exclusion not just from communion but from the civil community as well; these sin-crimes required not just supernatural restitution but natural restitution.[36]

Thomas Tentler observes the rough continuity between the earlier, public form and the later, private form of sacramental confession. Tentler notes the four substantive elements of the sacrament expressed in each form: sorrow for sin; explicit confession of sins; penitential exercises performed by the sinner; and an ecclesiastical ritual of absolution or reconciliation with the community of believers, done with the aid of priests.[37] These four elements were present in both the public and private systems, as were penances that could last years. Another similarity in practice was that even the public penance was already often private in nature, given that many people delayed canonical penance until their deathbed.[38] One other notable similarity between the two systems was the conviction that "forgiveness rested most securely on works of expiation."[39] Penance was not simply about feeling sorry, but about performing satisfaction; this effort indicated sorrow, and, whether the penance was public or private, the penitent engaged in such satisfaction could be confident in God's forgiveness expressed through the church.

The penitentials flourished until the tenth century, when the *Summae confessorum* began to take their place. Gallagher describes these as a product of Gregory VII's "papal revolution," which began to distinguish between the church and secular society, prioritizing the church in conjunction with the development of canon law as a codification of decretals—the legal decisions from the papal chancery.[40] Gratian's *Concordance of Discordant Canons* (or *Decretum*, as it is more commonly known) indicates the development of the Scholastic method. Gratian presupposed the authority of certain books, and he compiled and synthesized the relevant content, applying the Scholastic method to the study of law.[41] As canon law emerged, it detailed proper Christian conduct in regard to marriage, inheritance, property, and contracts. Canon law described

36. Ibid., 9.
38. Ibid., 10.
40. Gallagher, *Time Past*, 14.
37. Tentler, *Sin and Confession*, 3.
39. Ibid., 12.
41. Ibid., 15.

these issues in legal rather than ethical categories, and so the *Summae confessorum* surfaced in the eleventh and twelfth centuries as pastoral handbooks drawing upon the canonical and theological achievements of the time period and guiding confessors in the administration of the sacrament of penance.[42] Both the *Summae confessorum* and Celtic penitentials were legalistic as regards morality and the administration of the sacrament of penance, and they assumed repeated, auricular confession. The *Summae*, however, were intended for secular priests rather than religious monks, and hence they emphasized the sacramental authority of bishops.[43]

Tentler notes a few major changes in the theology and practice of confession between the ninth and thirteenth centuries: penances were lightened and became arbitrary rather than standard; contrition became the essential element for the penitent; and the meaning of the priest's role was more carefully defined.[44] Another significant event occurred when the Fourth Lateran Council of 1215 sanctioned the practice of private, repeatable penance and instructed the faithful to confess during Lent in preparation for their reception of the Easter Eucharist.[45] According to Katherine Jansen, the new emphasis on sacramental penance brought on a "penitential fever, or wave of evangelical penance that was being preached popularly in the streets."[46] As in the past, penitential acts were not limited to those constituting the sacrament or external actions prescribed to the penitent by the priest. Though any penances from the traditional triad of fasting, prayer, and almsgiving might be given to fulfill the satisfaction part of the sacrament of penance, there were communal penitential acts of the church, some according to the liturgical season, such as the great fast of Lent. Medieval pilgrimages and self-

42. Ibid., 18. 43. Ibid., 20.
44. Tentler, *Sin and Confession*, 16.
45. Canon 21, Lateran IV, in *Decrees of the Ecumenical Councils*, vol. 1, *Nicaea I–Lateran V*, ed. Norman P. Tanner, SJ (Washington, D.C.: Georgetown University Press, 1990), 245. Tentler notes elsewhere that it is well-known that books for confessors antedate Lateran IV, as did the obligation to confess. Moreover, Tentler describes Lateran IV's mandate as the result of a long religious movement that sought to emphasize confession; see Tentler, "Response and Retractio," in *The Pursuit of Holiness in Late Medieval and Renaissance Religion*, ed. Charles Edward Trinkaus and Heiko A. Oberman (Leiden: Brill, 1974), 134.
46. Katherine Ludwig Jansen, *The Making of the Magdalen: Preaching and Popular Devotion in the Later Middle Ages* (Princeton: Princeton University Press, 2000), 200.

flagellation were also popular as penitential acts in making satisfaction for one's sins.⁴⁷ Hence, even with this new obligation of annual reception of the sacrament, penance was not solely identified with the sacrament, but rather extended beyond the sacrament, which was supported by this penitential culture.

But there was also a more academic aspect relating to sin, penance, and morality as theology found its home in the university. Gallagher names this an "intellectual apostolate" and notes that theologians like Thomas were concerned with summarizing and systematizing many of the ideas of others, including Greek philosophers like Aristotle as well as the writers of the patristic period. So while sin and the administration of the sacrament of penance remained topics of pastoral concern for those involved in preaching and hearing confessions, the literature for what might be called moral theology went beyond the practical guide for morality found in penitentials and the *Summae confessorum* to more academic and less pastoral writings geared toward educating clergy, like Peter Lombard's *Libri quatuor sententiarum* and Thomas's *Summa theologiae*.

Peter Lombard and Thomas Aquinas lived at a time when the sacrament of penance was practiced in both forms, the public, canonical form and the private form, and this fact affected their thinking and writing about the sacrament of penance as a response to sin. In particular, the rise of the repeatable sacrament led to a change in how penance was considered theologically. Philipp Rosemann notes that the Lombard did not use certain terms systematically, partly because of the simultaneous existence of the public and private forms of the sacrament present at the time. The public form of penance had fallen into disuse, but the theory behind it remained and had not yet been supplanted by a theory supporting the prevalent practice of private penance: "Peter Lombard's frequent hesitations ... have everything to do with the fact that, in the middle of the twelfth century, a new doctrine of penance was taking shape in the western Church."⁴⁸ Rosemann explains that Peter the Lombard's distinctions on penance are nonetheless a confirmation that the church's understanding of penance had evolved to the point where private auric-

---

47. For an excellent account of penitential practices during the later Middle Ages, see the entirety of Jansen's part 3, "Do Penance," in *Making of the Magdalen*, 199–245.
48. Philipp W. Rosemann, *Peter Lombard* (Oxford: Oxford University Press, 2004), 162.

ular confession to a priest was becoming widely accepted even beyond the monastery.[49] Further evidence of this approval of private penance in the following decades is the aforementioned instruction of Lateran IV in 1215 for the faithful to receive the sacrament of confession annually.

It was clear that the sacrament of penance no longer seemed to correspond to the sacrament of baptism as a unique, decisive event in the life of the believer; a different narration of the sacrament of penance was needed to make sense of its repeatability. Public, canonical penance was still present and reserved for great sins, according to Lombard, but his conviction was that ordinary penance could and should be repeated. Hence Lombard's great contribution to this development was his explanation of penance as a habit of atoning for sin; those who possessed such a habit of penance would be indicated by their repeated recourse to the sacrament of penance. Lombard stated that penance is both a sacrament and a virtue of the mind, like all other virtues. Though nonsacramental penitential practices such as confessing sins, fasting, almsgiving, prayer, wearing ashes, and weeping were practiced regularly (as habits) throughout Christian and Jewish history, this seems to be the first time that penance was described as a virtue exhibited in those who practiced penance regularly through frequent use of the sacrament of penance.[50]

The three aspects of the sacrament of penance described by Lombard are compunction of the heart, confession of the mouth, and satisfaction by means of work. There was great debate in the twelfth and thirteenth centuries as to when God's forgiveness was imparted: at the moment of contrition (contritionism); following confession (confessionism); or at the time of the priest's absolution (absolutionism). Though Lombard believed sins were forgiven when the sinner was contrite, he nonetheless emphasized the importance of the sinner's intentions to express his interior penance exteriorly in the acts of confession and satisfaction. Circumstances might arise when a penitent was truly contrite but had no access to a priest in order to receive the sacrament properly; nonetheless, the normal procedure was for exterior acts to signify interior intention and the priest's absolution to declare the sins absolved.[51] The

49. Ibid.
50. Marcia L. Colish, *Peter Lombard* (Leiden: Brill, 1994), 2:601–2.
51. There is debate as to whether Peter the Lombard was truly a contritionist. Marcia Colish

Sin and Penance

virtue of the mind that was penance, like interior contrition, was always expressed outwardly in acts of penance when possible. These exterior acts were indications of the person's interior penance—that is, the virtue of penance. Though Lombard did not make a connection between the nonsacramental and sacramental acts of penance, the repeatability of the acts of contrition, confession, and satisfaction associated with the sacrament now seemed to bear greater similarity to the nonsacramental acts of penance so frequently practiced at the time.

In many ways, Thomas Aquinas followed in Peter Lombard's footsteps when he considered penance in the *Summa theologiae*. The sacrament of penance was particularly important for Thomas, as it was for all Dominicans, because of mandates from Pope Honorius III, who entrusted the Dominicans with the mission of hearing confessions in addition to their preaching service. This task was set by Honorius four years after he first allowed Dominic's band of local preachers to become the Order of Preachers (OP) in 1217.[52] Simultaneous with his work on scriptural commentaries, Thomas was responsible for forming friars in moral theology and the pastoral work of confession, and it was reportedly Thomas's dissatisfaction with the narrowness of available manuals that gave rise to his undertaking the project of the *Summa theologiae*.[53] Thomas himself made frequent use of the sacrament of penance; it is known that at least during the time period of 1252–59 he received the sacrament of penance daily before Mass.[54]

Jansen notes that the Dominican translator Domenico Cavalca argued in his tract on preaching that the apostolic life was predicated on the preaching of repentance.[55] Numerous texts emerged in order to prepare the Dominicans both to preach and to hear confessions; among the many texts were the *Summa de casibus* of Raymond of Peñafort and the

---

answers yes; Colish, *Peter Lombard*, 601–2. With an emphasis on contrition, the actual sacrament is not of great importance, but is more of a formality. Rosemann says a qualified no; Rosemann, *Peter Lombard*, 165. Tentler supports Colish's view, seeing Thomas Aquinas as in between Lombard's contritionist stance and Duns Scotus's absolutionist stance; *Sin and Confession*, 22–23.

52. Leonard E. Boyle, *The Setting of the Summa theologiae of Saint Thomas* (Toronto: Pontifical Institute of Mediaeval Studies, 1982), 1.

53. Jean-Pierre Torrell, *Saint Thomas Aquinas: The Person and His Work* (1996; repr. Washington, D.C.: The Catholic University of America Press, 2005), 144.

54. Ibid., 287n94.

55. Jansen, *Making of the Magdalene*, 201.

Summa vitiorum and *Summa virtutum* of Willelmus Peraldus. These works prepared the Dominicans to evangelize about the virtues while guiding them in the pastoral skills associated with hearing confessions.

Thomas's treatment on sin is valuable as a context for understanding his perspective on penance; this part comprises questions 71–89 of the *Prima secundae* in what is known as the "Treatise on Habits." Drawing from the Augustinian definition, Thomas describes sin as a thought, word, or deed contrary to eternal law. Thomas also acknowledges the effects of sin by drawing upon the biblical language of stain, burden, and debt. But perhaps what is most remarkable about this account is the positive role that sin and its effects can take as an opportunity for grace, healing, and growth in virtue, particularly when punishment is voluntarily accepted by the sinner. Sin was certainly not seen as a good, nor was punishment prima facie viewed positively, and yet, in another sense, punishment voluntarily accepted was beneficial, providing a healing medicine, allowing the soul to be reunited with God.

This positive perspective is apparent in article 7 of question 87, where Thomas distinguished two ways of understanding punishment. Simply speaking, a punishment is always in relation to a sin in the one punished, whether in relation to actual sin or original sin. On the other hand, a satisfactory punishment is voluntary. One can bear punishment bitterly and with resentment, or one can accept it willingly; the latter can be rightly identified as an act of penance. Moreover, sometimes a thing seems penal, but is only relatively so, as Thomas explained. Punishment is an evil, a privation of good, but sometimes a punishment entails the loss of some good in order to gain a greater good. Such a loss is only an evil to the person relatively speaking because the person actually benefits from the sacrifice. In short, Thomas saw punishment as medicinal—that is, as a way of restoring health. He also recognized that the Fall of Adam and Eve destroyed the gift of original justice; hence the virtuous person might have to sacrifice goods not on account of his own sin, but rather as a result of original sin.[56]

56. *ST* I-II, q. 85, art. 1. Cessario explains Thomas thus: "Simply speaking, satisfaction is voluntary, but in another and more literal sense of punishment, it remains involuntary. All in all, we should appraise the debt of punishment that exists after sin more as an opportunity for satisfaction than as an outright punishment"; Romanus Cessario, OP, *The Godly Image: Christ*

Sin and Penance

Evil has traditionally been understood as a privation of good, and so sin is a dearth of good. Thomas built upon Augustine's sense that a sin is a voluntary act that is disordered; it prioritizes a lesser good over a higher good, and in that sense it is a privation of good that is also identifiable. This act may be a thought, word, deed, or failure to act that is contrary to reason and eternal law. The species of sin is identified based on the object of the human act. The matter (act) and form (object) constitute the sin. Drawing on the biblical imagery, Thomas employed the language of stain and debt and cast a positive view of punishment accepted voluntarily. This satisfactory punishment is medicinal as well as retributive, restoring health by turning the faithful toward God and observation of the eternal law. The willing reception of punishment leads to a reconciliation with God, and penance is a way of restoring spiritual health for the ultimate good of the person. The concept of sin as a personal and communal reality is a crucial foundation for understanding the necessity and value of penance.

Thomas discussed the form of the sacrament in article 3, where he stated that the form of the sacrament is the words "I absolve thee." He noted that while the acts done by the penitent constitute the matter, the part done by the priest is the form of the sacrament; the sacrament is perfected by these words that signify the sacramental effect—namely, the removal of matter, the remote matter of sin. The priest is expressing the removal of matter, although "God alone absolves from sin and forgives sins authoritatively; yet priests do so ministerially."[57] Furthermore, this removal of sin (presumably mortal, rather than venial sin), "which cannot be done without the sacrament of Penance," is necessary for salvation on the supposition of sin, as discussed in article 5.[58] The *Baltimore Catechism*, so dominant in American Catholicism, was to draw upon the work of Thomas and the Scholasticism that followed him in its definition of sin and the sacrament of penance. Hence the Thomistic account is

---

and *Salvation in Catholic Thought from Anselm to Aquinas* (Petersham, Mass.: St. Bede's Publications, 1990), 120.

57. *ST* III, q. 84, a. 3, ad. 3.

58. *ST* III, q. 84, a. 4. Presumably, the use of "sin" here denotes mortal sin; as noted previously, Augustine and others throughout the history of the church have stated that venial sins can be forgiven by other penitential acts; this remains the teaching of the church. See q. 86 for more on this topic.

helpful for providing context as to how American Catholics understood sin and penance.

The practice of repeatable sacramental penance accorded with the conviction as to the necessity of the many repeatable nonsacramental acts of penance. The faithful penitentially abstained from meat on a regular basis; so also they were now to receive the sacrament of penance on a regular basis. The theology of penance at the time depended upon this coherence of sacramental and nonsacramental penance; the repetition of nonsacramental penances such as fasting and meat abstinence provided a context in which to understand the repetition of sacramental penance. Penance even became identified as "a virtue" by Peter Lombard, a concept that was followed by Thomas Aquinas. The idea was that the person who sought the sacrament of penance exhibited the virtue of penance—that is, a habit of making satisfaction for sin. Forgiveness of sins, according to Thomas, was an effect of the virtue of penance (the habit that led one to do penance) but even more so an effect of the sacrament of penance, wherein the priest absolved the person's actual sins.[59] The acts of the penitent in the sacrament of penance—contrition, confession, and satisfaction—constituted the matter of the sacrament and were acts of the virtue, and the penitents' acts were perfected by the form of the sacrament provided by the priest in absolving the sins.

According to Thomas, the grace of the sacrament strengthened all the virtues, including the virtue of penance. The *Summa theologiae* in fact ends with the sacrament of penance, without any further consideration from Thomas as to acts of the virtue of penance beyond those that constituted the matter of the sacrament. Yet it can be surmised that penances such as fasting and almsgiving would be considered acts of the virtue of penance as well, though the acts associated with the sacrament of penance would remain the quintessential acts of the virtue of penance. Drawing upon Thomas's work on penance, one could say that the acts of the virtue of penance, whether sacramental or nonsacramental, worked in concert for the person who possessed the virtue of penance. And as Jansen observed, the rise of the popularity of the sacrament of penance seemed to occasion a rise in the popularity of penance generally speaking. Though there might be variations in regard to which nonsacramen-

---

59. *ST* III, q. 85.

tal penitential practices were popular in a particular region, and there might have been a diversity of practice in terms of assigning penance in the sacrament of penance, nonetheless the idea of making satisfaction for one's sin was a Christian conviction, and more than just a conviction; engaging in penance was ubiquitous.

Sin and Penance and the Protestant Reformation

At the time of the Reformation, penance became a truly contentious topic. In the New Testament, the Greek word *metanoia*, which literally means turning away from something, is typically translated in English as "repent." Hence both John the Baptist's and Jesus' call for *metanoia*, for example, are translated "repent." The word *metanoia* seems to emphasize the interior dimension of penitential acts; an act of penance cannot be solely external but rather at its root is a change of mind, a conversion of heart. As was noted earlier, however, in the Old Testament, repentance was not typically portrayed as something interior; repentance was exhibited in exterior acts. The use of the word *metanoia* can be understood to imply exterior acts of penance accompanying interior conversion. And in the Vulgate translation of the New Testament *metanoia* was translated in this manner—as *poenitentiam agite*, or "do penance." This translation of *metanoia* no doubt obscures the interior dimension of the original Greek word by conveying the priority of external act constituting penance. The translation of *metanoia* as *poenitentiam agite* could also be understood to imply that penance is not mere sentiment without an outward sign; rather, the conversion represented by *metanoia* always spurs a person to action.

The danger of the translation "do penance" was a proclivity to turn the focus to the external action while neglecting the interior state of *metanoia*; in particular, some members of the church chose to focus upon almsgiving—not necessarily charitable giving to individuals living in poverty, but rather the giving of money to particular churches—as a preferred way of "doing penance" for the sins that would prevent them from entrance to heaven.[60] And this concern was what prompted Martin Luther to react to

60. On the history of almsgiving as a form of penance in early Judaism and Christianity, see especially Anderson, "Redeem Your Sins," 39–69.

problematic practices that he experienced in the Catholic Church. The first of Martin Luther's ninety-five theses in fact formally opened the debate as to the meaning of the phrase "do penance": "Our Lord and Master Jesus Christ, when he said *Poenitentiam agite*, willed that the whole life of believers should be repentance."[61] While Luther's third thesis stated that penance ought not only to be inward, nonetheless, the objective of the theses as a whole was to criticize the external penance that was exhibited in the apparently problematic indulgence system, which was always linked to the sacrament of penance.[62] It seemed that doing penance had become estranged from an interior attitude of repentance.

From that time forward, penance—especially sacramental penance—became one of the most contentious topics of the early modern period, calling into question the regulation of conventionally agreed-upon acts of external penance such as prayer, almsgiving, and fasting as well as penitential acts of popular piety such as pilgrimages. Ronald Rittgers argues that Luther's reformation of the late medieval penitential system was linked to the development of a new understanding of suffering in the life of the Christian. The trajectory of Luther's attack was to emphasize the internal nature of penance connected to the consolation of the penitent, in contrast to the external actions that addressed the temporal penalty or punishment for sin. Catholics in this time period (and later) were told that their sufferings on earth, both voluntary and involuntary, could be applied as a credit against the temporal penalties of their sins. Those who embraced daily sufferings and took upon themselves voluntary penance were acknowledging that sin had consequences and that

---

61. Martin Luther, "The Ninety-Five Theses on the Power and Efficacy of Indulgences" [1517], in *Works of Martin Luther*, trans. Adolph Spaeth, L. D. Reed, and Henry Eyster Jacobs (Philadelphia: Holman, 1915), 1:29, electronically developed by Mobile Reference, accessed at Google Books, January 20, 2012.

62. On reading the Protestant reformers' criticisms of penance and indulgences within the context of Thomas's discussion and traditional Catholic theology and seeing the reformers' criticisms of penance and indulgences as compatible with traditional Catholic theology, see Michael Root, "Aquinas, Merit, and Reformation Theology after the Joint Declaration on the Doctrine of Justification," *Modern Theology* 20 (2004): 5–22; David Steinmetz, *Calvin in Context* (Oxford: Oxford University Press, 1995), 117–18; Heiko A. Oberman, *The Reformation: Roots and Ramifications* (New York: T. and T. Clark, 1994), 176; Joseph Wawrykow, "John Calvin and Condign Merit," *Archiv für Reformationsgeschichte* 83 (1992): 73–90; and Oberman, *The Dawn of the Reformation: Essays in Late Medieval and Early Reformation Thought* (Grand Rapids, Mich.: Eerdmans, 1986), 215–38.

Sin and Penance

they or others deserved the punishment due to sin. This willingness to suffer on earth could benefit them or others after death; hence they were instructed to ask their confessors to apply their daily sufferings as penance to reduce their time in purgatory.[63]

Related to this was the system of indulgences, which had roots in Judaism and for Christians was initially connected to the canonical penitential system; indulgences matched the penances that were assigned for a particular sin. If someone were granted a seven-year indulgence by going on a pilgrimage, this would be the equivalent of performing a seven-year penitential fast, which was necessary to remit a mortal sin.[64] The practice of indulgences could assist the person in completing a difficult assigned penance.[65] Such a practice of indulgence began in the early eleventh century, but the roots of indulgences were much earlier. The biblical scholar Gary Anderson provides an excellent account of the practice of almsgiving described in the Old Testament as penance for a person's sins or even for others' sins.[66] More specifically Christian roots can be found in the practice of commutations and redemptions, which were part of the penitential system from at least the sixth century. Commutations allowed for one penance to be exchanged for another—for instance, fasting exchanged for prayers. Redemptions were commutations into the payment of alms. Directions for commutations were found in the penitential handbooks, such as that of Regino of Prüm; here one week's fasting on bread and water was equivalent to singing three hundred psalms while kneeling. Commutations were intended only for those penitents unable to fulfill the ordinarily prescribed penance, and they were not supposed to be easier.[67]

"Absolutions," or special prayers said by the priests, were another way of assisting penitents, and these actually lightened the penance. Absolutions might be granted to those performing a particular service to the

---

63. Ronald K. Rittgers, "Embracing the 'True Relic' of Christ: Suffering, Penance, and Private Confession in the Thought of Martin Luther," in *A New History of Penance*, ed. Abigail Firey (Leiden: Brill, 2008), 380.

64. Tentler, *Sin and Confession*, 328.

65. Ibid., 329.

66. Anderson, *Charity: The Place of the Poor in the Biblical Tradition* (New Haven: Yale University Press, 2013).

67. Ane Bysted, *The Crusade Indulgence: Spiritual Rewards and the Theology of the Crusades, c. 1095–1216* (Leiden: Brill, 2015), 75–76.

church or to those who had made payment of a certain amount of alms. Commutations, redemptions, and absolutions were the precursor to the formal practice of indulgence. The similarities among these practices can make it difficult to identify them as such in a particular case during the eleventh century, but most scholars agree that the first church-sanctioned indulgence was granted in 1035.[68] An indulgence was granted for a specific purpose, such as the building of a church. Unlike absolutions, indulgences remitted a specified measure of penance. Unlike commutations, indulgences were not simply for a pious work that substituted for an individual's penance, but rather were granted for a cause that would benefit the church as a community.[69] In 1343, Pope Clement VI affirmed the practice of indulgences in the papal bull *Unigenitus*: "For not with corruptible things, with silver and gold, did he redeem us, but with the precious blood of himself.... Now this treasure is not hidden ... but he entrusted it to be healthfully dispensed—through blessed Peter, bearer of heaven's keys, and his successors as vicars on earth—to the faithful, for fitting and reasonable causes, now for total, now for partial remission of punishment due for temporal punishment of sins, as well generally as specially (as they should understand it to be expedient with God), and to be applied to them that are truly penitent and have confessed."[70]

In itself, such an understanding was not necessarily problematic. However, the abuse of this practice by Luther's time was found in some bishops' acquisitive selling of indulgences billed as having the same effect as embracing daily suffering and voluntary penance. Luther's denial of these indulgences soon became a refutation of the idea that divine punishment could have a redemptive purpose. Instead, Luther regarded divine punishment simply as a summons to faith that people should not circumvent; suffering should be embraced not because it atoned for sin but because it enabled the person to become Christ-like and to grow in the trust of God's promise of salvation.[71] This highlights Luther's overall minimization of human effort in God's salvific plan and indicates how it would have undermined acts of penance.

68. Ibid., 77–78.
69. Ibid., 79.
70. Clement VI, *Unigenitus*, in *Documents of the Christian Church*, ed. Henry Bettenson and Chris Maunder (New York: Oxford University Press, 2011), 194–95.
71. Rittgers, "Embracing the 'True Relic' of Christ," 385–86.

Sin and Penance

Tentler states that Luther "must take primary responsibility for the situation in modern Christianity that allows a theologian to assert, by way of definition, 'a Protestant doesn't confess.'"[72] Luther and the other reformers saw confession as torment rather than consolation; indeed, it seems this was Luther's own experience. Luther undermined the necessity of confessing to a priest, arguing that the authority to forgive rested in the Word, not an ordained priest; in practice, however, clerical absolution early on became normative in Lutheranism.[73] Luther believed that reflection on past sins detracted from the focus on the new life ahead, and he rejected Lateran IV's mandate of annual confession, arguing that instead it must always be the freely willed choice of the penitent who desires the consolation of absolution. Luther also rejected examinations of conscience, replacing them instead with examinations of faith based on knowledge of the Lutheran catechism. In some sense, Luther was a contritionist, believing that forgiveness from God came with interior sorrow for sins, but he only promoted passive contrition. The penitent need not *do* anything to express contrition, but rather simply believe in the promise of forgiveness, and that in itself was forgiveness.[74] According to Tentler, Luther thought that those who mistakenly believed themselves to be pure as a result of sacramental confession were actually defiled by their belief in the sacrament of penance; what purified for Luther was faith, rather than the sacrament of penance. Related to this was the conviction that consolation came from faith rather than the person's acts (i.e., works) associated with the sacramental confession.[75]

In the face of this and other criticisms by the reformers, the Catholic Church sought to reaffirm its teaching on penance in the Council of Trent and to re-evangelize its members about the sacrament. Trent reaffirmed the list of the seven sacraments that had been recognized in the church since at least the twelfth century, when Peter Lombard enumer-

---

72. Tentler, *Sin and Confession*, 350; see also Favazza, *Order of Penitents*, 10–11, on this topic.
73. Rittgers, "Embracing the 'True Relic' of Christ," 392.
74. Tentler, *Sin and Confession*, 352–53.
75. Ibid., 358 and 361. Tentler says further, "For the Reformers, destruction of sacramental confession was an essential *means* to all of their goals. The leaders of the Counter-Reformation, on the other hand, reaffirmed sacramental confession with fervent devotion because they saw in its preservation a necessary condition of survival for the whole ecclesiastical order." Tentler cites Ignatius of Loyola and Bartolome de Las Casas as figures of the time who had powerful experiences of the sacrament; see Tentler, *Sin and Confession*, 367–69.

ated the sacraments in the fourth book of his *Sentences*.[76] Trent relied upon the Thomistic understanding that there were three acts required of the penitent to form what it named the quasi-matter of the sacrament: contrition, confession, and satisfaction.[77] The acts of the penitent "are required ... for the integrity of the sacrament, and for the full and complete forgiveness of sins."[78] Likewise, the Council of Trent stated that the form of the sacrament is expressed in the words of the minister when he says, "I absolve you."[79] Trent also noted that the faithful are able to make satisfaction in several ways: penances voluntarily undertaken; those imposed by the priest in the sacrament; and those by temporal afflictions imposed by God and borne with patience.[80] Trent therefore reaffirmed the value of both sacramental and nonsacramental acts of penance.

According to historian Robert Bireley, both the Catholic Reform and Protestant Reformation sought to deepen religious belief through knowledge and practice of the faith, and the Catholic Reform begun at Trent "was undoubtedly successful" by the early eighteenth century.[81] By the early seventeenth century, the devout generally practiced monthly, or at least quarterly, confession and reception of communion. Lateran IV's mandate for annual confession and communion was by that time universally observed, fostered by the church or government requirement that parishioners receive a certificate indicating that they had fulfilled this obligation.[82] Bireley states that "piety became more personal while retaining its communal character," and he cites the increased knowledge of the catechism and basic prayers, as well as more regular reception of the

---

76. Rosemann, *Peter Lombard*, 146–47.

77. Session 14, Council of Trent, Canon 4, in *Decrees of the Ecumenical Councils*, vol. 2, *Trent–Vatican II*, ed. Norman P. Tanner, SJ (Washington, D.C.: Georgetown University Press, 1990), 712.

78. Session 14, Council of Trent, chap. 3, "On the Parts and Fruit of This Sacrament," in Tanner, *Decrees of the Ecumenical Councils*, 2:704.

79. Ibid.

80. Session 14, Council of Trent, chap. 9 "On the Works of Satisfaction," in Tanner, *Decrees of the Ecumenical Councils*, 2:709.

81. Robert Bireley, *The Refashioning of Catholicism, 1450–1700* (Washington, D.C.: The Catholic University of America Press, 1999), 96.

82. Bireley, *Refashioning*, 105. Bireley does not specify what percentage of the population counted as "devout," but he does give the sense that the practice of Catholicism at this time was vibrant among most of the population.

Sin and Penance

sacraments of confession and Eucharist, the necessity of which had been restated by the Council of Trent.[83]

Anonymous confession with the person kneeling behind a screen with the confessor on the other side was common during the Middle Ages.[84] Charles Borromeo of Milan popularized the more deliberate arrangement of using a confessional following Trent, and this gradually spread across Europe, making confession both more private and more individual. The confessional structure also provided greater opportunity for conversation between penitent and confessor, serving as a forum for spiritual direction. Confession manuals became popular for assisting both the confessor and the penitent. According to Bireley, the greater frequency of confession brought the faithful into more regular contact with clergy, hence increasing the role of the clergy.[85] In addition to the increased popularity of the sacrament of penance, Catholics continued to engage in other penitential practices. Pilgrimages, for example, remained a common way of performing penance, as well as expressing thanks or seeking favors from God through the intercession of a specific saint. Hence there were various churches popular as pilgrimage destinations throughout Europe.[86]

In the midst of European confessionalization—the identification of a people with a particular form of Christian belief—certain aspects of the Catholic faith became important ways of identifying Catholics as different from Protestants. Bireley names several examples of this. Belief in the real presence in the Eucharist was one; this led to renewed vigor in the practice of Corpus Christi processions.[87] Belief in purgatory was another, and this was expressed in a commitment to having masses said for the dead.[88] In this context of confessionalization, sacramental confession and other

---

83. Ibid., 96, 50.

84. James F. White, "The Spatial Setting," in *Oxford History of Christian Worship*, ed. Geoffrey Wainright and Karen B. Vesterfield Tucker (New York: Oxford University Press, 2006), 813.

85. Bireley, *Refashioning*, 105. For more on Borromeo's project of promoting penance, see Wieste De Boer, *The Conquest of the Soul: Confession, Discipline, and Public Order in Counter-Reformation Milan* (Leiden: Brill, 2001).

86. Bireley, *Refashioning*, 110. Bireley notes that governmental leaders were eager to bring order to society and willing to apply Protestant or Catholic practices if they helped. Hence at times regions were re-catholicized; the imposition of specifically Catholic practices communicated that change to a region.

87. Ibid., 108.

88. Ibid., 114.

acts of penance also served as crucial identity markers for Catholics living among the new Christian pluralism of Europe. Despite the flaws in practice and ensuing controversy surrounding penance at the time of Luther, the longstanding conviction as to the need to acknowledge one's sins and to atone for them continued to be a feature of Catholic practice in the early modern period.

Sin and Confession in North America

The greater part of this work concerns penance among Catholics in the United States in the 1960s. Hence we turn now to considering sin and penance as they came from Europe to a different continent. Genealogically speaking, there were at least two beginnings of Catholicism in the land that was to become the United States of America. The first occurred when Catholicism came to North America through Spanish missionaries, who worked primarily in what would become Florida and California. As Roberto Goizueta notes, these missionaries brought with them the fifteenth-century Catholicism that had not been touched by the concerns of the Protestant Reformation or the reforms initiated by the Council of Trent.[89] By contrast, the colonial Catholicism of the seventeenth century, transplanted from England to Maryland in particular, was post-Reformation and thus essentially modern.[90] The Spanish saw themselves as cultural and religious missionaries to the native peoples, whereas the much later English Catholics such as the lords Baltimore had hoped to exist peacefully alongside Protestants, only to find themselves as a persecuted minority.[91]

Yet one commonality of these two beginnings of Catholicism was that both the Spanish missions of the fifteenth century and the English Catholics of the seventeenth century were largely priestless. Historian Patrick Carey states, "For almost three hundred years, Catholicism on the northern frontiers of the Spanish empire was much like a preparatory school

---

89. Roberto Goizueta, "The Symbolic Realism of U.S. Latino/a Popular Catholicism," *Theological Studies* 65 (2004): 258–60.

90. Goizueta attributes this use of "modern" to historian John O'Malley; ibid., 260.

91. Patrick W. Carey, *Catholics in America: A History* (1993; repr. New York: Sheed and Ward, 2004), 3–4; John Tracy Ellis, *American Catholicism*, 2nd ed. (1956; repr. Chicago: University of Chicago Press, 1969), 22–28.

Sin and Penance

that had no available higher education."⁹² Though the Spanish missions were temporarily successful, they failed to develop churches with native dioceses, bishops, parish priests, and all the sacramental and educational means necessary for sustaining a Christian community.⁹³ With the lack of native institutional strength in the church, the success of the Spanish missions was inextricably tied to the success of Spain itself, which soon found itself in financial difficulty and hence open to the attacks of Anglo-American military forces.⁹⁴ The remaining Catholics in these areas—whether converted natives or Spaniards—ultimately needed to sustain the faith without regular access to the sacraments of Eucharist and penance.

Likewise, the North American Catholics of the seventeenth and eighteenth centuries had very little contact with priests, in part due to the official establishment of various Protestant denominations in the original colonies and related persecution faced by Catholics.⁹⁵ In Maryland in 1780, for example, there were almost sixteen thousand Catholics, but only nineteen priests; in Pennsylvania, seven thousand Catholics and five priests; in New York City, fifteen hundred Catholics and no priests.⁹⁶ Catholic priests often ministered as circuit preachers, traveling from town to town celebrating Mass, baptizing children, and hearing confessions.⁹⁷ These largely priestless Catholic communities in the Northeast sought to maintain traditional Catholic penitential practices with some modifications. For example, instead of refraining from meat during all of Lent, in 1790 the Holy See allowed them to take meat on five of six Sundays of Lent, although they continued to follow the rule of fasting, which allowed only one full meal and two smaller collations, less than a meal, for every day of Lent.⁹⁸ Without the regular presence of priests and access to the sacrament of penance, the laity turned to examinations of conscience and contrition, a form of "spiritual confession," that served as an alternative when they were unable to confess to a priest. This practice of spiritual confession also prepared them to receive the sacrament whenever a priest did arrive in their locale.⁹⁹

92. Carey, *Catholics in America*, 4.
93. Ibid., 4.
94. Ibid., 5–6.
95. Ellis, *American Catholicism*, 1–40.
96. O'Toole, *The Faithful: A History of Catholics in America* (Cambridge, Mass.: Harvard University Press, 2008), 13.
97. Ibid., 15.
98. Ibid., 23.
99. Ibid., 31; see also O'Toole, "In the Court of Conscience, 132.

By the mid-nineteenth century, the greater presence of priests and the promotion of frequent confession in the United States had a noticeable effect, especially in cities that teemed with Catholics and now clergy available to hear confessions. The 1852 Plenary Council in Baltimore established a requirement for confessionals in a public and conspicuous place in churches. By the end of the nineteenth century, the sacrament was quite popular, especially in urban areas with large Catholic populations. The seven priests of St. Ignatius Loyola Church in Manhattan, for example, heard a total of approximately 78,000 confessions from July 1896 to June 1897.[100] This popularity continued into the twentieth century, up to the time period that is the subject of this book, and hence will be discussed in the following chapters in greater detail. At this point, it is enough to note that Catholicism in the United States maintained penitential practices as much as these were possible, including partaking of the sacrament of penance and continuing to observe the penitential practices of Europe, such as fasting and abstinence from meat on certain days.

100. O'Toole, "In the Court of Conscience," 133. O'Toole gives statistics from various parishes illustrating his claim that the sacrament of penance was popular, especially in urban Catholic communities. This topic will be discussed more fully in chapter 4.

2 From Actual and Personal to Relative and General

The Change in Lay Catholics' Conception of Sin

American Catholics who regularly participated in the penitential practices of their faith had been raised with a strong awareness of sin, and their conception of sin is beneficial for evaluating both sacramental and nonsacramental penance.[1] The concept of sin at the popular level during the mid-twentieth century in the United States can be described as a move from specific to general and from objective to subjective; sin had been used in the first half of the twentieth century to identify actual personal sin—that is, particular, discrete, confessable actions. As the 1960s progressed, however, sin understood as personal and actual lost its footing and became less important than it had been in the past. Sin had once

---

1. Much of the content of this chapter and an abridged version of the following chapter were published in Maria C. Morrow, "The Change in the Conception of Sin among Catholics in the United States, 1955–1975," *American Catholic Studies* 122, no. 1 (Spring 2011): 55–76. The article is used with permission.

been clearly defined and seemed tangible. More than an interior feeling, sin was seen as an exterior concrete reality that had identifiable effects on the individual and the community it ruptured. Sin was regarded as contrary to eternal law, and Catholics believed that sin was removed in the sacrament of confession. Sin was real, and its solution was located; the discrete actions of actual sin were addressed in the confessional. Failing to acknowledge and address sin had serious consequences, including eternal damnation.

Yet during the middle decades of the twentieth century sin became a much more elusive concept. Not only had the perception of the list of sins gradually changed for mid-century Americans, particularly in regard to matters of sex, but the very idea of sin itself seemed to have little grounding or meaning as something that might correspond to an eternal law. The former concept of sin as described by the *Baltimore Catechism* and memorized by generations of American Catholics in the nineteenth century and the first half of the twentieth century made little sense in the face of numerous changes in the lives of a new generation of Catholics. Though not generally denying sin as such, younger Catholics were less likely to know the *Baltimore Catechism*'s definition and less likely to agree with the church on the list of sins.

This decline in the sense of sin's reality among Catholics corresponded to a general decline of the concept of sin among Americans. In 1973, Dr. Karl Menninger attested to the near-disappearance of sin with the blunt title of his book *Whatever Became of Sin?* There Menninger wrote:

The very word "sin," which seems to have disappeared, was a proud word. It was once a strong word, an ominous and serious word. It described a central point in every civilized human being's life plan and life style. But the word went away. It has almost disappeared—the word, along with the notion. Why? Doesn't anyone sin anymore? Doesn't anyone believe in sin?[2]

Menninger's cultural observations about sin were apparently relevant enough to be published popularly, which is interesting because he was not a theologian or pastor, but rather a well-known psychiatrist, whose

---

2. Karl Menninger, *Whatever Became of Sin?* (New York: Hawthorn, 1973), 14. Menninger's frame of reference was primarily Western Christianity and Judaism.

From Personal to General

Calvinist background was not mentioned in the book.³ And, from a historical point of view, the question remains interesting today: what did become of sin in the United States? And in particular, what became of sin among Catholics in the United States?

By the 1950s, John Tracy Ellis described Catholicism in the United States as having matured; the church had "come of age" and reached "adulthood" as an American institution.⁴ At last the church seemed stable and prosperous. The 1960s, however, were eventful for Americans, particularly for Catholics. In addition to the political and social turmoil in their homeland, American Catholics also lived through important church events, most especially the Second Vatican Council and the liturgical changes that followed it, as well as the promulgation of Paul VI's encyclical *Humanae vitae*. Perhaps even more important was the dissolution of the Catholic subculture, coupled with the upward mobility of many American Catholics. These crucial socioeconomic changes conditioned the American reception of the significant ecclesiastical and political events.

This chapter contextualizes the change in the concept of sin among Catholics in the United States in regard to four key contributing factors. The first is the dissolution of the Catholic subculture that occurred as many American Catholics left their close-knit urban communities for more religiously diverse suburbs. Although Catholics continued to constitute the majority of the working class, greater assimilation to the larger American culture challenged traditional Catholic understandings on such matters as sin. Second, the rise of counseling and psychology brought reconsideration of the notion of personal actual sin by proposing other ways to address and solve people's problems. Third, the shifting notions of sexuality and sexual sins brought a reassessment of what acts in which circumstances constituted sin. Last, the newfound partiality to the concept of freedom, which Philip Gleason names the "contagion of liberty," accelerated the change in the understanding of sin. In partic-

---

3. Calvin's name is included in a footnote wherein Menninger states that theologians regard the sin of sensuality as second to the sin of pride: "Augustine, Luther, Pascal, Aquinas, Calvin, and others are in general agreement about this. Niebuhr says the ways in which other sins are derived from pride is seen differently by different theologians"; Menninger, *Whatever Became of Sin?*, 135n3.

4. Ellis, *American Catholicism*, 124. Notably, his post–Vatican II addendum indicated that the coming of age was short-lived; see especially 164–66.

ular, college-aged Catholics' view of freedom complicated and even undermined the traditional Catholic understanding of sin while allocating primary importance to conscience. In conjunction with this I will discuss how laity sought to move from fear to love in a Catholicism that often felt too rigid. With so many factors contributing to their experience of Catholicism, some laity responded to external constraints by looking for independence from church authority structures in their personal decisions and in lay organizations.

From Ghetto to World: Vatican II and Dissolution of U.S. Catholic Subculture

Historian Patrick Carey notes that, "between 1945 and 1965, American Catholicism experienced a phenomenal growth, one significantly unmatched during the previous twenty years and one not repeated in the post-1965 period."[5] Like their compatriots, American Catholics' participation in religious activities increased, indicating a revival of piety.[6] Moreover, Catholics felt at home in the United States and had a spirit of confidence and optimism that Jay Dolan identifies as "Catholic boosterism."[7]

The European immigrant Catholics of the nineteenth and early twentieth centuries had worked hard to make a home in the United States. By the 1940s, their dedication and efforts had resulted in the construction of a Catholic subculture involving parishes, schools, hospitals, and other organizations, and this shared religious culture protected them to some extent from the religious pluralism of the United States.[8] Particularly in the East, but elsewhere as well, Catholics lived in close-knit urban communities that both fostered and depended upon various Catholic institutions and organizations. William Portier observes that Catholics throughout the Unites States "learned similar practices of teaching and

---

5. Carey, *Catholics in America*, 93.
6. Ibid., 101.
7. Jay P. Dolan, *The American Catholic Experience* (Notre Dame: University of Notre Dame Press, 1985), 362.
8. William L. Portier, "Here Come the Evangelical Catholics," *Communio* 31 (Spring 2004): 45.

From Personal to General

praying that added to their demographic distinctiveness."[9] Despite a difference in devotions according to region or nationality, Catholics knew many of the same prayers—for example, the Our Father, Hail Mary, and Glory Be, which combined to make up what was traditionally known as a "station" and which also featured in the familiar prayer of the Rosary. The Mass, meanwhile, provided a common experience for Catholics who regularly fulfilled their Sunday Mass obligation.

Much of Catholic beliefs and practices had been simply taken for granted in a subculture created by the hardworking Catholic immigrants responsible for making America into a home for their families. The structures, organizations, and practices present in the subculture contributed to a robust Catholic environment. Whether the communion of saints, the real presence in the Eucharist, novenas, frequent confession, First Friday devotions, Mass, or even parish events such as fish fries, Catholics knew and lived their Catholicism in a setting where the mix of ethnic and religious ways of life were seen as normal; social structures were in place to support their Catholic life. In such a location, they were unlikely to entertain skepticism or to interrogate and criticize the dogmas, doctrines, and practices ingrained in them as children. Moreover, the criticism and questions of America's Protestants were regarded as, and, indeed, often explicitly experienced as, attacks on Catholicism. Rather than undermining Catholic practices and beliefs, these attacks often acted to strengthen the Catholic community, making the faithful more committed to all that made them distinct and making them feel comforted by the Catholicism that surrounded them. While this reinforced and maintained the Catholic subculture, it also left Catholics unprepared for navigating their later immersion into religious pluralism.

The *Baltimore Catechism* was an important instrument in the formation and training of Catholic children. Originally compiled in 1885 following a decision of the bishops at the Third Plenary Council of Baltimore, this "staple of the Catholic Sunday school and of children's religious instruction in general" featured a question-and-answer format, which was accompanied in the classroom by the memorization of scholastic terminology.[10] In its 1941 revised form edited by Francis J. Con-

9. Ibid., 45.
10. Dolan, *American Catholic Experience*, 391.

nell, CSsR, the *Baltimore Catechism* remained the dominant catechetical tool in the United States until Vatican II.[11] Given its widespread national prominence, the definition of sin therein represents the commonly known Catholic conception of sin during this time period.

Sin was one among the many Catholic concepts taken for granted in the pre–Vatican II world. An unquestioned reality for Catholics of the 1950s and 1960s, the traditional notion of sin coming from Augustine and Thomas was described to children by one version of the *Baltimore Catechism*:

> [Actual sin] is a sin which we actually commit *ourselves*. Actual sin is any *willful thought, desire, word, action or omission* which God forbids us to do. Actual sins may be *mortal* or *venial*. Mortal sin is the worse of the two, because it is a *grievous* offense against the law of God. Moreover, it takes away grace in our souls. *Venial* sin is not as big a sin as mortal sin. But God hates it also.[12]

Both children and adults were taught to be constantly on guard, vigilant for the occasion of sin.

Moreover, there were structures and practices in place to deal with sin, most notably the sacrament of confession. Frequent examinations of conscience helped Catholics to determine their sins, and the regular confession of sin was a part of Catholic life at this time. Novenas such as the Sorrowful Mother novena with its focus on sorrow nurtured a sense of guilt and compunction for that sin in the context of the difficulties of the early twentieth century, such as World War I and the Great Depression.[13] Priests reinforced the danger of sin, especially mortal sin, by enumerating various acts that could be in the category of mortal sin so the laity would have a clear list of sins. The importance of determining whether a sin was mortal or venial was at the forefront of the sinner's mind, and the knowledge of the reality of sin as matter convinced the Catholic of the importance of sacramental forgiveness, which was just as real as sin. Sin was a grounded concept because it was addressed in a specific location—namely, the confessional—and it was, furthermore, a concept shared by

---

11. Richard P. McBrien, ed., *The HarperCollins Encyclopedia of Catholicism* (New York: HarperCollins, 1995), 131.

12. Michael A. McGuire, *Father McGuire's The New Baltimore Catechism and Mass No. 1* (Cincinnati: Benziger Brothers, 1942), 25; emphases in the original.

13. Dolan, *American Catholic Experience*, 385.

From Personal to General

an entire Catholic culture. Socially constituted penitential practices such as the Friday meat abstinence and Lenten fasting, as well as the constantly promoted attitude of bearing patiently the ills of life by not complaining in the midst of suffering, further indicated a conviction in the pervasive and ongoing effects of sin in the life of every Catholic. These effects of sin necessitated ongoing penance—both penances chosen and those received by the vagaries of life. The embracing of penance also provided an embodied way of interpreting everyday sufferings.

Writing in 1966, Fr. John Reedy and James Andrews described the former distinctiveness of the American Catholic in this way:

He felt quite secure in his knowledge of how he stood with God at each moment of his life. Although he recognized that he couldn't be absolutely certain, still he felt he could discern for practical purposes, whether he was living in God's friendship ... or was cut off from that love by sin. He felt reasonably sure that he could determine, by the moral standards of his religion, whether his soul would be saved or lost if his life were to end at this moment.

Much of this security came from his specific, detailed knowledge of sin. From his first-grade catechism through his college religion textbooks, his understanding of complex, subtle patterns of sin deepened like an attorney's understanding of criminal law.

He learned about grave and light matter, about free and necessary occasions of sin, about the natural law, the divine positive law and the ecclesiastical law. He learned about invincible ignorance, the mitigating effects of powerful emotions, and especially about all the fascinating applications of the principle of double effect.[14]

Reedy and Andrews noted the practicality for this knowledge of sin, given the influence of the confessional. Though most Catholics have great respect for the sacrament, they "find the confessional itself naturally unpleasant," simply due to the dislike for confessing faults. Pedagogical instruction for the confessional, then, was aimed at helping the penitent to make a "good, efficient confession, with the minimum of embarrassment and confusion."[15] The authors recognized that Catholics were

---

14. John L. Reedy, CSC, and James F. Andrews, "Morality: A Concern for the Person," in the "Perplexed Catholic" series, *Ave Maria*, November 19, 1966, 16. My thanks to Thomas Grady for his exceptional hospitality at Ave Maria Press.

15. Ibid., 16.

becoming more confused as to the presence and gravity of sin in their own lives; the American Catholic distinctiveness in relation to the understanding of sin, previously described, weakened.

Transformations in Catholic communities occurred mid-century as the largely working-class population extended into other classes. Many of these Catholics left their cohesive urban parish communities for more religiously diverse suburbs, which did not assume or sustain beliefs and practices such as sin and confession as had their Catholic parish neighborhoods.[16] In the words of historian John McGreevy,

> The strength of the Catholic subculture ... concealed a historic transformation in the various Catholic communities. In retrospect, the end of mass immigration in the 1920s and the lack of economic mobility (at least upward) during the Depression imposed a false sense of stasis on Catholic life; a notion that the sense of order imposed on heavily Catholic, urban neighborhoods by priests, nuns, and politicians would endure indefinitely.[17]

McGreevy explains that following the war, much of the distinctiveness of the early twentieth-century experience of Catholics, which had seemed almost permanent, in fact "faded into the larger American kaleidoscope."[18] Joseph Chinnici and Angelyn Dries corroborate this when they state that "Catholics' collective identity appeared shattered."[19]

This description finds affirmation in the first published book of sociologist Andrew Greeley, who in 1959 observed the change as follows:

> For in the suburb the Catholic is regarded, at last, as a full-fledged American. The ghetto walls are crumbling. The old national parishes are breaking up. The Catholic suburbanite rides the same commuter train, wears the same brand of suit, reads the same paper, and does the same kind of work as does his non-

---

16. John T. McGreevy, *Parish Boundaries: The Catholic Encounter with Race in the Twentieth-Century Urban North* (Chicago: University of Chicago Press, 1996), 79. It is also important to note, however, that Catholics continued to constitute a large percentage of the working class, especially given the new Spanish-speaking immigrant population, including especially Mexicans and Puerto Ricans; see Dolan, *American Catholic Experience*, 362.

17. McGreevy, *Parish Boundaries*, 79. This raises the question of the role of the laity played in the decline of the sacrament, which is discussed in more detail in chapter 4.

18. Ibid., 80.

19. Joseph P. Chinnici, OFM, and Angelyn Dries, eds., *Prayer and Practice in the American Catholic Community: Original Documents From More Than 200 Years of Catholic History* (Maryknoll, N.Y.: Orbis, 2000), 182.

From Personal to General

Catholic neighbor. He may not be completely accepted by Protestants; but he is well on his way.[20]

It is difficult to pinpoint a date for any gradual, multivalent cultural transformation such as that described by Greeley; hence it is not easy to identify the end of the predominance of Catholic subculture. But by the end of the 1960s, "the demographic differences between Catholics and other Americans became statistically negligible."[21] This dissolution of Catholic subculture, in many cases a geographic diaspora in suburbia, as well, was a change that immersed Catholics in American religious voluntarism; the new configurations of suburban housing did not integrate the parish as had urban Catholic communities. Belonging to the local Catholic parish (or a particular ethnic Catholic parish) was no longer a foregone conclusion in these religiously diverse settings. The traditional Catholic beliefs and practices became isolated from the Catholic communities in which they had been rooted, and in the transplant they seemed to lose some of the meaning that they had in the original context. In the words of Joseph Chinnici, "The Catholic community experienced the tremendous mutations in their public conception of themselves and their relationship to American society."[22]

The changing demographics of the Catholic population were complex, and they cannot be identified as simply positive or negative in nature. On the one hand, Catholicism of the postwar decades in the United States seemed to be at a zenith with the people's increased involvement in the church and sense of belonging in the country. Catholics' expansion to the suburbs seemed a positive indication of growth; McGreevy notes that across the country four parishes were built each week in the early 1950s. On the other hand, it was a somewhat different sort of Catholicism as it moved away from urban centers. Parish communities had to start from scratch, and there was not as much generational diversity or ethnic Catholic culture. McGreevy observes that "parking lots replaced processions, and upwardly mobile parents demanded schools even be-

20. Greeley, *The Church and the Suburbs* (New York: Sheed and Ward, 1959), 56.
21. Portier, "Here Come the Evangelical Catholics," 46.
22. Chinnici, "Changing Religious Practice and the End of Christendom in the United States 1965–1986," *U.S. Catholic Historian* 23, no. 4 (Fall 2005): 75.

From Personal to General

fore the church building itself."[23] Moreover, what had at times been comforting and felt supportive in the city could now seem rigid or even restrictive in this new environment.[24]

Greeley dramatically expressed one of his concerns for Catholicism transplanted to the suburbs when he criticized what he regarded as the dangerous materialism in the suburbs: "Wherever he lives and whatever his home is like, there is one thing that characterizes the life of the suburbanite—material abundance. It is prosperity that made the post-war suburbs possible, and it is the promise of further prosperity that keeps them going and furnishes the vision of an ever better life for the suburbanite."[25] How might this comfort and materialism affect Catholicism?, wondered Greeley: "In the midst of plenty, does not prayer become extremely difficult, if not impossible? Does mortification have any meaning to people who have never known material want? ... Can man, when he has so many things in this world, seriously long for the next?"[26]

Although perhaps overly dramatic, Greeley's book implied the rewards granted to those who had endured the struggles of the past, and it also reflected his understanding that many Catholics had finally realized the American dream of financial stability and success. They had hoped their hard work would pay off in the end, bringing them greater financial and social stability. Now that they had achieved this dream, they were not eager to take on hardships or to forfeit the results of this hard work, which they wanted to hand on to their children. Carey suggests that these Catholics were influenced by "spiritual bankruptcy of bourgeois-mindedness." Only a few Catholics protested what they saw as the superficial consumer culture or objected to the lifestyles of the many people who had separated their religious principles and values from everyday life in their capitulation to consumer culture.[27]

At the heart of Greeley's concerns was the idea that Catholics were

23. McGreevy, *Parish Boundaries*, 84.
24. See, for example, Robert A. Orsi's description in chap. 3, "Imagining Women," in *Thank You, St. Jude: Women's Devotion to the Patron Saint of Hopeless Causes* (New Haven: Yale University Press, 1996), 70–94.
25. Greeley, *Church and the Suburbs*, 33.
26. Ibid., 149. It is not clear how Greeley's book was received, though it was republished at least once, in 1963. Regardless of its reception, however, the book does not seem to have dissuaded Catholics from continuing to enter suburban life during the 1960s.
27. Carey, *Catholics in America*, 103.

From Personal to General

losing sight of their supernatural end—that is, beatitude in God. Whereas adversity could foster yearning for God and eternal rest, material comfort might breed complacency and contentment with the natural ends celebrated by the ethos of the American dream of success and prosperity. The ultimate end of hard work on earth from the Catholic perspective was supposed to be heaven, not social mobility or financial stability. Of course, poverty had its own crushing effects, and so adversity did not guarantee sanctity, nor did suburbanite life doom one to hell. The concern was simply that Catholics in the United States were failing to recognize material abundance as a potential handicap for the spiritual life and instead were seeking these natural ends to the detriment of their supernatural end. In both the case of severe poverty and great affluence, more focus can be turned to the comforts of temporal life on earth rather than eternal life in heaven.

In the midst of the upward mobility of many Euro-American Catholics, Vatican II, which began in 1962, was, in Carey's words, "another major symbol in the age of Catholic confidence and transition."[28] Just as Catholics in the United States had finally caught up to and even improved upon America, so now the church was catching up to and improving upon the world. And the dissolution of Catholic subculture in the United States was the context in which Vatican II was received and interpreted.[29] Although there is debate as to whether the Second Vatican Council represents historical continuity or rupture, in the United States the faithful experienced it as a time of abrupt changes in longstanding traditions, especially those of a liturgical nature.[30] Peter Steinfels suggests that such conciliar changes "accelerated the Catholic population's cultural assimilation and the erosion of a distinctly Catholic subculture and its supportive institutions."[31]

And, of course, in addition to this important ecclesiastical event,

---

28. Ibid., 111.
29. Portier, "Here Come the Evangelical Catholics," 47.
30. See Massa, *American Catholic Revolution*, chap. 2, for a discussion regarding the liturgical changes as implemented in the United States. For two opposing perspectives on Vatican II, see David G. Schultenover, ed., *Vatican II: Did Anything Happen?* (New York: Continuum, 2007), and Matthew L. Lamb and Matthew Levering, eds., *Vatican II: Renewal Within Tradition* (Oxford: Oxford University Press, 2008).
31. Peter Steinfels, *A People Adrift: The Crisis of the Roman Catholic Church in America* (New York: Simon and Schuster, 2003), 32.

American Catholics also lived through the numerous American political events of the time period. The Catholic community experienced simultaneously social and religious reforms, and the corresponding transformation occurred during a time of great change in American cultural and political life.[32] During this tumultuous time for American Catholics, the clearly defined Catholic understanding of sin was weakened by the residential shifts and the church's new openness to pluralism and ecumenism. Dolan describes the tumult for Catholics during this time period:

> For the first time in modern history, Catholics no longer agreed on an answer to the question of what it meant to be Catholic. Vatican II was largely responsible for forcing Catholics to rethink the meaning of Catholicism in the modern world. In all likelihood, the church would have undergone a period of reform and renewal even if the Council had never taken place.... What the Council did was to unlock the gates and let the currents of reform burst forth with much greater force than would have been otherwise true. A church council not only sanctioned reform, it accelerated it.[33]

Despite the complex history of the church and the papacy, preconciliar American Catholics had been presented with an image of the church as the one stable, permanent institution in a world that was chaotic and constantly changing.[34] Now Catholics experienced twofold pluralism: great diversity within the American church in the midst of change, as well as an immersion in religiously pluralistic American society. And this was in addition to international and national political upheaval. The decline in the concept of sin must be understood within this context of immense changes for Catholics in the United States.

In what follows, we have three examples of how Catholics became more like their compatriots in ways that directly influenced their conception of sin and their identification of sin in their own lives. The next section observes Catholics' altered opinions regarding counseling and psychology. The section after that notes shifting beliefs concerning what constituted sexual sin. Both of these changes coincided with the demographic changes of Catholics in the United States; as Catholics became

32. Carey, *Catholics in America*, 114.
33. Dolan, *American Catholic Experience*, 428.
34. Carey, *Catholics in America*, 113; see also Massa, *American Catholic Revolution*, 8.

From Personal to General

more like other Americans, their distinctive understanding of sin declined. The final section discusses how what Philip Gleason identifies as the "contagion of liberty" resulted in a challenge not only to civil authorities but also to ecclesiastical authorities. No longer taking for granted long-held beliefs like the teaching of sin, the Vatican II generation questioned such beliefs and found that these teachings did not always resonate with them.

From Confessional to Couch: The Rise of Counseling and Psychology

In a 1966 broadcast, the radio and television superstar priest Fulton Sheen invited his viewers to consider the story of two couches. In the case of the first couch, the patient is on the couch, the patient is passive, merely answering questions, and, finally with this couch, "No guilt, no sin, no one ever does anything wrong. One may have a complex, but one has never committed a sin."[35] In contrast to this critique of the psychoanalytic method, Sheen presented a second couch: the couch on which Jesus reclined when he was approached by a woman who had a sense of sin and sorrow. No passive patient, this woman anointed Jesus' feet and sobbed in his presence; she was contrite and repentant. This woman came to the couch to have her sins forgiven; she did not come to have them explained away, as Sheen insinuated happens in the counseling sessions where the psychoanalytic method is employed.[36]

This segment of Sheen, as well as his earlier 1957 broadcast entitled "Psychology and Psychiatry," which includes a more extended explanation and critique of various psychologists, indicates that there was an early concern among Catholics for the effects that psychology and counseling were having on the concept of sin.[37] Sheen and other Catholics feared that the rise of counseling, particularly Freud's psychoanalytical

35. Fulton Sheen, "Psychoanalytic Couch," *The Fulton Sheen Program*, original broadcast 1966, http://www.youtube.com/watch?v=09c6rX3UQmo; accessed February 5, 2010.
36. Ibid.
37. Sheen, "Psychology and Psychiatry," *Life Is Worth Living*, original broadcast 1957; http://www.youtube.com/watch?v=ChF4P7PIx4I (part 1), http://www.youtube.com/watch?v=V4lAgxidT4w&feature=related (part 2), and http://www.youtube.com/watch?v=uYzYVr8xCTs&feature=related (part 3); accessed February 5, 2010.

method, explained away sin by attributing people's actions to the influences of their childhoods, thus removing the reality of culpability for sins. Writing in 1949, Sheen addressed Freud's "psychoanalytic doctrine of human nature" in the opening pages of his book *Peace of the Soul*:

> The most important feature of this doctrine is the belief that man's conscious mental life, his experiences, and his conduct are determined, not by what he knows, feels, or intends, but by forces largely hidden from his consciousness. His ego, or consciousness, is only the battlefield where an incessant war is fought between his biological, primitive urges and the powers embodied in the super-ego. These powers take the place of conscience; they originate, not in an awareness of a natural law and of man's obligation in the face of the divine law, but from social pressure, environmental influences brought to bear on the plastic mind of the small child....
>
> According to such a modern conception of the subjective life, man appears as a captive within his own mind and as a victim of forces which he cannot recognize.[38]

Sheen was expressing a common Catholic concern that people were beginning to transfer the blame for their personal sins from themselves to those who had treated them hurtfully in their childhoods. This denial of culpability for personal sin was detrimental because it prevented the sinner from seeking forgiveness from God and amending his or her behavior.

Sheen's presentations serve as examples of historian James O'Toole's claim that there was an early hesitance of Catholics to embrace psychology. The confessional and couch were seen as rivals wherein the confessional clearly had the advantage; it was a sacrament of grace and forgiveness—and it was free of charge, in contrast to the new and expensive psychological treatments. O'Toole poses the question as, "More practically, why would anyone pay money for something that was available for free every Saturday afternoon from 3:30 to 6:00 at the local parish?"[39] Psychology, which etymologically means "the study of the soul," had, in the early nineteenth century, been associated with philosophy. The "new psychology" had its origins in the experimental laboratories of Europe

---

38. Sheen, *Peace of the Soul: A Magnificent Message of Hope and Inspiration for All Men* (1949; repr. Garden City, N.Y.: Doubleday, 1954), 3.
39. O'Toole, "In the Court of Conscience," 176.

From Personal to General

and sought to establish psychology as a science with objective methods of measurement.[40] The coincident emergence of psychoanalysis "led to a clinical psychology that placed great emphasis on unconscious motivations, thereby relegating to second place the rational choices of the mind." It was this new psychology that was a concern to Catholics.[41] Catholics worried that the minimization of rational choice undermined the Catholic teaching of free will.

The psychoanalytic method of psychology "prompted the quip that psychology had first lost its soul and then its mind."[42] It was no longer a study of the soul, and now it seemed not even to be the study of the conscious mind. One particular Catholic objection to the new psychology was regarding the sexual focus of Freudian psychoanalysis. In 1952, Pope Pius XII "strongly asserted his arguments against psychotherapeutic treatments that [sought] to unleash the sexual instinct for seemingly therapeutic reasons."[43] Though his concerns about such treatments may have remained, by early 1953 the pope had an expanded view of the new psychology and was more positive about it in general, going so far as to encourage European and American Catholic psychologists to interact with and even use much of the new psychology.[44]

In the early twentieth century, there were several U.S. Catholics who worked in the area of psychology. Thomas Verner Moore, E. Boyd Barrett, Charles Bruehl, and Rudolf Allers all engaged the new psychology.[45] Amidst an American Catholicism trying to define itself, Moore believed that Catholics could make an important contribution to psychology by emphasizing psychology's relationship to philosophy.[46] Barrett and Allers both critiqued psychoanalysis. Barrett criticized the psychoanalytic method as unoriginal, materialistic in focus, obsessed with sex, and morally dangerous in its use of free association and hypnotism.[47] Allers, meanwhile, concurred that psychoanalysis was materialistic, but also saw it as

---

40. C. Kevin Gillespie, SJ, *Psychology and American Catholicism: From Confession to Therapy?* (New York: Crossroad, 2001), 1.
41. Ibid., 1.
42. Ibid., 1.
43. Ibid., 19.
44. Ibid., 26.
45. Moore and Barrett were formally trained in psychology and practiced as psychologists. Bruehl was trained as a theologian and used psychology to address pastoral issues. Allers was a medical doctor engaged in psychiatry, as well as in the last class taught by Freud; see Gillespie, *Psychology and American Catholicism*, chap. 3, for more information on each person.
46. Ibid., 43.
47. Ibid., 46.

hedonistic and deterministic to the point that it left no room for freedom, the objectivity of values, or even the existence of a substantial soul.[48] Bruehl, on the other hand, did not see a fundamental conflict between the rational psychology of neo-Scholasticism and Freudian psychoanalysis; he noted that the classical psychology of neo-Scholasticism did not say anything about pathologies that could affect the will, and this was where psychoanalysis could complement neo-Scholastic psychology.[49]

These scholars' engagements with psychoanalysis were the forerunners to the gradual acceptance of psychology and counseling by Catholics. By the time of Vatican II, the council fathers who authored *Gaudium et spes* were willing to mention psychology favorably, listing psychology among the sciences that could bring hope of human self-knowledge and help people to influence social groups.[50] Moreover, in this same document, the fathers hoped that those who were learned in psychology and the other sciences could be a service to marriage and family.[51] Suspicion of psychology was replaced by at least a degree of approval for some schools of psychology. From 1954 to 1973, St. John's College in Collegeville, Minnesota, held an institute for mental health, covering a wide range of psychological and religious concerns in an attempt to address the interface between psychology and religion.[52]

Gillespie suggests that there was a definite positive development in the relationship between psychology and Catholicism during the time period that the St. John's Institute for Mental Health existed. While initially there was a clear division between the two, by the end psychology and Catholicism were more collaborative.[53] Gillespie describes a narrative wherein Catholics attempted to assimilate American values as informed by professional psychology, which he defines simply as the "experimental and clinical disciplines whose central project revolves around understanding the mental states and processes." The initial ten-

---

48. Ibid., 52.
49. Ibid., 49.
50. *Gaudium et spes*, no. 5, accessed at http://www.vatican.va/archive/hist_councils/ii_vatican_council/documents/vat-ii_cons_19651207_gaudium-et-spes_en.html.
51. *Gaudium et spes*, no. 52. In particular, this reference was in the hopes that the sciences "explain more thoroughly the various conditions favoring a proper regulation of births."
52. Gillespie, *Psychology and American Catholicism*, 13.
53. Ibid., 20.

From Personal to General

sion in the narrative of psychology and Catholicism involved discerning how to appropriate the "attitudes, insights, and methods of psychology without accommodating the emerging secularization which many of psychology's leaders tended to promote."[54]

The sacrament of confession, generally regarded by priests and laity as the better alternative to counseling, often became understood and described sometimes in psychological terms as Catholics became more open to psychology during the late 1960s. Applying psychology to the sacrament, for example, some understood the scrupulous behavior of the faithful in the confessional as obsessive-compulsive behavior. As another example, the earlier claims of penitents' sense of relief could now be interpreted as an indication that the sacrament was "therapeutic" and the purpose of amendment could be described as "preventative of disorders."[55] Hence it seemed by the 1960s that psychology and Catholicism were reconciling for good. Gillespie notes that, "in the decade prior to the Council, there were signs that psychology was beginning to have a significant impact on American Catholicism ... psychiatrists, psychologists, and even psychoanalysts helped to train American Catholic clergy and religious to address pastoral concerns though special symposiums."[56] And while the sacrament of penance was often interpreted in psychological terms, Gillespie states that the confessional was indeed replaced to some extent by the counseling couch as Catholics looked to therapists, rather than parish priests, for wisdom and guidance.[57]

---

54. Ibid., 6, 8. It would be valuable to have a more precise notion of the different schools of psychology and which ones were especially problematic or helpful here. Gillespie, author of the standard text on the topic, *Psychology and American Catholicism*, does name particular individuals and schools, but I follow his lead in making generalized statements regarding the relationship between psychology and Catholicism.

55. O'Toole, "In the Court of Conscience," 175–76.

56. Gillespie, *Psychology and American Catholicism*, 106.

57. Ibid., 108. Unfortunately Gillespie does not cite statistics indicating the number or percentage of Catholics seeking counseling. Gillespie does, however, mention the importance of Charles A. Curran's book *Religious Values in Counseling and Psychotherapy* (New York: Sheed and Ward, 1969) as an example of a new approach integrating theology and psychology. Gillespie contrasts this with Curran's earlier *Counseling in Catholic Life and Education* (New York: MacMillan, 1952), seeing a shift from Thomistic virtue to value and use of post–Vatican II catchwords (122). Note that this is not Charles E. Curran, the student of Bernard Häring, but rather Charles A. Curran, who served as a *peritus* at Vatican II and taught pastoral counseling at Loyola of Chicago.

By 1973 psychiatrist Karl Menninger more or less confirmed Catholics' initial fear, expressed by Sheen, that psychiatry was explaining away sin. Echoing Sheen's critique, Menninger suggested that because scientific methodology and research viewed bad behavior as symptomatic, the opinion of many psychiatrists was that the offender was not to be blamed for the action.[58] In this account, the behavior was merely an indication (a symptom) of an existing condition for which the person was not accountable. An action that in the past had been labeled a sin, with culpability assigned to the perpetrator, had importance only to the degree that it pointed backward, assigning blame to others in one's past.

With such an explanation, sinners who might have become penitents in previous years turned elsewhere for help. Instead of seeking forgiveness for sins and striving to sin no more, people were learning to "work through" their issues, forgive those who had hurt them in years past, and "forgive themselves" in order to improve their self-esteem as well as their relationships with others.[59] They were explaining away their sins by transferring the blame to others, while working on self-improvement in a manner that circumvented the confessional. Nor were such attitudes found solely among those who frequented the psychoanalyst's couch; rather, such opinions about reassigning responsibility for a person's actions became common currency, as is indicated by the growth of the new literature of pop psychology in the United States.

Norman Vincent Peale was perhaps the first of the self-help pop psychology genre to make it big in this time period. Published in 1952, *The Power of Positive Thinking* stayed on the *New York Times* bestseller list for 186 consecutive weeks.[60] But this Methodist minister's blatant anti-Catholicism, expressed vociferously less than a decade later in his objections to electing the Catholic John F. Kennedy as U.S. president, could hardly have made him popular with Catholics.[61] Less than two de-

58. Menninger, *Whatever Became of Sin?*, 43.
59. O'Toole, "In the Court of Conscience," 176.
60. Ron Alexander, "Chronicle," *New York Times*, May 31, 1994, http://www.nytimes.com/1994/05/31/nyregion/chronicle-254657.html; accessed on September 13, 2011.
61. "The Religious Issue: Hot and Getting Hotter," *Newsweek*, September 19, 1960. Some have compared Fulton Sheen to Norman Vincent Peale, for example, linking Sheen's *Peace of Soul* to Peale's *The Power of Positive Thinking*; see Dewey W. Grantham, *The United States Since 1945: The Ordeal of Power* (New York: McGraw-Hill, 1976), 151.

From Personal to General

cades after Peale, however, came the paradigmatic example of self-help psychology in the bestselling nonfiction book *I'm OK—You're OK* by psychiatrist Thomas Harris. By this time, Catholics were in a different place demographically and already looking elsewhere than the confessional to address their problems.

One colorful example of this was Timothy Leary, the former Catholic who became a psychologist perhaps best known for his advocacy of psychedelic drugs. Leary was an important figure in popular culture and friends with the likes of John Lennon. Leary also received some attention among Catholic audiences. A 1966 interview with Leary was published in the magazine *Ave Maria*, wherein Leary claimed that sin had to be dealt with by a religious act of contrition, penance, and sacrifice, which is what the LSD experience was for him. But Leary also noted that when he was Catholic, the act of confession was not powerful enough to stop him from sinning, which he suggested was true of most Catholics. Leary blamed it on failures of the church, especially the clergy, in not promoting LSD usage, and he made the bold prediction that within fifty to a hundred years, the church would accept LSD as a sacrament.[62]

But if Leary was more exceptional, Harris's *I'm OK—You're OK* was increasingly normative, indicative of the embrace of the genre of pop psychology. In 1973, the year that Menninger published his book on sin, Harris's book held the number-three spot in nonfiction bestsellers, having just come down a notch from being the second-bestselling book of 1972.[63] Harris followed on the heels of his mentor Eric Berne's popular book *Games People Play*, which remained on the bestseller list for two years. Harris used an accessible explanation of transactional analysis in order to provide a psychological resource that was much more affordable than pricey counseling sessions with psychotherapists. *I'm OK—You're OK* perhaps stands as the quintessential guide to improving self-esteem and relationships, and it came at a time when Catholics were more amenable to popular psychology, so it likely had more influence than previous similar books.

62. Joe O'Sullivan, "God and Timothy Leary," *Ave Maria*, December 17, 1966, 10–11.
63. Thomas A. Harris is identified as a "church-going Presbyterian" in "Dr. Thomas Harris, a Reported Suicide, Spikes Rumormongers: 'I'm OK—You're in Trouble,'" by Nancy Faber, *People Magazine*, April 21, 1980, http://www.people.com/people/archive/article/0,,20076291,00.html; accessed on August 17, 2015.

In *I'm OK—You're OK*, Harris utilized Berne's concept of transactional analysis in order to advise and guide readers in making positive changes to their self-esteem and interactions with others. Harris expounded transactional analysis, known in the book as P-A-C, where each letter stands for a set of data to be processed. "P" indicates the Parent or the early influence and standards impressed upon a child during his childhood. "A" signifies Adult data, which represents external reality of the present as well as data from the past that is independent of the Parent and Child. "C" stands for the experiences and impressions of the child that continue to exert influence.[64] For each decision, the person must work through the various sources of data, and the "emancipated adult" is one who can discern the best decision without simply obliging the voice of Parent and the fears of the Child. "We Can Change" is the title of chapter 4, and the ultimate goal is for the person to change so as to recognize both her own worth (I'm OK) and the other person's worth (You're OK). In an American culture that prized voluntarism, Harris provided a valuable way to conquer those voices that seemed to be inhibiting freedom and choice.

At the end of the book, Harris addresses P-A-C and moral values, suggesting that sin (or, anyway, something vaguely defined as a flaw in human nature) is apparent in every person and that the primary problem can be expressed as a position other than I'm OK—You're OK, and the person takes up this harmful position early in life.[65] Harris identifies "original sin" (or, as he also names it, "the flaw in our species") as primarily an issue of self-esteem, which, we might note, is distant from the Catholic theological concept of original sin. It also bears little resemblance to Thomas Aquinas's definition of actual sin as a human act, a thought, word, or deed contrary to eternal law that serves as remote matter for the sacrament of confession. Additionally, Harris further relates religion and transactional analysis, comparing dogma to the authoritarian voice of the Parent and describing the grace of Christ's ministry as "a theological way of saying I'm OK—You're OK."[66] Apparently, the salvation brought by Christ is the natural benefit of the ability to achieve "adult-

---

64. Thomas Harris, *I'm OK—You're OK* (1967; repr. New York, 1973), 79.
65. Ibid., 259.
66. Ibid., 261.

From Personal to General

hood" by relating to others from the framework of I'm OK—You're OK. It is a sort of secular version of the sacrament of confession—without the guilt.[67]

Of course, the missing relationship in Harris's transactional analysis, as well as in the counseling and therapy offered by many psychologists at the time, was the relationship featured in the confessional—namely, the relationship with God. In the words of Fulton Sheen, "Sin is not just the breaking of a law. Guilt is the breaking of a relationship, the hurting of someone we love."[68] Sheen's perspective also echoes the Thomistic conviction that the virtue of penance follows under the category of justice, indicating a relationship with God. While the confessional was often understood primarily in legalistic and juridical terms to the detriment of God's mercy and forgiveness, there was nonetheless the sense that a sin was an offense against God and not just an issue of self-esteem.

Limiting and narrow though the confession manuals might have been, they could not be accused of representing an abstract or elusive concept of sin. Rather, they were filled with lists of sins, case studies, explanations, and appropriate penances. In the 1950s, no Catholic would have questioned the importance of distinguishing between mortal and venial sins; specificity was of utmost importance in the confessional. But by the 1970s, sin no longer seemed so concrete or useful as a category, and even priests would feel the need to consider carefully the psychological aspect of a problem when giving pastoral care. The growing elusiveness of sin was indicated by both Menninger's and Harris's struggle to define the concept in a culture where psychological explanations of behavior seemed more compelling and where counseling and self-help books were more popular than the sacrament of confession.

The psychological explanations of behavior may have been more compelling because of the turn to human relationships. This focus resonated with many people who believed that sin ought to be understood primarily in the context of human relationships rather than as a thing to be counted and a matter to be confessed. One Catholic author, writing in 1968 on the topic of training catechists in the new morality, suggested that sin was a failure to respond with love to God and others. He insisted

---

67. Thank you to Sandra A. Yocum of the University of Dayton for this observation.
68. Fulton Sheen, "Psychoanalytic Couch."

that sin may be seen as an individual sharing in the failure of the community, but "this must not lead us to speak of sin as a thing, but as referring to persons."⁶⁹ This author stressed that the awareness of failures was not about counting individual actions or deeds so much as trying to grow in love for God and neighbor.⁷⁰ The emphasis was on relationship rather than discrete thoughts, words, and deeds opposed to eternal or ecclesiastical law. While the emphasis on relationship was a helpful corrective to confessional sin counting, it also minimized the important objective of removing or destroying sin in the sacrament of confession.

From Confessional to Bedroom: Difficulties in Identifying Sexual Sin

Besides Catholics' newfound accommodation of psychology and counseling, their immersion into the American mainstream also brought a review in the conventional list of sins. The change in Americans' list of sins was apparent to psychiatrist Karl Menninger, among others. In *Whatever Became of Sin?*, he quipped, "How quaint and puritanical it is to feel guilty about working on Sunday or for having a sexual fantasy—or, if we are Catholics, eating meat on Good Friday and, if we are Jews, eating bacon and eggs for breakfast!"⁷¹ This indicates that Menninger, at least, seemed to think the United States had largely moved beyond the preoccupations with naming certain "insignificant" acts as sins; in the previous quotation he highlighted ritual acts.

In Menninger's perspective, the harshness of punishments for small and basically unimportant sins were in part to blame for the decline in the concept of sin; for too long religious Americans had exaggerated the minor offenses. The severity of punishments made people reconsider whether certain actions really were sins. Such was the case with masturbation, in Menninger's opinion. He summarized the history by noting that for years, the youth had been warned about the dangers and punishments of "self-abuse," but now, instead of acknowledging a mistaken

---

69. Ken J. Bernard, "Let's Teach Christian Morality," *Homiletic and Pastoral Review* 69, no. 2 (November 1968): 131.
70. Ibid., 132.
71. Menninger, *Whatever Became of Sin?*, 133.

From Personal to General

labeling of sin as the past and simply recognizing this particular act as morally acceptable, people had declined use of the word "sin" altogether. If masturbation, so well established as a sin for so many years, was now deemed normal and acceptable, then how useful was the language of sin, anyway?

For Catholics, there was additional confusion because of changes to certain church laws that had been regarded by many laity as immutable: changes in the Eucharistic fast, the Lenten fast, and the obligation to send a child to Catholic school were listed by authors Fr. John Reedy and James Andrews as they discussed the Catholic understanding of morality in the magazine *Ave Maria*. Reedy and Andrews were concerned that the faithful failed to understand the reasons for the change: "Too often, the ordinary Catholic gets the impression that these laws (which must have had some good reason for existence) are being dropped simply because too many people are ignoring them. And, somehow, that doesn't seem to be a very good way of dealing with law."[72] Yet there was no denying that many church officials were doing an about-face on other issues, as well, such as racial segregation and praying with Protestants; this led to confusion for some of the faithful, giving the impression "that this whole dimension of moral law has been thrown wide open for discussion and private interpretation."[73]

Reedy and Andrews might have been partly responsible for some of this confusion as to what constituted a sin. In an earlier article in this "Perplexed Catholic" series, the authors addressed the problem of birth control, ultimately concluding that the general question of birth control should not be raised; rather, individual couples must seek personal spiritual guidance and then, "reconciling ... all of their obligations, they should make, for themselves, the most responsible Christian decision of which they are capable. And they should go ahead and act confidently, without the agonies of scrupulosity."[74] The authors certainly were not threatening the readers with claims of mortal sin and the corresponding loss of heaven.

72. Reedy and Andrews, "Morality: A Concern for the Person," 17.
73. Ibid., 17.
74. Reedy and Andrews, "The Problem of Birth Control," in the series "The Perplexed Catholic," October 22, 1966, 30.

Many sexual acts once considered sinful by the majority of Americans were no longer identified as sins; Protestants seemed to be updating the list of sins, though official Catholic teaching had not.[75] The issue of contraception had gradually been moving off the sin list and into the realm of expected, if not acceptable, behavior for most Americans, including many American Catholics. Beginning with the Anglican's Lambeth Conference of 1930, non-Catholics had officially become more amenable to contraception for limiting family size.[76] Then with the 1965 court case *Griswold v. Connecticut*, contraception was deemed protected by right of privacy, and it was clear that states no longer had the ability to make laws reflecting this particular moral code.[77] But for Catholics in the United States, contraception remained an ambiguous issue. Leslie Woodcock Tentler notes that in the 1940s, U.S. Catholics were "acutely conscious of standing alone in most of the nation's battles over law and sexual morality."[78] The teaching on artificial birth control was, for many Catholics, "a kind of tribal marker—a proud if onerous badge of Catholic identity."[79]

At the same time, however, Catholics in the early twentieth century were already concerned about limiting family size, since they often found it financially and emotionally difficult to raise large families. Studies show that Catholics were engaging in contraceptive practice prior to the 1960s; 30 percent of Catholic wives in 1955 admitted to it.[80] This was despite Pius XI's 1930 encyclical *Casti connubii*, which had maintained that the use of contraceptives was against nature and that the primary end of sexual intercourse was procreation.[81] *Casti connubii* found a respectful reception in a formal sense; Catholic periodicals, many secular publica-

---

75. Refer again to Karl Menninger's discussion of masturbation in *Whatever Became of Sin?*, 31.

76. "Resolution 15: The Life and Witness of the Christian Community—Marriage and Sex," Resolutions from 1930, the Lambeth Conference; http://www.lambethconference.org/resolutions/1930/1930-15.cfm; accessed on March 14, 2013.

77. McGreevy, *Catholicism and American Freedom: A History* (New York: Norton, 2003), 239.

78. Leslie Woodcock Tentler, *Catholics and Contraception: An American History* (Ithaca, N.Y.: Cornell University Press, 2004), 9.

79. Ibid., 9.

80. Ibid., 10.

81. Pius XI, *Casti connubii*: Encyclical on Christian Marriage, December 31, 1930, ¶54; http://www.vatican.va/holy_father/pius_xi/encyclicals/documents/hf_p-xi_enc_31121930_casti-connubii_en.html; accessed on May 14, 2010. For more on *Casti connubii* in context, see McGreevy, *Catholicism and American Freedom*, 162.

From Personal to General

tions, and Catholic clerics greeted the encyclical warmly.[82] Tentler finds, however, that many Catholic couples effectively rejected *Casti connubii*, judging by their behavior. Though not given to public dissent, the context of the Depression made the teaching seem too difficult for some Catholics to observe for the whole of their marriages in the 1930s and 1940s.[83]

By the early 1960s, the dissent of many Catholics had moved from private practice to the public forum, in anticipation of an official change to the church's stance against artificial birth control. According to Tentler, the topic became popular in Catholic lay periodicals such as *Jubilee*.[84] The difficulty of adhering to the teaching and the stress this placed on marriage was a constant theme, and the debate was intense. In the cultural context of the sexual revolution and distrust of authority, the Catholic position seemed out of place.[85] Moreover, with the advent of Vatican II, where so many traditional church stances seemed to be undergoing examination and modification, it seemed likely that a change was on the horizon. Contraception was broached in 1964 at the Second Vatican Council in the context of the debate of the document that would become *Gaudium et spes*.[86] While numerous bishops raised the contraception question from time to time, discussion was kept to a minimum because John XXIII had already established a Papal Commission to study the problem, and Paul VI did not want it discussed on the floor.[87]

The Papal Commission on this issue continued to meet, and Paul VI even expanded it to include three married couples. The commission did not reach a unanimous conclusion, however; rather, a majority report was submitted to the pope recommending a modification of the church's stance, and an unofficial minority report, in part drafted by Fr. John C. Ford, SJ, urged no change in the teaching against contraception. The pope ultimately sided with the minority report and issued his encyclical *Humanae vitae* in 1968, restating the Catholic stance against birth control. It was met with a negative reaction in the United States. According

---

82. Tentler, *Catholics and Contraception*, 74.   83. Ibid., 230.
84. Ibid., 220.   85. Ibid., 210–11.
86. Ibid., 198.
87. John O'Malley, *What Happened at Vatican II* (Cambridge, Mass.: Harvard University Press, 2008), 237–38.

to Mark S. Massa, "many American Catholic moral theologians in 1968 felt that the theological arguments seemed implausible, or at least appeared dated, and easy to refute."[88] A lack of clerical support for the encyclical, and at times outright dissent, affected the laity's reception of the statement. Polling data in 1970 confirmed that many Catholics were disregarding the encyclical, with more than 75 percent of married women in their twenties using a form of birth control.[89]

Moreover, Catholics could not be wholly immune to the sexual revolution in their country, which brought to the bestseller list books such as Helen Gurley Brown's *Sex and the Single Girl*, George and Nena O'Neill's *The Open Marriage*, William Masters and Virginia Johnson's *Human Sexual Response*, Phyllis Diller's *Marriage Manual by Phyllis Diller*, David Reuben's *Everything You Ever Wanted to Know about Sex but Were Afraid to Ask* and *Any Woman Can!*, *The Sensuous Woman* by "J," Marabel Morgan's *Total Woman*, and Alex Comfort's *Joy of Sex*.[90] In regard to premarital sex, for example, 74 percent of Catholics in 1963 deemed it always wrong, whereas only 35 percent in 1974 agreed.[91] While the change in regard to birth control was not quite as drastic, nonetheless Catholics more closely reflected the view of their compatriots than that of their pope on sexual issues. Effective contraception further facilitated the possibility of nonprocreative premarital sex, hence the attitudes toward both issues were related.

Catholics in the United States were not prepared to accept Paul VI's conclusions expressed in *Humanae vitae*. Immersed in a religiously pluralistic American society, these Catholics had become more like their non-Catholic peers in many ways, including their views on contraception. The Catholic perception on these issues was influenced by the larger American societal understanding of sex and increasing medicalization combined with the growing availability of oral contraceptives. As Carey notes, "From the 1960s onward, a veritable revolution took place in American society on a variety of moral and lifestyle issues that seriously challenged official Catholic Church teachings."[92] Premarital sex, abor-

88. Massa, *American Catholic Revolution*, 31.
89. O'Toole, *The Faithful*, 242.
90. There is no data available about how popular these books were in Catholic circles. I merely note their presence on American bestseller lists.
91. Greeley, *Catholic Revolution*, 38.
92. Carey, *Catholics in America*, 131.

From Personal to General

tion, and homosexuality—in addition to artificial contraception—had become increasingly accepted by the American population but created divisions both within the church and within society.[93]

The pope's insistence on contraception as contrary to eternal law when most Americans had concluded it was morally acceptable called into question the whole concept of authority, obedience to the church's teachings, and assent to the conventional list of sins. Although it was something new for them, American Catholics found themselves simply ignoring or even outright protesting what the magisterium had clearly communicated. In O'Toole's words, "The very undermining of authority that some church officials hoped to prevent had become a reality."[94]

Those who disobeyed *Humane vitae* either did not think that they were succumbing to sin or were not concerned with the effects of committing it. Many sincerely believed that the pope was mistaken and that the church's teaching was out of touch with reality. Here the concept was best captured in the phrase "freedom of conscience." In seeking to follow their consciences regarding birth control, many Catholic couples found that they had no problem turning to artificial means of preventing birth. No longer constrained by ingrained obedience buoyed by a strong Catholic subculture, they made their own decisions about birth control, and these decisions did not mark their Catholic religious identity as unique. In the words of Tentler, "It was precisely in the context of birth control, an issue that intimately affected nearly all adult Catholics, that a remarkable generation—better educated and perhaps more devout than any before it—came to a sense of moral autonomy."[95]

One indication of the sense of moral autonomy can be found in the American Catholic Psychological Association's response to *Humane vitae*. Drawing on their knowledge from the science of psychology, the members raised fifteen questions about the encyclical in a statement made at their annual convention in September 1968. These questions indicate a

---

93. Ibid., 131.
94. O'Toole, *The Faithful*, 242; see also McGreevy, *Catholicism and American Freedom*, 245–46. McGreevy notes that the Jesuit moralist John C. Ford feared that a change in church teaching would undermine church authority. Ironically, "reaffirming Catholic opposition to contraception had had exactly the diminishing effect on papal teaching authority that Ford had anticipated would follow from permitting contraception."
95. Tentler, *Catholics and Contraception*, 3.

genuine concern for the good of Catholic laity in regard to sexuality and marriage, but they also reveal that Catholic psychologists—as well as many theologians and other laity—saw themselves in a position of knowledge and autonomy wherein they were able to criticize *Humanae vitae*. "Does the encyclical give evidence of an understanding of the complex of conscious and unconscious psychological factors operative in the total experience of marriage?" was one such question, implying that the encyclical was limited in its understanding of marriage. Another, drawing on the now popular notion of conscience, asked "Does the history of the encyclical's development and promulgation conflict with the church's teaching that responsible human beings must develop a mature conscience?"[96] As Gillespie notes, the ACPA statement was a sign of widespread public dissent and private disobedience of the birth-control ban: "A critical consciousness toward the church and its authority soon emerged."[97]

Along with the sense of moral autonomy, and seemingly related to dissatisfaction with *Humanae vitae*, came a decline in the sacrament of confession.[98] Some Catholics stopped going to confession since they intended to continue their use of contraception; for some it was avoidance and for others a confirmation of how the ritual of confession made little sense in the context of their lives.[99] Others merely stopped mentioning contraception in the confessional as Catholics' views on sexual matters became more similar to others in the United States. Still others turned to guidance elsewhere, as Gillespie notes: "Rather than confessing an action that church authorities believed to be sinful, but they did not, many chose not to go to confession at all. Instead, they chose to see a counselor or therapist."[100]

In general, Catholics encountered a lack of clerical instruction on sexual matters during this time period, and, because Paul VI had spoken against birth control so completely, there was little room for a discus-

---

96. "Report: The American Catholic Psychological Association Meeting," *Bulletin of the National Guild of Catholic Psychiatrists* 16 (June 1969): 45–46, as cited in Gillespie's discussion in *Psychology and American Catholicism*, 100–101.
97. Gillespie, *Psychology and American Catholicism*, 101.
98. O'Toole, Tentler, and Gillespie all see the contraception issue as an important cause for the decline of confession.
99. O'Toole, "In the Court of Conscience," 179.
100. Gillespie, *Psychology and American Catholicism*, 100.

From Personal to General

sion on a moral use of contraceptives in limiting family size.[101] For the church's hierarchy, it was regarded as a sin—an act contrary to eternal law—and for many American members of the church, it was not recognized as a sin. In a sense, the challenge to the Catholic moral code was a disagreement that undermined church authority, leaving the church voiceless on matters of sexual morality and leading Steinfels to describe it as "missing in action" on this topic for over thirty years.[102] This debate in defining sexual sin weakened the concept of sin itself. A sin that had once been concrete and tangible now was perceived by priests as theologically ungrounded and abstract. The focus of debate on contraception shifted from the morality of its use to the morality of dissenting from the Holy See. Many priests and lay people saw the choice to use contraception as a morally neutral decision of one's own self-legislating conscience, appropriate to one's situation rather than accountable to some abstract eternal law expressed concretely in a myriad of official magisterial difficult-to-follow rules. Though the encyclical was greeted with incredulity and anger, the actual contraceptive practice among the laity seemed unaffected by the encyclical. Tentler states:

> the trend toward nonconformity with Church teaching continued unabated. This was especially true among the young. Fully 78 percent of Catholic married women aged twenty to twenty-four ... were limiting their families by a means other than abstinence or rhythm. ... One could hardly offer more definitive evidence of *Humanae Vitae*'s nonreception on the part of most laity."[103]

Though some Catholics considered contraception sinful and kept to the longstanding moral norms, the widespread dissent from Paul VI's encyclical gave rise to other considerations from those who disagreed with *Humanae vitae*. Assuming that the church was wrong to maintain that contraception was sinful, some people wondered if the church might also be mistaken on other acts identified as sins. If dissent from this teaching was possible, was it not also feasible to dissent from other offenses delineated by the church as contrary to eternal law?

---

101. For additional perspective on this, see Avery Dulles, "'*Humanae vitae*' and the Crisis of Dissent," *Origins* (April 22, 1993): 774–77.
102. Steinfels, *A People Adrift*, 268.
103. Tentler, *Catholics and Contraception*, 267.

From Obedience to Freedom: The Contagion of Liberty and the Vatican II Generation

Particularly when considering the influence of the Second Vatican Council in causing change in U.S. Catholicism, it is crucial to recognize the context in which implementations were received, not only demographically, but generationally. It was not simply the spirit of Vatican II, but also the timing of Vatican II; Steinfels observes that it ended "just as the most radical part of the 1960s was beginning."[104] The context in which Vatican II was conducted was different from the context in which it was implemented. This Catholic assimilation was also an immersion in a particular climate, specifically for educated youth and young adults, who were beginning to challenge various established authorities. In a culture of criticism, the church and its longstanding beliefs would not be immune.

In a 1966 Advent reflection on obedience for *Ave Maria*, Dorothy Day recognized this: "What the American people ... now feel free to do is to criticize, speak their minds. They have always been accused of a lack of diplomacy, or at least of bad manners, and they have felt it a virtue in themselves, the virtue of honesty, truthfulness. Freedom has meant searching and questioning."[105] Day found this tendency to be troubling and suggested that cradle Catholics were in need of a second conversion that would bind them with "a more profound, a more mature love and obedience to the Church."[106]

That such a "second conversion" of younger cradle Catholics did not occur for most seems indicated by others from the time period seeking to describe the situation. Fr. John Reedy and James Andrews, in the tenth of their "Perplexed Series" for *Ave Maria*, noted in regard to the youth:

> These young men and women (including young priests, seminarians and religious) have been trained to challenge all assumptions, to rely on their own judgment, to be independent and critical in their dealings with every kind of academic authority.
>
> These people, who are often very vocal and very well educated, simply refuse

---

104. Steinfels, *A People Adrift*, 37.
105. Dorothy Day, "Obedience," *Ave Maria*, December 17, 1966, 21.
106. Ibid., 23.

From Personal to General

to be controlled by the system of ecclesiastical administration which worked in the past.[107]

Reedy and Andrews observed that part of this challenge to the teaching authority of the church was based on the feeling that the trust and confidence of Catholics in the past were misused by "unjustified reverence for all the acts and opinions of religious spokesmen."[108] The younger generation was wary of making the same mistake. And many of the older generation were also cautious of emphasizing the obedience of ecclesiastical authority to the younger generation. Reedy and Andrews ultimately advocated that the Catholic "accept the fact that this teaching authority and responsibility, by divine institution, reside primarily in the college of bishops under the leadership of the pope."[109]

Although they also noted the importance of the living experience of God and the necessity of differentiating the authority of various statements, Reedy and Andrews were met with backlash from none less than *Ave Maria*'s former managing editor, William Jacobs. Jacobs wrote, "There is entirely too much concern in the Church about 'disturbing the faithful.' I think perhaps our greatest sin has been that we have not disturbed and been disturbed enough."[110] Rather than assuring people that everything was going to make sense, Jacobs suggested describing the scope of the challenge and acknowledging the importance of attitudes of flexibility and acceptance. Using the liturgical changes an example, Jacobs noted, "Too many Catholics are still looking for a complete set of rules, a comfortable way of worship, a freedom from the awful demands of real personal freedom and responsibility, and especially a dispensation from a certain amount of intellectual exercise without which life has become largely impossible."[111]

Whether this generational inclination in celebration of freedom and corollary criticism of authority was perceived as positive or negative by the older generation, it had great practical effect. Writing in regard

---

107. Reedy and Andrews, "The Teaching Church," The Perplexed Catholic, *Ave Maria*, November 26, 1966, 19.
108. Ibid., 18.
109. Ibid., 23.
110. William J. Jacobs, "Backtalk," *Ave Maria*, December 10, 1966, 22.
111. Ibid., 23.

to the sacrament of confession, O'Toole notes that "the decline among particular segments of the Catholic population was especially steep, and college-age young adults seem to have led the way."[112] By pointing to the generational differences, O'Toole's comment corroborates the observation that the change in the concept of sin occurred most rapidly among the younger generations of cradle Catholics. College-age young Catholics began to see themselves as independent and religiously autonomous in a way that their parents had not been.[113] When it came to confession, these new Catholics were not as likely to want to submit themselves to the judgments of priest-confessors but rather had confidence in their own ability to make moral decisions and to discern morality for themselves rather than rely upon the hierarchy's interpretation of eternal law.

The older generation of Catholics—those who had made the flight to the suburbs, hoping to give their children a better life free from the worries of the city—often brought their Catholic subculture with them, inasmuch as it was embodied by them because of their solid Catholic upbringing that for many had included parochial education as well as numerous religious practices, such as saying the Rosary and attending Sunday Mass. The children who were post–Vatican II and post-dissolution of the Catholic subculture, however, were raised in the midst of religious pluralism at a time when the church was undergoing reform, experienced dramatically in the liturgical changes, and often profoundly in catechetical developments. They were less likely to have memorized church doctrines, more likely to ask questions about church teachings than their parents had been, and more likely to be disappointed in the plausibility of the answers. The credibility of authority in general, and the church's authority in particular, had been seriously undermined by this time, and so instead of banking on established tradition, these post–Vatican II Catholics sought to come to their own conclusions.

This attitude is similar to what Philip Gleason names "the contagion of liberty." Writing in regard to Catholic higher education, Gleason describes the phenomenon wherein Catholic intellectuals were captivated by the idea of freedom. The concept of freedom meshed well with the

---

112. O'Toole, "In the Court of Conscience," 170.
113. Ibid., 173.

From Personal to General

growing emphasis on individual subjectivity and was "the polar opposite of rigidity, formalism, and authoritarianism that had become so distasteful to American Catholic intellectuals."[114]

In the United States, the government came under fire in regard to both civil rights and the antiwar movement; protests were common, particularly on college campuses. To some degree both a confrontational tone and confrontational techniques were also employed in internal church debates, such as those over contraception.[115] Hence Greeley identifies the postconciliar movements in the United States as a "revolution within Catholicism," wherein lower clergy and laity created their own reform that swept away the Catholic "rules" that no longer made sense to them.[116] Peter Steinfels further supports this when he notes that many people took the "spirit of the Council" as an opportunity to challenge all established practices and teachings of the church.[117] Carey notes that Vatican II had opened up the church to reform and criticism, and following its close, very little in the church's tradition was immune to criticism or questions. Church conflicts reflected and were exacerbated by the American cultural revolution that protested against institutions. There was little presumption in favor of the side of tradition and the church.[118]

In particular, it was the Vatican II generation that both challenged the authority of the church and questioned the teachings that had long been accepted. These Catholics were not likely to be swayed by a natural law argument against contraception, nor were they likely to choose confession over pop psychology as a solution for any feelings of guilt they might have had. They were educated and inquisitive, ready to fight against what they viewed as injustice, including injustice that they detected within the church. O'Toole's description of Patty Crowley, a founder of the Christian Family Movement and a member of the papal commission on birth control, is illustrative. Describing one meeting of the commission, O'Toole writes:

114. Philip Gleason, *Contending with Modernity: Catholic Higher Education in the Twentieth Century* (Oxford: Oxford University Press: 1995), 306.
115. Steinfels, *A People Adrift*, 38.
116. Greeley, *Catholic Revolution*, 8, 2. Note that Massa also uses the language of revolution to describe American Catholicism in the 1960s, hence his *American Catholic Revolution*.
117. Steinfels, *A People Adrift*, 32.
118. Carey, *Catholics in America*, 123.

During the deliberations, one incident encapsulated all the changes that had come to the church with the Second Vatican Council. Father Marcelino Zalba, a formidable Spanish Jesuit, was insisting one day that the church's policy simply could not be changed. To do so would call into question the validity of the earlier teaching and thereby undermine all church authority. If the condemnation of artificial contraception had been wrong, he asked, "what, then, with the millions we have sent to hell" for disobeying it? Buoyed by confidence in the new understanding of the church and her role in it, Patty Crowley blurted out, "Father Zalba, do you really believe God has carried out all your orders?" It was apparent in that one moment how much had changed. Fifty years earlier—perhaps even five years earlier—a lay woman would not have dared to speak to a priest in that way. That Patty Crowley felt capable of doing so was a measure of what it was like to be an American Catholic in the church of Vatican II.[119]

Zalba's comment indicates the greater context for the problems in understanding the church's authority; too often moral theologians had simply appealed to authority itself as an explanation, rather than seeking the explanation behind the authority's position. Such an appeal now appeared dissatisfying and distasteful, if not also theologically problematic to post–Vatican II Catholics such as Patty Crowley.

O'Toole sees the "People of God" language as indicative of the change in sentiments for Catholics of this time period. This democratically interpreted phrase, added to the "universal call to holiness," contributed to the laity's growing sense that they were equally part of the church as clerics and that they had responsibility for their faith and their church.[120] The laity were not second-class citizens in the people of God, but rather were called to participate more visibly; hence the emphasis was on "universal" rather than "holiness." There was a sense of newfound freedom in this perspective. To some degree, this contagion of liberty or exaltation of freedom echoed the trends in pop psychology as expressed by Harris in *I'm OK—You're OK*. In particular, there was again a turn to the language of maturity, associated with freedom. O'Toole states that the laity's confidence in their intelligence was a widely held sentiment, "one that was often described as a passage from childhood to adulthood."

119. O'Toole, *The Faithful*, 201.
120. *Lumen gentium*, chaps. II and V, respectively; see O'Toole's discussion, *The Faithful*, 198, 200.

From Personal to General

Catholics no longer had to attend church out of obligation or to feel good, which were seen as childish motives. Instead, these mature, adult Catholics could appreciate the "real reasons for going to Mass."[121]

O'Toole notes that priests often reinforced this view that mature and thinking Catholics were now being acknowledged by the church. Priests sometimes indicated that the laity had grown up, moving beyond the religious world of their parents and grandparents, and hence they rightfully expected a degree of freedom and autonomy unknown to these previous generations of Catholics. Writing in *America* in 1967, one college teacher of pastoral theology emphasized the importance of encouraging freedom rather than imposing external morality. He suggested that the most important thing was not keeping college students from doing or saying bad things, nor helping them to do and say good things, but rather, "the most important thing on a college campus is that people be helped to grow in freedom, in inner freedom, to get the confidence and zest and strength to determine themselves and their lives, to make themselves at the core and, working organically outward, make their lives."[122] Notice that freedom was not understood particularly in terms of freedom from sin, but in terms of choice and self-determination.

To many, this change was regarded as a move from fear to love, from obedience and obligation to freedom and responsibility, with the latter motivated by true charity and free will rather than the dread of hell that found a place of importance in cultural Catholicism of the early twentieth century. The pre–Vatican II Catholicism in the United States had a rich Catholic subculture, but its hegemony for those who lived amidst it could make it seem too rigid and hence limiting of flexibility and freedom. The subculture reinforced Catholicism as the rightful status quo and made its continuance possible while there was a stasis, wherein the subculture's strength was equal to the outside cultural and societal American forces. The upward mobility of many Catholics, including a geographical transition away from insulated Catholic communities, destabilized the assumptions and presumptions granted to Catholicism. Along with their compatriots, Catholics were captivated by the idea of freedom and in-

---

121. O'Toole, *The Faithful*, 210.
122. John G. Milhaven, "Be Like Me! Be Free!" *America* 116, no. 81 (March 18, 1967): 336.

creasingly applied notions of liberty when thinking and speaking of the church. In particular, the notion of their role as laity within the church was understood in terms of freedom from clerical control by means of inflexible church law and punishment for those who failed to adhere. Crucial to this sense of independence was the notion of conscience as a self-legislating faculty providing moral guidance, in contrast with the law of the church, which was expressed chiefly in manuals and catechisms and practiced primarily in the confessional.

Like many other beliefs taken for granted in the Catholicism of the ghetto, the concept of sin as a thought, word, deed, or omission contrary to eternal law per the *Baltimore Catechism* was no longer given a place of importance in the Catholic understanding of how the world worked. There was a general sort of decline in the concept of sin in the United States, perhaps among Catholics inadvertently facilitated by the open and positive language of Vatican II, which contained no anathemas. This conviction of sin as personal and actual had long been reinforced by various practices such as the examination of conscience to identify and name sin, the sacrament of confession to destroy the matter of sin, and practices of penance to reinforce the importance of the penitential element of Christian life. The decline of the notion of sin in terms of one's own personal, actual sin occurred most rapidly amidst the younger generation. Though the language of sin continued to be used at least in liturgies, for many it became an elusive, empty, and even forgotten concept, with little reference to the actions in young adults' own lives.

The church's authority in delineating sins became less compelling throughout the 1960s because of multiple changes in the world of U.S. Catholics, such as the dissolution of Catholic subculture, the acceptance of counseling and psychology, the changing conception of sexual morality and accompanying revision to the conventional list of sins, and the new generation of Catholics raised post-dissolution of the subculture and in the midst of and after Vatican II. All of these challenged the hegemony of the confessional as the primary location for naming actions as sins and addressing them in relation to God and the church.

From Personal to General

3 From Responsibility to Freedom

Changes in the Conception of Sin among Theologians

Just as the laity's concept of sin became increasingly elusive and lacking in meaning as the 1960s progressed, so also a similar change in the conception of sin took place among many Catholic academics—mostly priest-teachers at seminaries. Priest-theologians were influenced by the same trends as the laity—for instance, by the acceptance of psychology and counseling, the debates about sexual morality, and the "contagion of liberty," as Philip Gleason names it. In academic moral theology of the 1950s through the 1970s there was a newfound emphasis on certain concepts that facilitated the move toward a more general notion of sin, in contrast to the more specific and detailed account of sin as a thought, word, deed, or omission contrary to eternal law serving as the remote matter for the sacrament of penance.

Concepts such as freedom, fidelity, conscience, liberation, and creativity were all needed and valuable correctives to the manualist-based morality, which tended toward minimalism and legalism in its catalog of sins and emphasis on distinguishing between mortal and venial sins. However, the concepts of freedom, fidelity, conscience, liberation, and creativity often had little practical instantiation, aside from one particular usage common in the late 1960s and into the 1970s. Ultimately those who favored these concepts employed them regularly to dispute the moral reasoning and moral positions of the manual-based moral system and hence to challenge the authority represented by the church's magisterium, which manualists regarded as crucial for moral theology.

Underpinning the move away from a manual-based morality, wherein the person sought to recognize, confess, and avoid sin, was an emphasis on meaningfulness and interior disposition. The focus on intention and sins in thoughts as well as deeds had a long history; Peter Abelard, for example, in the late eleventh and early twelfth centuries, argued that action itself, apart from intention, did not necessarily damage or benefit anyone.[1] The focus on interior disposition was used to undercut earlier teachings on obedience and obligation to the external rules of the church, and in the United States of the 1960s this view was persuasive to many Catholics, both clergy and lay. Rather than seeing obedience to the church's rules as an external manifestation of the interior disposition, many Catholic theologians tended to view obedience to these laws as preventing the proper interior disposition by causing undue concern with the law. This chapter focuses upon the debates in moral theology surrounding the terms "freedom," "responsibility," "obedience," and "obligation," recognizing that the alterations in the language of morality set the stage for the bishops' interpretation of *Paenitemini* as well as the laity's reception of the letter from the National Conference of Catholic Bishops that changed the rules of penance and fasting in the United States;[2] all of that will be discussed in chapter 5.

This chapter will begin by discussing the decline of neo-Scholasticism and confession-based manuals, with particular regard to how Vatican II seemed to accelerate this decline. After this general consideration, the chapter turns more specifically to authors of the time who represent the

1. John Marenbon and Giovanni Orlandi, eds., "Introduction," in *Collationes*, by Peter Abelard (2001; repr. New York: Oxford University Press, 2003), lxxxii.
2. The National Conference of Catholic Bishops was a predecessor to the United States Catholic Conference of Bishops (USCCB).

From Responsibility to Freedom

traditional stronghold in comparison with those who challenged the status quo and changed the focus of moral theology. The Jesuit priest team of John C. Ford (1902–89) and Gerald Kelly (1902–64) stands as an example of the last great American neo-Scholastics in moral theology; the German Redemptorist priest Bernard Häring (1912–98) signifies the dissatisfaction with the minimalism and legalism inherent in such a neo-Scholastic manual-based system, as well as the turn to other resources for understanding and describing morality. By exploring Häring's use of the terms "obedience," "obligation," "responsibility," and "freedom," in contrast to Ford and Kelly's usage, we see Häring's dissatisfaction with Catholic practice and can understand why he turned to more Nominalist and Kantian notions of freedom and responsibility. Häring hoped both for greater moral meaning and greater sanctity for the Catholic faithful, rooted in a sincere interior orientation toward God.

The chapter will conclude by returning once again to changes in the concept of sin, noting that Häring's usage of the concepts of freedom and responsibility minimized the role played by obedience to authority or at least located that obedience elsewhere in some abstract universal norm. This change relativized the "eternal law" aspect of the Augustinian-Thomistic definition of sin by challenging the church's authority to interpret that law; hence Häring's emphasis on freedom and responsibility facilitated a perceived revision in the conventional list of sins. Häring did not view obedience and obligation to church as habits that could serve as virtues aiding the person to his or her supernatural end of beatitude. Rather, obedience and obligation engendered unthinking routine and hence became externally imposed constrictions to freedom, which was here understood as choosing between contraries. Meanwhile, the turn to "new values," as they are named by James Keenan, and the concern with social sin further undermined traditional practices such as the examination of conscience and the sacrament of penance.[3]

---

3. James F. Keenan, *A History of Catholic Moral Theology in the Twentieth Century: From Confessing Sins to Liberating Consciences* (New York: Continuum, 2010), 115–18; chap. 5 on Häring discusses these "new values."

Dissolution of Neo-Scholasticism

The previous chapter described the dissolution of the Catholic subculture and the move of many urban Catholics to a more suburban, religiously pluralistic setting. Catholic moral theology can analogously be described as abandoning a Catholic ghetto, one that had been rooted in seminaries and based on the presumption of the sacrament of penance as the primary location of moral theology. The formation of confessors had been a chief occupation of moral theology, and there was a degree of uniformity of method in this education, even if there was a diversity of opinion in identifying sin and occasions of sin. Neo-Scholastic priests trained with manuals that cataloged sins were initiated into a casuistry that was a sort of case law, a practical application of objective rules to be used in order to respond to penitents and to exhort the faithful to avoid sin and make satisfaction for the sins that they acknowledged they had committed. As Catholic laity were becoming immersed in religious pluralism in the suburbs, Catholic moral theology in the United States was undergoing a transition to the university, where that field stood as one among many sciences, as opposed to its previous standing as the cornerstone of its own independent world.[4]

Those Thomists that looked suspiciously upon modern philosophy had found support for their position in Leo XIII's 1879 *Aeterni Patris*, which had revived the study of Thomism.[5] In the first half of the twentieth century, Thomism enjoyed a certain popularity among Catholics

---

4. Charles E. Curran suggests that there was no "academic" moral theology before the 1960s. He states that Catholics who taught theology were opposed to research and were mostly priests and professed religious. Academic freedom, professional societies, increased numbers of advanced degrees in theology, more doctorate programs, more publishing, and the diversity and complexity of moral theology in the late 1960s indicate the onset of "academic" moral theology; Curran, *Catholic Moral Theology in the United States: A History* (Washington, D.C.: Georgetown University Press, 2008), 93. Keenan echoes Curran's claim, saying that there was no "academic" moral theology prior to this move to the university; Maria Morrow conversation with Keenan, July 2011. This claim is accurate to the extent that it rightfully reflects a notion of "academic" in reference to the academy, characterized by debate in academic settings such as professional societies, doctoral programs, and publications and identifies a dearth in regard to Catholic moral theology. On the other hand, it can be argued that this claim unfairly minimizes the extent to which the seminary-based manual debates were both intellectual and subject to study. An argument in either direction is tangential to the current project.

5. Fergus Kerr, *After Aquinas: Versions of Thomism* (Malden, Mass., and Oxford: Blackwell, 2002), vii.

From Responsibility to Freedom

in the United States, as Philip Gleason explains: "Indeed, it came to be regarded as axiomatic by educated Americans that Thomism provided a rational justification for religious faith, supplied the principles for applying faith to personal and social life, and thus constituted their basic resource in the campaign to reorder society and culture in accordance with the Christian vision."[6] Gleason credits the uniformity of Thomistic teaching at seminaries and colleges for this popularity, and he attributes the decline of Thomism in the middle decades of the century to the disagreements among schools of Thomism.[7] Nonetheless, this neo-Scholastic Thomism reigned among Catholics in the United States and abroad prior to Vatican II.

Manualism was a particular expression of neo-Scholasticism, one that focused upon the legal aspect of morality, as conveyed in the sacrament of confession. Though the historical origins of manualism are no doubt complex, Servais Pinckaers traces the legalistic tendency to William of Ockham in the fourteenth century and the Nominalist school. Ockham and the Nominalists understood freedom as "freedom of indifference"—that is, the freedom to choose between contraries.[8] The manuals that followed Ockham's critique of Thomas omitted the discussion of the happiness and the final end of beatitude and focused instead upon law and obligation. This truncated version of Thomas failed to communicate the main point that virtue-based morality aimed toward the person's happiness and final end in God. Pinckaers notes that despite their weaknesses, these manuals, which were dominant up to the first half of the twentieth century, fulfilled the role assigned to them of educating priests and laity on essentials of Catholic morality.[9] During the Thomistic revival, when scholars rediscovered the importance of beatitude and the supernatural end in Thomas's work, there was an attempt to reinsert the importance of the final end. A dearth remained, however, when it came to discussing happiness in relation to morality. When Thomas was systematized by the manualists with an eye to identifying sin and assigning penance, this was to the detriment of the whole of Thomistic

---

6. Gleason, *Contending With Modernity*, 115.
7. Ibid., 116.
8. Servais Pinckaers, OP, *The Sources of Christian Ethics*, trans. Mary Thomas Noble, OP (1985; repr. Washington, D.C.: The Catholic University of America Press, 1995), 256, 329.
9. Ibid., 279.

teaching. This systematization removed the concepts of sin and penance from the larger context of morality wherein happiness, virtue, grace, and heaven were crucial.

Priests had been educated primarily as Thomists with a neo-Scholastic outlook. Dissatisfaction with the narrowness of that training, as well as with the legalism inherent to the manual system, led them to find other ways to relate their Thomistic training to theology, as well as to make this neo-Scholasticism more pastoral for the contemporary situation. The rise of Transcendental Thomism provides one example of a response to the dissatisfaction with neo-Scholastic training.[10] The tone of Vatican II, paradigmatically expressed in *Gaudium et spes*, was one of openness to the world. Bolstered by Vatican II's apparent openness to the world, many priest-theologians sought to break free from the monolithic and constricting education they had received, similar to the way that Catholic laity in the pluralistic suburbs sometimes sought to break free of the traditional Catholicism in which they and their parents had been raised. Priest-theologians found the manualist system inadequate to address many of the problems in the modern world and wanted something more personal, practical, and pastoral, as well as something more able to address social problems. Meanwhile, those who adhered to casuistry found themselves to be a criticized minority in the years following the Council.[11]

Pinckaers notes that openness to the modern world following Vatican II resulted in "an allergy to traditional positions" among moral theologians.[12] While fighting against concepts like obedience and natural law, moral theologians simultaneously, and often uncritically, welcomed modern thought in areas of philosophy, psychology, sociology, and history, subjecting everything to reexamination in light of Hegel, Freud, Marx, and Nietzsche. Pinckaers notes three characteristics of what he identifies as this "Secular Christianity": (1) radical openness to the world, with primacy given to love of neighbor over love of God; (2) the critical spirit,

10. Romanus Cessario, OP, explains that Rahner's Transcendental Thomism was an eclectic selection of Thomas that assumes that Kant's critical turn rendered obsolete Aquinas's use of Aristotle; Cessario, *A Short History of Thomism* (Washington, D.C.: The Catholic University of America Press, 2003), 88.

11. Cessario, *The Moral Virtues and Theological Ethics*, 2nd ed. (Notre Dame: University of Notre Dame Press, 2009).

12. Pinckaers, *Sources of Christian Ethics*, 304.

From Responsibility to Freedom

particularly in the criticism of the church's authority; and (3) reinterpretations in light of human values, which defend pluralism and emphasize human values at the expense of traditional Christian values.[13]

These characteristics are useful as context for this chapter as we consider several major theologians of the period. While Gerald Kelly did not live post–Vatican II, John Ford's negative reception, particularly following the release of *Humanae vitae* and, by contrast, Bernard Häring's popularity with moral theologians at that same time, make sense in a theological world that took a perspective such as that described by Pinckaers. Like the firmly entrenched cultural Catholicism then undergoing a transformation in the midst of pluralism, the Catholic neo-Scholasticism associated with manualism was reexamined and found wanting. While a few, like Ford, remained loyal to traditional teachings, the authority of the papacy, and the privileged locus of the confessional, most, like Häring, sought other ways to think about morality, and Häring's approach was compelling for secular Christians as described by Pinckaers. In the midst of such a transition, the denigration of manualism and casuistry led to the concept of sin becoming detached from the sacrament of confession. Words like "obedience" and "obligation" were associated with the neo-Scholastic and manualist outlook; to many they implied a judgmental legalism and an unthinking faith of the past. Words such as freedom and responsibility, on the other hand, became the touchstones of a morality that turned away from the restrictive legalism of the past in an attempt to bring greater meaning to Catholic life and morality.

The Last Stand of the Old School: John C. Ford, SJ, and Gerald Kelly, SJ

In his book *A History of Catholic Moral Theology in the Twentieth Century*, James Keenan identifies Jesuits Ford and Kelly as neo-manualists, the classicist resistance to the advent of historical-mindedness in moral

---

13. Ibid., 307–9. For another view of this time period, see Keenan, *History of Catholic Moral Theology*, chap. 7, "New Foundations for Moral Reasoning, 1970–1989." Keenan's take is surprisingly similar to Pinckaers, although more positive in tone with an emphasis on the pastoral motivation of the changes in moral theology; see also Charles E. Curran, *Catholic Moral Theology in the United States*, especially chap. 4, "The Setting of Moral Theology After Vatican II," 83–101.

theology. Keenan makes the ultimate failure of this resistance palpable: while Kelly did not live to see the end of Vatican II, Ford's support of *Humanae vitae* led to the boycott of his classes and his resignation from the Weston School of Theology.[14] And yet despite the criticism toward the end of their careers, John McGreevy suggests that these two "should be ranked among the period's most influential American intellectuals, with a reach extending from the confessional to Catholic hospitals, bishops, theological journals, and even the Vatican itself."[15]

Both Ford and Kelly entered the Society of Jesus after graduating from Jesuit high schools, and they met in Rome while studying at the Gregorian University. Following this education, both became seminary instructors of moral theology; Kelly taught at St. Mary's in Kansas, and Ford spent most of his career in Weston, Massachusetts.[16] As individuals, Kelly came to be regarded as the father of medical ethics because of his work on life support, while Ford became well-known because of his essay against obliteration bombing, which he wrote in the midst of World War II.[17] Ford and Kelly, often working as a team, were also known as the editors of the moral theology section of the journal *Theological Studies*. In this role from 1941 to 1954, they annually authored the comprehensive surveys of their field in a section called "Notes on Moral Theology."

With an eye to a multi-volume series, Ford and Kelly published their first volume of *Contemporary Moral Theology*, subtitled *Questions in Fundamental Moral Theology*. Here they reorganized, synthesized, and expanded upon their work that had appeared in the *Theological Studies* notes section. The result is a worthwhile survey addressing contemporary topics in accessible prose. Originally published in 1958, the book was unique at a time when manuals were still popular. Ford and Kelly's text goes far beyond the manualist format, almost as if anticipating Pinckaers's criticism of that form. From the first pages, these Jesuits established the supernatural aspect of moral theology, stating that ethics was the science of morality based on reason, whereas moral theology included ethics but

---

14. Keenan, *History of Catholic Moral Theology*, 115–18; chap. 5 is on Häring, and Ford and Kelly's theories are a section of chap. 6.
15. McGreevy, *Catholicism and American Freedom*, 217.
16. Ibid., 216.
17. Keenan, *History of Catholic Moral Theology*, 117.

From Responsibility to Freedom

went beyond it by "studying man in the supernatural order, possessed of a supernatural destiny."[18] Despite being inheritors of the casuist system, Ford and Kelly described a sort of freedom for gaining virtue and the final end of beatitude, dependent especially upon the guide of authority, which for them was synonymous with the church as an interpreter of revelation. And perhaps it is this last point that gained for *Contemporary Moral Theology* a reputation of being the outdated, old style of legalistic and minimalistic Catholic morality.

Ford and Kelly's series never proceeded beyond the second volume, subtitled *Marriage Questions*, because Kelly suffered a fatal heart attack in the same year of this volume's publication. Moreover, the rapid changes in moral theology during the time period meant that their work was no longer as highly regarded as it had been in the 1950s, as a review by the young layman Daniel Callahan indicated. In *Commonweal*, Callahan described the authors as "years behind the [theological] revolution now in progress."[19] The subsequent rejection of Ford by his students at Weston was further evidence that Ford and Kelly's reprise of manualism was no more popular than manualism itself.

For their part, Ford and Kelly were aware of the dissatisfaction that many had with the status quo of contemporary moral theology; to some extent they shared in the criticism. In the decades preceding the Second Vatican Council, changes in moral theology were becoming evident; for example, the publication and use of confession manuals that had long guided confessors were on the decline. In their first volume of *Contemporary Moral Theology*, the authors noted that "a feeling of uneasiness about moral theology has been in the air for some years. It is a feeling which cannot be brushed aside as mere murmuring by malcontents."[20] In chapters 4 and 5, entitled "Modern Criticisms of Moral Theology" and "New Approaches to Moral Theology," respectively, Ford and Kelly surveyed critics of Catholic moral theology, and they noted in particular the widespread discontent with a manualist tradition that appeared to be legalistic and minimalistic and not sufficiently focused on the virtue of charity.[21]

18. John C. Ford, SJ, and Gerald Kelly, SJ, *Contemporary Moral Theology: Questions in Fundamental Moral Theology* (1958; repr. Westminster, Maryland, 1960), 1:3.
19. Daniel Callahan, "Authority and the Theologian," *Commonweal*, June 5, 1964, 322.
20. Ford and Kelly, *Contemporary Moral Theology*, 1:42.
21. Ibid., 1:42–43, 1:60.

Ford and Kelly saw the criticism as justified, particularly in regard to the neglect of charity. But they also worried that Catholic morality represented by the manuals was being replaced by a morality based too much on the subjective judgment of the faithful at the expense of the law and universal principles. After an exposition of Louvain's Jacques Leclercq, Ford and Kelly noted the "dangers of a personalistic morality which rejects traditional norms as being too abstract to be adapted to the exigencies of the concrete man," and they observed that this tendency turned away from casuistry in favor of situation ethics.[22] The authors stated that modern criticisms of Catholic moral theology should be welcome; there certainly was a need for a change in emphasis, as well as a more positive approach to the moral life. At the same time, however, Ford and Kelly insisted that "the welcome we extend to critics should itself be a critical one."[23]

At the heart of their defense of objective morality, casuistry, and the manuals was the sense that moral theology, whether cases studied at the seminary or matter heard in the confessional, was about sin and salvation and hence was practical; moral theology dealt with applying moral laws to possible and actual specific situations. Salvation was not something elusive, but rather was attainable for the person who sought to do God's will. In contrasting moral theology with ethics, then, Ford and Kelly emphasized that moral theology "studies man in the supernatural order, possessed of a supernatural destiny," which is based on revelation and the teaching of the church.[24] The reason for hope in a supernatural destiny also provided a motivation to study laws and moral principles; these laws and principles were an aid for those seeking to do God's will and attain salvation. Moreover, the laws and principles were not simply abstract ideas, but rather were embodied concretely in the everyday life of believers. Priests communicated these laws in practical terms from the pulpit, and the ministry of the confessional was a particularly important place to explain the moral principles pastorally. Hence Ford noted in an exam for his Jesuit seminarians that he did not want to test "*abstract knowledge*" but wanted to gauge "the student's ability to *apply correctly* and *prudently* to concrete human situations the law and the moral prin-

22. Ibid., 1:58–59.
23. Ibid., 1:80.
24. Ibid., 1:3.

From Responsibility to Freedom

ciples and concepts he has studied for two years."[25] This important skill enabled priests in their ministry of judging and healing; they assisted the faithful in identifying their sins, assigned appropriate penances, gave counsel, and granted absolution. Thus the confessor played an important role in guiding the laity toward their supernatural destiny.

One of Ford and Kelly's chief concerns with the new trends in moral theology was the damage to a healthy understanding of obligation that could be caused by an emphasis on love. Ford and Kelly noted modern critics' impatience with "obligationism," stating, "People can speak beautifully of the law of love casting out fear. But sometimes it leaves one with the uneasy feeling that they are casting out the restraints of objective morality along with the fear."[26] Ford and Kelly acknowledged that this turn to love was to some degree motivated by the problem of "private teachers," lay and cleric, who constantly belabored various obligations of the faithful by enumerating a multitude of actions they classified as mortal sins.[27] In the face of seemingly impossible moral standards, it was easier for the moralist to invoke an abstract law of love in order to trump specific objective moral guidelines.

Ford and Kelly recognized that some moral theologians saw an outright incompatibility of the ethics of love and the ethics of obligation, with a priority to be given to the supposed ethics of love.[28] The dissatisfaction with obligationism could become dissatisfaction with obligation; irritation with legalism could become irritation with law; and fondness for the concrete, personally creative, and subjectively satisfying could tend toward a belittling of the abstract, universal, and objective values of morality applied to specific cases.[29] In particular, it seemed to them that critics of obligationism contended that sanctity only began where obligation ends: "One would think that obedience to the obligations of the law of God is somehow incompatible with generosity, liberty, joy, and the flowering of one's spiritual personality." Perhaps thinking of the concept of blind obedience, Ford and Kelly noted that some Catholic authors

---

25. Cited in McGreevy, *Catholicism and American Freedom*, 218; Some Notes on the Exam, "Ad Audieindas Confessiones" [1950s], Audiendas Confessiones, 1940–62 file, box 18 from the John C. Ford papers at the College of the Holy Cross.

26. Ford and Kelly, *Contemporary Moral Theology*, 1:87.

27. Ibid., 1:88–89.   28. Ibid., 1:40.

29. Ibid., 1:102–3.

"speak as if obedience were somehow an irrational abdication of the self, as if authority were somehow the enemy of one's personal liberty and perfection."[30] Ford and Kelly thought this was an unfair depiction of obedience as lived by many of the faithful. For them, obedience and obligation to the established moral norms facilitated freedom, rather than restricting it, as seemed to be implied by those who protested the legalism of the church. The Sunday Mass obligation, for example, was a moral norm aimed at facilitating freedom for those who obeyed this command of God.

Ford and Kelly also detected a "Quietistic distortion." They observed that the criticism of obligation devalued particular actions and obligations in favor of a general orientation of love, wherein the person was not responsible for particular deviations from the law; this tended toward the heresy of Quietism, the absorption of the soul into the divine during earthly life.[31] In contrast, the authors emphasized that the concept of freedom in no way contradicted obedience to an obligation. As a particular illustration, Ford and Kelly considered the example previously mentioned concerning whether it would be better to attend Sunday Mass "freely"—that is, without obligation—than to attend because the law imposes a grave obligation to do so. They answered that of course it is better to do something by choice (a voluntary action) rather than by coercion, but, nonetheless, "there is no absolute value or special spiritual merit in choosing to do a good thing precisely because one is not morally forced, that is, not morally obliged, to do it."

The authors noted that when one fulfills a moral obligation in observation of God's law, he is free to do the opposite. But this free choice, made with God's help, is the means of perfection. Here Ford and Kelly distinguished between obligatory works and supererogatory works, which go beyond the call of duty. At times, the person may have to choose between the obligatory and the supererogatory, but the obligatory work is not less valuable to God merely because it is obligatory. In fact, to make a free choice to perform the obligatory might be more perfect than an act of supererogation. Consider as an analogy a student who fails to attend class or complete any required assignments but does delve into all the

30. Ibid., 1:92.
31. Ibid., 1:90.

From Responsibility to Freedom

texts listed under "Suggested Further Reading" on the syllabus. This student has performed a supererogatory act by going beyond the syllabus, but he or she has simultaneously failed to meet the course requirements. From the professor's point of view, it would have been better for her to have attended class and completed the required assignments. The fact of these assignments being obligatory does not detract from their worth. Rather, the professor designates them as requirements because they are regarded as being more important for effective learning of the material. It is precisely these requirements that first facilitate freedom in the knowledge of the subject at hand, and the further reading enriches that knowledge.

Ford and Kelly saw it as important to recognize that moral obligation is not a barrier between God and man, but a unique necessity binding God and man and uniting man with his final end of beatitude: "The law of God is our truest good, and conformity to His will is our highest perfection."[32] Ford and Kelly acknowledged that the perfection of freedom involved conformity to God's will, not because, in a Nominalist perspective, God was an exterior will imposing arbitrary regulations on human beings, but rather because conforming to God's law and will was best for human beings, who had been given a supernatural destiny.

Ford and Kelly had another concern about the devaluing of obedience to obligation—namely, that in the attempt to transcend minimalist, legalistic morality, it left behind the vast majority of Christians who "will not be spiritual heroes." While it was obviously important constantly to call Christians to a higher degree of sanctity, moral rigorism could be harmful in its effects. As long as they partook of the sacraments, the faithful need not have "perfect charity" in order to be justified; even with venial sins and imperfections they could stay in the state of grace.[33] Hence the obligations imposed on the faithful were beneficial in maintaining a degree of sanctity that was attainable for the majority of the people in the pew and a good starting point for seeking greater perfection. While obviously it was better for the faithful to fulfill obligations out of love than out of fear of punishment, this was a matter of motivation and hence should not detract from the need for obligations.

32. Ibid., 1;94.
33. Ibid., 1:82–84.

To act out of grave obligation was not necessarily to act out of fear of punishment, and Ford and Kelly believed that the sense of obligation could keep the faithful on the right track as concerned their supernatural destiny. Additionally, Ford and Kelly believed fear of punishment and love of God did not have to be contradictories.[34] Rather, they could and did exist simultaneously, as exemplified by the standard Act of Contrition, which stated it in these words: "Oh my God, I am heartily sorry for having offended Thee, and I detest all my sins because I dread the loss of Heaven, and the pains of Hell, but most of all, because I have offended Thee, my God, Who art all good, and deserving of all my love."[35] Both to dread the loss of heaven and to regret offending God were important, and not mutually exclusive.

When it came to the concept of responsibility, Ford and Kelly espoused a traditional understanding in which responsibility was synonymous with imputability or culpability. This meant that responsibility was a word to describe a person's relation to his or her personal, actual sin. Catholic morality, they argued, presupposes recognizable serious responsibility in a large number of acts.[36] The authors' concept of freedom was closely related to that of responsibility, for it was the extent of a person's free will that allowed for a designation of culpability for a particular act. In the face of a psychoanalytical attack on freedom proposing diminished responsibility for actions, Ford and Kelly wrote that Catholic moralists must defend the notion that "normal men and women per se have sufficient freedom in the concrete circumstances of daily life to merit great praise or great blame before God."[37] To these authors, morality as a concept made no sense unless voluntary choice was granted. On the other hand, they acknowledged a complexity wherein there were degrees of freedom and therefore corresponding degrees of responsibility. And yet, even the acknowledgment of various influences, conscious or unconscious, external or internal, experienced by a sinner did not necessarily denote that the agent had insufficient freedom to be accountable for a

34. Ibid., 1:95.
35. "Act of Contrition," standard prayer, here cited from *My Sunday Missal Explained*, compiled by Joseph Stedman, Latin-English ed. (1938; repr. Brooklyn: Confraternity of the Precious Blood, 1941), 333.
36. Ford and Kelly, *Contemporary Moral Theology*, 1:183.
37. Ibid., 1:200.

From Responsibility to Freedom

mortal sin.³⁸ Again, we see that, for these authors, responsibility was a word defined in relation to sin and was a concept addressed practically in terms of culpability within the context of the sacrament of confession.

The understanding of freedom and responsibility was also reflected in the authors' understanding of maturity, a notion that was gaining ground in popular currency. Ford and Kelly saw the confessional as the place for growth in maturity. In no sense did maturity liberate one from the law or from the confessional; rather, it was in seeking the sacrament that the person became mature.³⁹ Maturity denoted the continual growth in identifying one's freedom for actions and hence one's responsibility for one's sins and the willingness to bear punishment for them. Those who took their sins to the confessional succeeded in acknowledging their responsibility for their sin and grew in freedom as they became more aware of their culpability for sin and more able to avoid sin. Here again, it is possible to identify a notion of freedom tending toward virtue. The ability to avoid sin was an advance in freedom; the *habitus* that was established and strengthened in the confessional was not a limit to freedom; rather, it was a step toward seeking freedom through the development of virtue. Though the voluntary nature of action remained crucial, virtue was not a hindrance to freedom, but rather supported the person's freedom of perfection and conformance to God's will.

Ford and Kelly represent the last stand of a Thomistic-based neo-Scholastic model of moral theology. Keenan describes their book *Contemporary Moral Theology* as "an example of the classicist's resistance to the historical-minded model."⁴⁰ These Jesuits were distinguished by their belief in the teaching authority of the church—in particular as it was represented by the pope—and hence they also emphasized the corresponding notion of obedience to moral obligations set forth by the church. The call

---

38. One case study Kelly examined in 1947 is that of a Catholic African American family that is shunned at each of the nearby white parishes. Kelly rightly criticizes the lack of hospitality of these white parishes and states that those treating the African Americans in this way are in serious sin. However, despite the difficulty of circumstances, the African Americans in question are still morally obligated to attend Sunday Mass. Though they may have diminished freedom, they maintain enough freedom that, should they choose *not* to seek out a more accepting (albeit farther away) parish, they are responsible for the sin of not attending Mass; Gerald Kelly, "Notes on Moral Theology," *Theological Studies* 8 (1947): 112–14.

39. Ford and Kelly, *Contemporary Moral Theology*, 1:99.

40. Keenan, *History of Catholic Moral Theology*, 116.

to such obedience did not inhibit freedom, in their opinion, but rather assisted freedom and allowed one to remain in a state of charity with God. The notion of freedom furthermore implied responsibility; a person who maintained free choice was also culpable for sins. Each of these terms was related to the understanding of a person's supernatural end, and the sacrament of confession was instrumental in assisting a person toward that supernatural end. Maturity marked progress in the spiritual life and, again, advancement to the supernatural end; rather than an autonomous will, it denoted obedience to God's will (set forth by the church, in many cases) and the perfection of charity in ascribing to God's law. All of these convictions were expressed concretely as Ford and Kelly tackled moral issues in their "Notes in Moral Theology." That which might seem to be ridiculous, legalistic hair-splitting was in their minds connected to a larger, supernatural picture. The method of case study and the hours spent by priests in the confessional attested to a belief in the nature of sin as something that hindered the penitent on the journey of her supernatural destiny. Hence there was a need to remove sin for the benefit of each person seeking sanctity. Maturity came from identifying and confessing one's sins and by amending the will so as to sin less; this maturity was associated with growth in freedom and progress toward the supernatural end.

As heirs of the casuist system, Ford and Kelly believed in the value of case studies and the skill that emerged from applying laws to actual situations that might be brought to the confessional. These two prioritized the supernatural end for human beings while also asserting that moral obligations did not detract from spiritual life. They did not, however, describe adherence to moral obligations in terms of strengthening virtue, nor did they emphasize the spiritual value of going beyond the minimum requirements.[41] The resulting emphasis was, then, on solving cases according to rules rather than on strengthening virtue. Even this more su-

---

41. It is interesting to think about four examples presented by Joseph Chinnici in *Living Stones*—namely, Virgil Michel, Dorothy Day, James Keller, and Thomas Merton, about whom Chinnici writes, "While accepting the values of obedience and discipline, they argued for a more affective, interior sense of prayer, a unity between action and contemplation, the role of conscience in the spiritual life, and the primacy of love." This suggests that even during the time period there were those who maintained aspects emphasized by Ford and Kelly, while also highlighting love, as would Bernard Häring; Joseph P. Chinnici, OSF, *Living Stones: The History and Structure of Catholic Spiritual Life in the United States* (New York: MacMillan, 1989), 212.

From Responsibility to Freedom

pernatural casuistic model would not satisfy those who objected to Catholic moral theology being portrayed primarily as a legal system.

Ford and Kelly's approach could be further criticized as lacking a personal element and emphasis on love that would make the sacrament of confession meaningful for the laity. Their approach failed sufficiently to address the personal and relational dimension of the sacrament because it focused upon moral judgment of the situation based on the objective moral law. The approach might have been more compelling if it had appealed to the lives of the faithful by conveying the value and meaning of the sacrament of penance and confession-based morality as intrinsic to a relationship with God. As it stood, however, the ultimately quick decline of the manualist system is evidence of the widespread judgment that it was insufficient for addressing the moral problems of the times.

A New Approach to Morality: Bernard Häring, CSsR

Bernard Häring (1912–98) was a German who joined the Redemptorist community in 1934. Hoping to be a missionary, Häring was disappointed in his assignment to study moral theology, and he did not find his academic study to be beneficial because of the way it was structured at that time, focusing on morality understood primarily in relation to canon law.[42] In his mind, the well-established link between canon law and moral theology only served to reinforce the legalism of moral theology and make it unhelpful for the laity. Nonetheless, Häring persevered at Tübingen, despite a suspension of his studies due to World War II. While teaching at the newly founded Academia Alphonsiana in Rome, he wrote *The Law of Christ* that in 1954 secured his fame as a moral theologian.

In place of the primacy of obedience and obligation found in moral theology at the time, Häring emphasized the concepts of freedom and responsibility, grounded first and foremost in love, which was the law of Christ on which his book was based. For Häring this change in emphasis was not simply intellectual, but rather grew out of his experience of Germany, and the church in Germany, during World War II. Häring attested:

42. Kathleen A. Cahalan, *Formed in the Image of Christ: The Sacramental-Moral Theology of Bernard Häring, C.Ss.R.* (Collegeville, Minn.: Liturgical Press, 2004), 5; Keenan, *History of Catholic Moral Theology*, 89.

Unfortunately I ... experienced the most absurd obedience by Christians—God have mercy—toward a criminal regime. And that ... radically affected my thinking and acting as a moral theologian. After the war I returned to moral theology with the firm decision to teach it so that its core concept would not be obedience but responsibility, the courage to be responsible. I believe I have remained true to this decision—of course not to the damage to genuine obedience, that is, to an obedience that is responsible and joined to openness and a critical sense.[43]

Responsibility was, for Häring, a concept that implied much more than culpability or imputability. First and foremost, responsibility denoted the "personal-essential characteristic of religion. This is the relation of dialogue, word and response, in a community ... responsibility means that in a community between man and God, man responds to God's word with the responsibility of his personal decision and action."[44] While not entirely shirking the more usual usage of responsibility, Häring nonetheless insisted that responsibility primarily implies interaction with God, with the ability to remain open to the word of love and respond in love.[45] Häring used etymology to explain the word "responsibility," and hence he defined it just as its word parts suggested: the ability to respond—in this case, to respond to the love of God. One difference between Häring's understanding of responsibility in contrast to that of Ford and Kelly's was chronological. For Häring, responsibility was more like a motivation or reason for acting in a particular way prior to the action, whereas for Ford and Kelly responsibility allowed for an assessment and designation of merit or blame after the action.

Häring's concept of freedom was closely tied to this concept of responsibility: "The personal autonomy of the Christian is based in his personality and especially in the freedom heightened by grace by virtue of which he is not only irreplaceable and unique, but also personally responsible to the Father in heaven."[46] Häring saw responsibility and freedom as interdependent, with freedom being an expression of response

---

43. Bernard Häring, *My Witness for the Church*, intro and trans. Leonard Swidler (Mahwah, N.J.: Paulist Press, 1992), 23–24; originally published in German in 1989.

44. Häring, *The Law of Christ*, vol. 1, *General Moral Theology*, trans. Edwin G. Kaiser (Westminster, Md.: Newman Press, 1961), 47.

45. Ibid., 1:157.

46. Häring, *Christian Maturity*, trans. Arlene Swidler (New York: Herder and Herder, 1967), 51.

From Responsibility to Freedom

to God.⁴⁷ Human freedom, by virtue of participation in divine freedom, allowed for the person either to accept or reject God's call.⁴⁸ Employing the conventional meaning of responsibility, Häring noted the importance of freedom when he said, "Freedom which makes man responsible for his actions is itself a noble trust committed to man, a tremendous responsibility."⁴⁹

The language of "freedom" and "responsibility" were in vogue as theological words of the time. In his dissertation, which in 1968 was published as a book, Albert Jonsen explored the theme of responsibility in the works of Karl Barth, Dietrich Bonhoeffer, H. Richard Niebuhr, and Robert Johann, in addition to Häring.⁵⁰ By the time of Vatican II, this language of freedom and responsibility was reflected in the council documents, most notably *Gaudium et spes*. Häring was the coordinating secretary for the editorial committee for *Gaudium et spes*, and his input in that document becomes apparent when comparing it with his own theological work, particularly the focus on responsibility and freedom.⁵¹ *Gaudium et spes* employs the word "responsibility" twenty-seven times and the word "freedom" thirty-two times, in addition to the word "liberty," which appears ten times. Meanwhile, the word "obedience" occurs only three times in *Gaudium et spes*, and one of these references bears a negative connotation, as it is part of the phrase "blind obedience."⁵²

With Häring's assistance, the notion of obedience—so often exalted in the history of the church—took a backseat to responsibility and freedom, which had risen in popularity in the midst of international power struggles and in the European post-fascist context. The church in the modern world would not be understood through the traditional language of obedience, which indicated an authoritative (and perhaps authoritarian) leader. Rather, *Gaudium et spes*' panegyric approach confirmed and even celebrated the modern commitment to responsibility and freedom, both

---

47. Häring, *Law of Christ*, 1:49.   48. Ibid., 1:101.
49. Ibid., 1:103.
50. Albert Jonsen, *Responsibility in Modern Religious Ethics* (Washington, D.C.: Corpus, 1968), 100.
51. Häring, *My Witness for the Church*, 61.
52. *Gaudium et spes*, accessed on March 15, 2010, at http://www.vatican.va. "Blind Obedience" is in paragraph 79, under section 1, "The Avoidance of War." Even the title of this section indicates that the larger context for concern about blind obedience grew out of a post-Nazi and post-fascist European context.

of which evoked interior motivation rather than the imposition of external authority and necessity of obedience.[53] The general negative reaction toward obedience was understandable in the wake of World War II, but it easily tended toward a problematic overreaction that undermined the traditional importance of obedience.

Häring himself did not abandon the concept of obedience but rather emphasized its essential compatibility with freedom: "Freedom and obedience ... are not contradictories: rather, they require one another and complement one another. Christian freedom lives from its union with obedience in faith. But in the same way obedience proceeds from the virtue of freedom."[54] He noted that an emphasis on the virtue of freedom should not conflict with the "esteem" for obedience in following Christ; rather, obedience seeks and enhances freedom, and freedom grows out of obedience in faith.[55] Despite this seemingly affirmative portrayal of freedom, Häring nonetheless generally minimized a positive understanding of obedience in his discussion of that topic. His theology was haunted by the association with unthinking Nazi obedience and the knowledge that Christian obedience was so rarely understood to demand disobedience to injustice. This practicality prevented the notion from securing an important place for Häring.[56]

Moreover, despite his occasional positive comments about obedience based in the church's tradition, Häring's was a particular understanding of obedience at variance with other moralists of the time, such as Ford and Kelly. The Jesuit team saw the potential of freedom as proceeding from obedience to God's law expressed by the church. To be free was to be obedient to God and hence church law; freedom resulted from obedience. Häring, meanwhile, was more apt to describe it the opposite way: obedience proceeded from freedom. To be free in this account was

53. The conviction that the language of Vatican II was epideictic or panegyric (in contrast to earlier ecclesiastical councils that favored anathemas and canons) is stated most convincingly by John W. O'Malley in chap. 2, "Vatican II: Did Anything Happen?," in *Vatican II: Did Anything Happen?*, 52–91.

54. Häring, *Christian Maturity*, 53.

55. Ibid., 57, 65.

56. Cahalan, *Formed in the Image of Christ*, 19. Cahalan states that Häring's concern for blind obedience to both Nazi and church law convinced Häring "of the need to move moral theology away from legalism and minimalism toward personal freedom and responsibility in relation to God."

From Responsibility to Freedom

to be able to choose to be obedient. To be obedient necessitated a choice between contraries, made after careful consideration and discernment, and this meant that not all obedience was good; freedom did not guarantee a correct decision in favor of obedience. In short, for Ford and Kelly, obedience to the church was the first step to freedom, but for Häring, freedom came first and enabled one to choose whether or not to be obedient to a particular authority.

Häring's specific concern was about what he called "blind obedience," and often his use of the word "obedience" seemed to imply that adjective, even when it was absent. This blind obedience was, first and foremost, the obedience that Häring ascribed to the German followers of Hitler, but it was also a flawed obedience that he sometimes recognized in the church, perhaps because church and government were often intertwined in his experience of World War II Germany. In 1967, Häring proclaimed, "That era of Christianity which can be roughly characterized by the narrow vision of the hierarchy and the blind obedience of the faithful—and often the unenlightened faith of both—has come to an end."[57] Published just a year earlier was a book that compiled a series of lectures, entitled *Liberty of the Children of God*. Though these lectures concerned both civil and ecclesiastical authority, Häring did not take pains to distinguish the two or any potential difference in how a Christian might approach these authorities in different manners. Focusing on the problem of blind obedience, rather, Häring explained that

> Blind obedience is never a Christian obedience. God does not want blind obedience but intelligent obedience, an obedience that sees all things in the light of love. He does not want a forced obedience but rather desires that obedience which flows from one's free will and personal evaluation of each concrete situation in which he is asked to obey.[58]

Whenever he turned to a discussion of obedience as such, Häring was apt to distinguish blind obedience from the true Christian obedience, which he often associated with maturity and the free choice to be obedient. The circumstances of the time also contributed to his view on maturity and obedience: "The responsibility of Christians in the modern democratic

---

57. Häring, *Christian Maturity*, 7.
58. Häring, *Liberty of the Children of God* (Staten Island, N.Y.: Alba House, 1966), 85–86.

state and the increased maturity of the laity so vitally necessary to the Church today force us to re-think the essence of authority and the corresponding question of obedience."[59]

As Häring saw it, this maturity of the laity meant that all obedience must now be a discerning, thoughtful obedience wherein Christians were willing to criticize if they believed it was necessary. Moreover, Häring seemed to think that laity's criticism *would* be necessary. In fact, he suggested that a lack of criticism for authority was not a "true and dignified kind of Christian obedience." Rather, the one who fails to criticize, whether intentionally or unintentionally, is "actually guilty of foolishness and lust for power."[60] Häring had found in the Second Vatican Council an affirmation of the laity's maturity and sanction of their more active participation in the church.[61] He viewed this, first and foremost, in contrast to that "blind obedience" manifest toward Hitler, but also, secondarily, toward the obligations set forth by ecclesiastical authority, which had lost credibility to some extent through complicity in European fascist regimes.

At the heart of his concern was Häring's experience of a Catholic morality that tended to be both legalistic and minimalistic, fostering the development of a laity overly focused on a narrow set of rules and on following those rules to avoid God's punishment. Even his own training, which explained morality in terms of canon law, was an indicator of the propensity for Catholicism to define behavior in terms of law. The moral theology represented by the manualist tradition reinforced such an attitude because manualists tended to focus on laws of morality and encourage the easiest way to avoid violating those laws, rather than calling Christians to aim higher. A sense of duty toward obligation conceived legalistically was problematic because it failed in recognizing that the ultimate "law of Christ" was the law of love. Häring's concern was that the external actions of those operating under "blind obedience," wherein they adhered to the bare minimum of the moral law, lacked the necessary

---

59. Ibid., 7.
60. Ibid., 48. It is possible that by authority here, Häring thought only of civil authority, not ecclesiastical, but this is not clearly specified.
61. Häring, *Road to Renewal: Perspectives of Vatican II* (New York: Alba House, 1966), 83, 117, 135.

and more crucial interior disposition of love toward Christ and others. In the *Law of Christ*, he explained:

> Love is the center, the very heart of all religious and moral good.... No one denies, of course, that an action can possess a formal ethical correctness without the impulse of love, but the perfection of good in the religious sense can be formed only in the thought and action which are in some measure sustained and ennobled by the divine power of love.[62]

The spirit of morality, therefore, should not revolve around duty as the obligation to perform certain actions. "Mere awareness of duty, set exclusively on the 'must' and the 'must not' of obligation, is the very antithesis of inner disposition and right intention, which as such are grounded on consciousness of true value."[63] Häring worried that the emphasis on obligation would detract from the inner disposition of love. Häring's thought on this developed such that in 1966 he would write that "what is imposed is never or seldom loved."[64]

Crucial to Häring's understanding of morality was the presence of choice and personal discernment; freedom was to choose between contrary actions. Häring was confident that the truly mature Christian with a strong interior life would not simply choose the easiest route in a particular situation, but would make the more valiant decision.[65] Hence the free will acting on the law of love would naturally go above and beyond the obligations imposed by an external authority. In contrast to this was the faithful's preoccupation with following a multiplicity of laws and obligations imposed on them by the church, which Häring believed often distracted the faithful from acting out of love. Ford and Kelly might have interpreted such an emphasis as granting priority to supererogatory,

---

62. Häring, *Law of Christ*, 1:207.
63. Ibid., 1:196.
64. Häring, *Liberty of the Children of God*, 131. There is some evidence that Häring looked to Immanuel Kant during this time period as an alternative explanation to a Thomistic manualist system experienced as external law imposed as obligation on the individual. Häring's use of the Kantian understanding of freedom as self-legislating empowered the faithful to criticize authority. Chronologically speaking, the first action of the will's assent was to love, not to obedience. While this love made obedience to an external authority possible, it also made criticism of that external authority possible, as both actions depended on the individual's autonomous choice between contraries.
65. Häring, *Law of Christ*, 1:176.

spontaneous moral actions rather than to those required by obligation. While Ford and Kelly no doubt regarded the supererogatory actions to be excellent as one strove to perfect one's spiritual life, they still saw these actions as supererogatory—that is, above and beyond obligation, and hence not in place of obligation or in preference to obligation. Häring could be read as highlighting the intention of love or charitable interior disposition in order to determine the merit of an act, in contrast with the more Thomistic notion that human acts take their meaning from their objects.

The differing trajectories of the two convictions can be supposed by considering various responses to the problem of Sunday Mass obligation for the reluctant.[66] Ford and Kelly no doubt recognized that obligations of this kind could be fulfilled in more or less meritorious ways depending upon intention, but they could not be knowingly and purposely omitted without sin. If the person's Mass attendance resulted from habit or the sense of fulfilling an obligation, one could view this as an opportunity for improvement, for rectifying intention. It would not be a sufficient reason for choosing to miss Mass. The person who recognizes that this law facilitates freedom should strive rather to perfect one's interior disposition or intention of love in obediently performing this act of obligation; the person would never use an imperfect intention as an excuse to avoid fulfilling an obligation.

Häring, on the other hand, worried that the very law of Sunday Mass attendance caused undue concern as to whether missing Mass was a mortal or venial sin when the real issue at hand was always responding to God's love, not splitting hairs in identifying sin. One possible trajectory of Häring's position was to gauge the value of an act based on the person's perception of response to God's love without consideration of the law. Going to Mass on Sunday was no more or less important than other acts simply because it was required, and in fact the concern with fulfilling this duty could detract from a genuine loving response to God. The person might be so worried about getting to Sunday Mass that it would

---

66. This example is mostly speculative, although Häring did comment, as noted later in this chapter, that there is no objective borderline between mortal and venial sin in the case of missing Sunday Mass. I am concerned here more with the trajectory of the two positions than the conclusions they made explicit.

From Responsibility to Freedom

become a distraction, causing her to fail to examine how her racist attitudes detract from his or her ability to respond lovingly to God.

Ford and Kelly saw laws and obligations as facilitating freedom—that is, a freedom for excellence presuming a supernatural end. In contrast, Häring believed what he had witnessed in Catholics was that, practically speaking, the concern for law and obligation actually hindered the freedom engendered by the ultimate law, the law of love, which allowed one to make the better choice between contraries. In his 1967 book concerning the sacrament of reconciliation, Häring wrote, "Legalism caters to routine and conformity, not to the individual."[67] Thus he argued that confessors should adopt what he saw as an Alphonsian line wherein confessors need not necessarily remedy the invincible ignorance of a penitent. Häring believed that the penitent should not be counseled immediately as to the extent of his sin as regards the law, but rather should be gradually introduced to the truth over time. He saw this as a dynamic approach to morality, "moving the person ever onward toward a fuller realization of Christian life."[68]

Häring clearly did not want this dynamic approach identified with situation ethics, which had a bad reputation. Hence he noted that "the older form of situation ethics erects its altars to human precepts and human traditions with a total carelessness with regard to fundamental divine commandments and a blindness to the exigencies of the natural law and of present opportunities conforming to 'what truth demands.'"[69] In contrast, in this dynamic approach, the role of the confessor was to motivate the penitent to a deeper faith, to "help him establish a personal relationship with God, a more personal prayer life, and encourage him to exercise fraternal charity."[70] Häring hoped that the person would become more mature and responsible and hence able to make good moral decisions on questions of proximate occasions of sin and the influence

---

67. Häring, *Shalom: Peace; The Sacrament of Reconciliation* (1967; repr. Garden City, N.Y.: Image Books, 1969), 54.

68. Ibid., 60.

69. Ibid., 60. On the next page, Häring states that "Situation ethics ... in its pejorative sense, refers to a standard of conduct that permits a person who has or could have full knowledge, as opposed to one in invincible ignorance, to seek his happiness and salvation outside the golden circle of Divine Law. It is as 'static' and 'minimum-oriented' as the legalistic morality."

70. Ibid., 61.

of cultural trends. He wanted confession to be meaningful and helpful for the penitent. Hence in forming the Christian conscience, Häring suggested that the penitent be taught to see that the question should not be, "Is this a mortal sin?" but, "Is this the right response to the loving will of God?"[71]

Häring was clear that the spirit did not contradict the law; however, the moral value of the law proceeded from the inner spirit of love, which was creative.[72] Häring had high hopes that the faithful would use freedom to seek perfection:

> Freedom can also attain the stage in which man surrenders entirely to the guidance of the Spirit.... There is no greater freedom than that of the children of God, who have freely risen above the impotence of sin, thrown off the shackles of the slavery of Satan, and voluntarily submitted to the law and yoke of Christ ... they have freed themselves from the universal law as the sole and ultimate norm of morality and without constraint of law have accepted the joyous responsibility of seeking what is most perfect in the situation in which God has placed them; they have cast aside all desire of resisting the guidance of the Holy Spirit and have thus arrived at the very summit of freedom in obedient service to God.[73]

This quotation, from the *Law of Christ*, can be taken as an example of what Ford and Kelly feared was Quietism at work. Though such language was used in various contexts, Häring's words could be interpreted as denigrating the law while suggesting Quietism, a sort of absorption of the soul into the divine, a false mysticism wherein the mind and will are inactive and God alone acts.[74] The seventeenth-century heresy of Quietism was viewed as a threat to morality and the embodied practices of the church, such as the sacraments.[75] For those moralists like Ford and Kelly, who prized authority and saw it as a special gift of Catholic moral theology in contrast with Christian ethics, the suggestion that law constrains freedom and that perfection transcends law, rather than embodies it, was worrisome.

---

71. Ibid., 147.
72. Häring, *Law of Christ*, 1:207.
73. Ibid., 102–3.
74. The work of the Jesuit Jean Pierre de Caussade (1675–1751), *Abandonment to Divine Providence*, for example, consisted of letters written to Nuns of the Visitation in Nancy, France. The publication of these letters was delayed and even then edited to protect Caussade from the criticism that his writings were Quietist in nature.
75. E. Pace, "Quietism," in *The Catholic Encyclopedia* (New York: Robert Appleton, 1911).

From Responsibility to Freedom

Gerald Kelly said as much in his "Notes on Moral Theology," from 1963. In a subsection entitled "Magisterium and Natural Law," Kelly began by discussing morality courses for the laity, agreeing that such classes lend themselves to what he identified as "new approaches." Kelly emphasized the importance of the magisterium, even in this context: "It seems to me that no theological textbook is properly orientated unless it makes clear from the beginning that the first argument of Catholic theology is the teaching of the magisterium. This is especially important today, when people have so much 'freedom' to think and when they are definitely inclined to accept only what they see and agree with."[76] Kelly continued by introducing Bernard Häring as the best-known example of the new approaches. While stating that Häring's treatise on virtue and faith was extensive and generally excellent, Kelly also criticized *The Law of Christ* for not explicitly stating the church's authority, specifically in the teaching of natural law. Kelly saw the magisterium as filling an important role given the apparent moral impossibility of knowing the natural law; special divine guidance was necessary to understand natural law adequately.[77] The guidance provided by the magisterium's interpretation and communication of natural law assisted in freedom, rather than constraining it. Hence even with an extensive and excellent treatment of the virtues, this missing piece of magisterial authority in Häring's work could indicate a potentially problematic trajectory.

Moreover, by the late 1960s and early 1970s, Häring's concept of responsibility had fully absorbed a conviction as regards the necessity of criticism, wherein responsibility was associated with obedience flowing from love. This notion of responsibility was strikingly similar to Thomas Harris's transactional theory in *I'm OK—You're OK*, discussed in the previous chapter. Rather than thinking of Catholic formation in a positive light as his words had indicated in the past, Häring seemed to be simply associating the external authority of the church with the often oppressive "Parent" voice, which could be identified as a constraint on freedom because it caused immense worry about trivial acts. Borrowing Harris's terms, we might say that Häring was looking for the "Adult" Christian to move beyond simple allegiance to the "Parent" voice and the hurts expe-

---

76. Kelly, "Notes on Moral Theology," *Theological Studies* (December 1963): 632.
77. Ibid., 634.

rienced by the "Child" who had been obliged to follow the parent's rules. Häring was looking for discernment on the part of the mature Catholic; moral actions were to be motivated by love rather than the result of unthinking conditioning or indoctrination. Hence Häring observed that the formulations of preconciliar catechisms "are surely not adequate for the formation of a mature conscience."[78] To his mind, maturity required going beyond the memorization of catechisms and might even be inhibited by learning such rules and regulations. Like Harris, Häring was looking for the mature adult Christian to engage responsibly in a discriminating synthesis of various influences of authority. Again, borrowing Harris's words, it was a case of seeing that "I'm OK" but the church was "Not OK."

This theological conclusion played out practically in Häring's work in various ways. For instance, Häring emphasized that most "sins" that Catholics had been obliged to confess in the preconciliar age were "sins against the laws of the Church rather than against the law of God proclaimed in the Gospel and inscribed in man's innermost being."[79] From this perspective, the penitent was mistaken in thinking that she was "Not OK" when she ate meat on a Friday; the church, in instilling such a fear of mortal sin over such minor acts, was actually at fault. The conditioning and habituation of meatless Fridays and the fear of mortal sin that came from violating this church-imposed law hindered a Catholic's ability to determine a circumstance—for example, dining at a Protestant friend's home on a Friday—in which it might be a more loving action to eat meat, rather than to refuse it. The focus on these church-imposed laws could also distract the faithful from recognizing their larger sins. What good was obsessing over Friday meat abstinence if one was knowingly harboring hatred for a neighbor?

Kelly also noted this aspect of Häring's theology. In the same "Notes on Moral Theology" previously discussed, Kelly addressed Häring's discussion regarding a priest not praying a "small hour" from his ecclesiastically required daily office. Kelly interpreted Häring as saying that such

---

78. Häring, *Sin in the Secular Age* (Garden City, N.Y.: Doubleday, 1974), 178. Ford and Kelly may have agreed on this point about the catechisms not providing for adequate conscience formation, but might have seen them as a good starting point, especially when learned in conjunction with frequent recourse to the sacrament of confession.

79. Ibid., 198.

From Responsibility to Freedom

an omission was likely not an objectively grave sin, but, in the case that a priest omitted the small hour with full deliberation and consciousness that God, through the church, had required it, the priest would certainly be committing a venial sin, and as a free and basic decision to contravene a commandment, the priest would be committing a mortal sin. If the priest doubted his omission was due to an inner evil disposition, then he could take the benefit of the doubt.

The problematic issue at hand for Kelly was typical in Häring's "responsibility-response approach to moral theology," as Kelly described it: "It is a morality which looks much more to inner dispositions than to objective norms. And though it is generally respectful to the objective standards, it shows a tendency to look upon them as 'external rules,' especially when human laws are concerned."[80] Kelly stated that more thought must be given to such a new approach before it was accepted. He worried that such a focus on inner dispositions could tend toward scrupulosity, an obsession with analyzing the interior as opposed to simply acknowledging the sinful transgression of an ecclesiastical law. Nor did Kelly think scrupulosity was averted through the supposedly comforting rule of recognizing the object of the act as slight and therefore not of grave matter.

While the tendencies toward an outlook of self-legislating mature laity and hence uncertainty of ecclesiastical teaching were already present in Häring's *Law of Christ*, no doubt the catalyst for the development in Häring's theology was *Humanae vitae*. Kelly seemed to realize the potentially problematic way that Häring's theology could tend toward an unsuitable stance against the church's teaching on contraception, should that position be reaffirmed. Kelly specifically raised questions regarding natural law, the importance of the magisterium's interpretation of natural law, and the necessity of observing ecclesiastical law in reference to contraception. He saw that all of this could be endangered by an emphasis on an abstract notion of love transcending law, coupled with a primacy of one's personal responsibility-response to God.

As late as 1966, Häring was toeing the church's line in opposition to contraception, advising people not to assume that the discussion around

---

80. Kelly, "Notes on Moral Theology," 642.

birth control was already an indication in favor of it, but rather advising that they wait for Paul VI's judgment: "The serious study that these problems are receiving at the hands of the supreme authorities of our Church is a further reason for us to give them full obedience."[81] While he privately seemed to have concluded in favor of some forms of contraception in certain circumstances, in 1966 Häring was confidently awaiting the official conclusion, to all appearances ready to back the magisterium's judgment.

It played out, however, in what Häring came to regard as "the crisis around *Humanae vitae*." Knowing he was in the majority of the members of the Papal Commission but would ultimately be unable to influence the final result, Häring did not attend the final session of the commission. Häring did not agree with the exceptionless norm prohibiting birth control for every marital act, yet he had determined he would remain silent no matter what followed the majority and minority reports of the commission. Having been leaked a copy of the encyclical prior to its release, Häring went on retreat in order to read and reflect on it. Ultimately, however, Häring did not keep his silence and instead issued a declaration, which ended up on the front page of the *New York Times*:

> Whoever can be convinced that the absolute forbidding of artificial means of birth control as stated by *Humanae vitae* is the correct interpretation of divine law must earnestly endeavor to live according to this conviction. Whoever, however, after serious reflection and prayer is convinced that in his or her case such a prohibition could not be the will of God should in inner peace follow his/her conscience and not thereby feel her/himself to be a second-class Catholic.[82]

Note that Häring did not present this statement in terms of sin or objective morality or obedience to the church's moral teachings. He did not dissent from the encyclical on its own terms, especially regarding Paul VI's explicit stance against contraception. Häring did not state that Paul VI was wrong and he himself was right, nor did he argue that there was no sin in contraception. Despite the fact that he did think the magisterial teaching was erroneous, Haring appealed to individual conscience and a sense of

---

81. Häring, *Bernard Häring Replies: Answers to 50 Moral and Religious Questions* (Staten Island, N.Y.: Alba House, 1967), 81–83.

82. Häring, *My Witness for the Church*, 82.

From Responsibility to Freedom

belonging to the Catholic community. This reflects the move from a clearer, objective understanding of what constituted sin and morality to a more subjective and individualized notion, where it was up to the discernment of the individual to judge whether or not the prohibition of contraception was the will of God. Conscience, Häring implied, very likely would view that the will of God was not identical with the magisterium's pronouncement.[83]

In his book, Keenan describes the synthesis of Bernard Häring by noting a change from fundamental morals to new norms through new values. Keenan quotes Häring to the effect that moral theology is not concerned first with decision-making and acts, but rather has the purpose of gaining the right vision, presenting truths and values that bear upon decisions taken before God.[84] This was known as the "fundamental option" and was popularized by Karl Rahner, becoming a key moral category following *Humanae vitae*. No doubt the rise of fundamental option was a reaction to the problematic aspects of a morality concerned chiefly with acts, identifying sin in those acts, and sacramentally confessing those sins. And while Häring saw fundamental option as dynamic morality, focused on a relationship with God rather than a fear of breaking rules and suffering eternal punishment, it nonetheless shifted attention away from the concrete guides of morality like those memorized by many American Catholics in their childhood.

The development of Häring's line of thought is evident in his second three-volume work, *Free and Faithful in Christ*. The title named what Häring saw as the leitmotif of the work, but the related concepts indicate Häring's understanding of being free and faithful in Christ: respon-

---

83. Interestingly, while debates about the morality of contraception in both academic and lay publications were numerous prior to *Humanae vitae*, after the encyclical's release, the discussion turned to the debates regarding magisterial authority. Once Paul VI had spoken on the issue, it became more important to minimize and question the authority of the encyclical than to engage his natural-law-based claims in *Humanae vitae*. This is particularly ironic given that the defenders of the stance against contraception argued that a change in the church's teaching would undermine its authority by indicating that the church of the past had gotten it wrong and might be wrong elsewhere in its moral teachings, as well. In fact, the restating of the church's position on contraception contributed to the undermining of magisterial authority. The church did not seem credible, having taken such an unpopular position opposed to the view of so many American Catholics.

84. Keenan, *History of Catholic Moral Theology*, 83, citing Häring, *Free and Faithful in Christ*, vol. 1, *Moral Theology for Clergy and Laity* (New York: Seabury Press, 1978), 6.

sibility, solidarity, personalism, a communal focus, and, perhaps the most frequently mentioned concept, creativity, which Häring describes as pneumatological. The definition of creativity, however, is not exactly clear, though Häring says a theology of responsibility characterized by liberty, fidelity, and creativity may cause a "rethinking of a number of doctrines, traditions, teachings and practices, and to distinguishing the deposit of faith from ideologies, taboos and other obscuring factors."[85] Like other concepts in this work, creativity exemplifies the degree to which Häring's theology had become lacking in substance. Expressed in negative terms, creativity becomes somewhat clearer: "One of the most uncreative approaches in the Church is to stress fidelity to certain negative commandments to such an extent that fidelity to Christ and his great affirmative commandments of justice, love and mercy is seriously neglected."[86] Häring associated the rigidity and legalism of the manuals and manual-based, authority-based moral theology with a lack of creativity. In contrast to this, creativity was about freedom and relationships and response.

One shortcoming of the moral theology represented by Ford and Kelly was its lack of rootedness in scripture. Häring's efforts to make use of the Bible are noteworthy. In particular, Jeffrey Siker notes that Häring tended toward a self-selected "biblical concept" approach, wherein he identified a concept such as sin or conscience in the Bible and then did what Siker calls a "word study," followed by discussion of the concept.[87] By the time he wrote *Free and Faithful*, Häring also freely borrowed from the field of psychology in elucidating the important concepts, including those he chose from the Bible. For example, Häring drew upon psychologist Erik Erikson, known for his theory of lifecycles, when he wrote that "the fundamental option is studied above all in the light of a psychology of development. As a consequence, a much more dynamic vision prevails which better meets the biblical perspectives."[88] Häring saw the theory of self-actualization as a good way of describing moral development, but

---

85. Ibid., 1:4.
86. Häring, *Free and Faithful*, 1:75–76.
87. Jeffrey S. Siker, *Scripture and Ethics: Twentieth-Century Portraits* (Oxford: Oxford University Press, 1997), 65.
88. Häring, *Free and Faithful*, 1:166.

From Responsibility to Freedom

he clarified that in true progress toward maturity, the person does not simply seek self-realization, but rather self-transcendence.[89] This self-transcendence fit with Häring's understanding of freedom in Christ, and such freedom could come contra an established authority. Noting Karl Marx's and B. F. Skinner's criticism of organized religion, Häring suggested that "it is not just a matter of being set free from some concrete fears but, rather, liberation from a system of religion that is built too much on sanctions, laws, controls: a system that unavoidably creates fearfulness, scrupulosity and lack of loving trust."[90]

Häring also sought to advance the recognition of social sins. "There has been a transition from a rather individualistic concept [of sin] to one characterized by solidarity."[91] Häring believed that original sin had been used too often to excuse people from their responsibility in structures of sin extant in the world as each Christian instead focused only on his own salvation.

As individuals and as members of the community, we all have to examine our consciences about whether we have any share in the oppression, manipulation and violence that persist around us. This terrifying share can fall to us not only through direct participation in criminal misuse of authority or of power, but also because of uncreative use of our freedom, a lack of commitment to the common good, or lack of initiative and creativity. One of the main causes of so many evils in society and Church is surely a legalistic morality that stifles the positive energies of liberty.[92]

In contrast to the legalistic morality, Häring believed that the church should be "a community of liberated people committed to the liberation of all, in response to the longing of all creation to share in the liberty of the children of God."[93]

Häring's new stress on social sin and structures of sin was a valid reminder to Catholics in the United States struggling with issues of racism, sexism, and war, among others. But while his later work drew attention to such concerns, it did not necessarily provide a method—as confession might have—for addressing moral problems at a personal level. Nor did

---

89. Ibid., 1:209.
91. Häring, *Sin in the Secular Age*, 106.
93. Ibid., 1:158.
90. Ibid., 1:134.
92. Häring, *Free and Faithful*, 1:81–2.

it address how one could understand complicity in social injustices. This concept could have been used to add a new dimension to a person's examination of conscience and offenses against God, inviting penitents to examine, repent of, and avoid formal or material cooperation in sins of racism, for example. Instead, however, social sin turned the focus to human relationships at the societal level and the need to fix them—a task that could seem impossible to the average Catholic. Moreover, sins of a social nature were often emphasized in opposition to personal actual sins. These social sins—even though they perhaps represented remote material cooperation with evil—were assessed as having a higher priority, in contrast to the formal cooperation with evil identified by the sinner as his actual sin.[94] Sins addressed in the confessional had in the past been overly narrow without consideration of these crucial social sins, and the limited focus on personal actual sin had not prevented or solved Catholic participation in structures of sin. The sacrament would hence seem to be of very little aid in solving these larger problems.

Moreover, the energy spent criticizing moral theology in the past prevented the structuring of a new moral theology that would be as relevant to the laity as manualism had been. Freedom, fidelity, conscience, liberation, creativity were all valuable concepts and useful as correctives, but they too often remained at the level of a concept, with no institutional structure or parish-level practices other than that which was a criticism of authority represented by the teaching office of the church and the manualism of the past.

Differing Viewpoints

For Ford and Kelly there was a real urgency tied to the recognition and confession of sins. Those who sinned knowingly and failed to confess their sins put themselves at risk for eternal damnation, but God's grace and forgiveness were available for those who sought it in the sacrament; it was possible for sin to become an occasion of grace and redemption. In

---

94. One example might be, "Don't worry about your sin of having missed Mass on Sunday! What really matters is your sin of using racial slurs!" In fact, the two might be connected, and both are formal cooperation in evil and hence sufficient matter to confess in the sacrament of penance.

From Responsibility to Freedom

short, what made moral theology so important to Ford and Kelly was that eternal salvation was at stake and that human beings could move closer to that supernatural end by conforming to God's will through the law of the church. There were subjective considerations in their application to sins confessed by penitents within the confessional, as casuistry was an attempt to take into account the complexity of actual events, not the abstraction of rules. The problematic tendency of casuistry was to continue making rules to address every situation while neglecting the importance of formation and development of virtue. Ford and Kelly recognized that objective moral laws were, after all, objective, and the outright refusal to follow them was dangerous. Heaven, hell, and purgatory were just as real as sin. Ford and Kelly's manualism, however, was perceived as inadequate to the task of modern moral theology, and the relevance of this critique is exhibited in the rapid decline of manualism's popularity.

Häring had in the past expressed concern about life after death, in 1966 describing the sacrament of confession as "a pre-judgment of mercy, a prelude to the final judgment, so that we may look forward to it with happy confidence."[95] Häring also argued for the meaningfulness of those condemned to hell because they stand as a testimony to the fact that God has not willed to save humanity without its cooperation or to make people happy without their free will.[96] By the mid- to late seventies, however, Häring had a slightly different emphasis wherein the value of the sacrament of confession was not described as tied to death and judgment but rather regarded as "proclamation of the messianic peace and as personal and communal commitment to the kingdom of justice, peace, and liberation."[97] Häring remained confident in God's mercy but seemed less certain of the church's knowledge of mortal and venial sin—for example, in the case of missing a Sunday Mass, which he did not generally regard as a mortal sin. Writing in *Free and Faithful*, Häring seemed to question the value of such categories altogether: "My conviction is that an objective border-line, valid for all, between mortal and venial sin can never be determined."[98]

Häring's teaching of morality was meant to call Catholics beyond

95. Häring, *Confession and Happiness* (Derby, N.Y.: St. Paul, 1966), 19.
96. Häring, *Bernard Häring Replies*, 170.   97. Häring, *Sin in the Secular Age*, 187.
98. Häring, *Free and Faithful*, 1:213.

minimalistic laws to perfection in Christ; these laws, enumerated by the church, could even be seen as constraints on freedom inasmuch as they prevented the person's free choice to worship and serve God out of love. For Häring, there needed to be a choice of contraries in order to make it real freedom. Many Catholics agreed with Häring's use of responsibility and freedom. One college teacher ridiculed the "old-fashioned" way that many educators used the word "responsible": "By 'responsible' they mean meeting one's obligations.... They mean some kind of conformity of the man to something outside him. The vision they have of man is not contemporary or relevant today, nor ... does it get to the heart of the human matter."[99]

And yet Häring's version of responsibility and freedom was, practically speaking, elusive. It made it more difficult to identify personal actual sins just as it also held the sinner accountable for a host of social sins in which material cooperation seemed ordinarily impossible to escape. Furthermore, while Häring maintained the concepts of heaven, hell, and purgatory, the final judgment seemed to have lost its place of importance. The emphasis was on mercy, but with so little importance and clarity given to identifying sin, even the concept of mercy seemed groundless. Sin had been used to identify specific actions that were confessed in the sacrament of penance. Now, the rare identification of actual sin indicated a sort of indefinable turning away from God that was difficult to address personally and therefore unlikely to be dealt with sacramentally.

In some ways, pre–Vatican II Catholic moral theology based in the seminary with an eye to forming confessors was too specific, too rational, and too rigid, without sufficient attention to the Thomistic conception of virtue and its importance for the moral life. With its numerous case studies, objective moral norms, intellectual debate, and manuals for responding to penitents, the moral theology of Ford and Kelly seemed out of touch with the new directions taken by Catholics in the United States; the context and circumstances of American Catholic lives had changed. Had their approach to moral theology been adequate and compelling, it would not have suffered such a quick rejection in the wake of Vatican II and *Humanae vitae*.

99. Milhaven, "Be Like Me! Be Free!," 334.

From Responsibility to Freedom

The great strength of Häring's work was to identify the "law of Christ" with the "law of love." Häring's work spoke to a generation of moral theologians and laity who had felt constrained by the manualist tradition, unable to grow in charity because of the preoccupation with the constantly multiplying rules of morality presented by manuals and often uncritically preached in terms of "mortal sin" to the laity. The weakness of Häring's work, much of which was read popularly by the faithful as well as by professional theologians, was that it tended to view this so-called law of love in opposition to obligation and obedience to moral rules held by the church. It also provided little practical guidance or guidelines for the growth in morality. Häring's work decreasingly valued magisterial teaching at the same time that it increasingly reflected the trends and opinions among the laity described in the previous chapter. Häring embraced psychology and relied upon it in his own work. He questioned the birth control prohibition in *Humanae vitae*, celebrated the idea of freedom, and challenged the past glorification of obedience and obligation to church law, understood as the authoritative representation of God's eternal law.

And as he moved away from the manual-based moral theology he had been taught, Häring increasingly viewed the law of love in opposition to the law of the church, discounting sins identified by the church and highlighting instead a response to God that was outside the conventional language and delineation of sin. The discernment of individual conscience was to take the place of rules and laws passed down from the magisterium through priests. This would allow for greater maturity of the laity in their moral decision-making as well as a more positive understanding of God's love, mercy, and forgiveness. With little reference to personal actual sin, however, these concepts were not sufficiently grounded. How important was God's forgiveness with such a weak account of sin? And what role could penance play in such a schema?

When comparing Ford and Kelly to Häring, there is no reason to assume a substantial disagreement between them in the 1960s or to assume that their moral theology was utterly contradictory. At the same time, however, Ford and Kelly clearly had different emphases than Häring when it came to the concepts of freedom, responsibility, obligation, and obedience. Both sides agreed that charity should be the foundation of morality, but Ford and Kelly did not see how this was possible with any denigration of the law, the objective moral norms that were obligatory and required obedience. These norms, and obedience to them, facilitated the freedom that led to the person's supernatural destiny. Yet despite the Jesuit team's admirable defense of a traditional understanding of obligation and obedience, the paucity of a personal element and diminished emphasis on charity made the sacrament of penance seem disconnected from the whole of a person's life.

We will see in chapters 5 and 6 the many criticisms aimed at the sacrament of penance and other penitential practices in the 1950s, indicating that they tended to be too routine and impersonal, not sufficiently fostering growth in the context of a loving relationship with God. In the midst of these criticisms, Häring's moral narrative, which had less emphasis on moral rules, sin, and penance and more emphasis on responsibility and freedom in the context of a loving response to God, was justifiably compelling, so much so that Häring's trajectory of freedom and responsibility, with the focus on the individual's interior disposition of love and desire for meaning, resonated with the U.S. bishops as they considered revising the practices of penance in the United States. The criticisms of both the sacrament of penance and other nonsacramental penitential acts highlighted the weakness of a manual and confession-based morality like that taken to be normative by Ford and Kelly. The Häring-style path depending upon individual freedom and responsibility with little reference to actual sin, eternal law, or practical ways for improving was ultimately an insufficient answer for the question of how to revitalize penance among American Catholics.

4   Penance in a New Land

Developments in Nonsacramental Penitential Practice

Today, the word "penance" is often narrowly identified with the sacrament of penance, and scholars investigating penance historically or even theologically tend to focus narrowly on the sacrament itself. This limited understanding has resulted at least in part from the dramatic decline of the many other penitential practices that once shaped and even defined Catholicism in America. Many younger Catholics have no experience of penance aside from the sacrament; even Lent is associated with resolutions rather than penances. The church's conviction in the reality of sin, practically embodied in the faithful's identification of their own personal, actual sin, has long been reinforced by numerous rigorous and regular penitential practices—even aside from the sacrament of penance—that were taken for granted as part of Catholic culture.

Sin and penance have a long and varied history, but they have always been present together as key aspects of the faith. The faithful in the United States performed numerous acts of penance outside the context of the sacrament of confession prior to 1966, which was when changes to penitential practices were implemented in the wake of the Second Vatican Council. The description of these nonsacramental penitential practices provides an important context for understanding the popularity of the sacrament of penance, as the popularity of nonsacramental and sacramental penance coincided.[1] The sacrament of penance, even when its popularity was at a zenith, was never alone as "penance," despite the current narrow identification. Rather, the sacrament was one among many penitential practices inherent in American Catholicism.

The nonsacramental penances stand out for their social element and provide an interesting comparison with the sacrament of penance. Theologically, the sacrament of penance is regarded as having an intrinsically social nature, but this is not readily apparent to observers, for whom the sacrament of penance may appear individualistic. In contrast, one of the most striking aspects of these nonsacramental penances is that, though they required individual commitment, they were inherently social. Practices such as Friday meat abstinence and Lenten fasting were obligatory, and they were done consistently by the majority of Catholics in the United States, reinforcing Catholic identity, including the penitential dimension of Catholic life. Catholics supported each other in the common practice of penance, and in many cases, the penances were even instituted structurally, as when Catholic schools did not serve meat on Fridays throughout the year or when parishes joined together for Friday fish fries.

Yet despite the profound social aspect of these nonsacramental penitential practices, they were not without flaw as performed by the laity. For many, in fact, these penances presented more of a practical problem than an ideal solution as regards making reparation for sin. Sources from the time period indicate the challenges that were recognized with regard to how these penances were performed; in particular, a tendency toward legalism often dominated the discussion, and unreflective habit seemed to detract from the sense of interior repentance. The perception of these problems is also indicated by proposed solutions from the time period. Some people believed that changes to penitential practice could make it more meaningful, facilitating an improved sense of interior repentance.

1. O'Toole, "In the Court of Conscience," 132–43.

Penance in a New Land

Among several key penitential practices that were part of Catholic culture in the United States prior to the Second Vatican Council, perhaps the most notable was the Friday meat abstinence, which was an important marker of Catholic identity in a religiously pluralistic country. There were other penitential days and seasons, as well; Catholics were supposed to fast every day of Lent, during Ember Days (three days, four times a year), and on the days prior to major feasts such as Christmas. All of these practices were obligatory and hence experienced communally. There was one other penitential practice that was a crucial part of Catholic culture—namely, the offering up of suffering in penance for one's sins.[2] "Bearing the ills of life" was involuntary in the sense that the faithful did not choose this suffering, but it was voluntary and individual in that this penitential practice depended on the person and how she chose to deal with suffering. Yet regardless of how well a person might, in practice, bear the ills of life as penance for his sins, it was nonetheless a part of the Catholic understanding of penance, frequently emphasized in homilies and popular periodicals. "Offer it up" was a common Catholic expectation for those undergoing difficulties of any sort, from poverty to illness to death of a loved one.

After describing the previously listed penitential practices, the chapter will identify the recognizable problems that arose in regard to these practices. Chief among these was the inherent legalism, given that most penitential practices were obligatory and rarely explained in terms of their role in facilitating growth in virtue and sanctity or aiding the individual and church toward the final end of the beatific vision. Rather than emphasizing the significance and meaning of penance, priests and theologians tended to speak of penance in legal terms, as evidenced by the numerous debates regarding the letter of the law. Given the legalistic tendency and dearth of spiritual exposition, the regular practice of these penitential acts could easily devolve into an unthinking routine, a criticism concurrently applied to the sacrament of penance as well as non-sacramental penance. Some people worried that these external penances were not accompanied by suitable reflection, an appropriate interior sentiment, or adequate contrition for sin. Others thought that the peni-

2. Benedict XVI, in his encyclical *Spe salvi*, no. 40, urged a return to this concept of "offering it up"; http://www.vatican.va/holy_father/benedict_xvi/encyclicals/documents/hf_ben-xvi_enc_20071130_spe-salvi_en.html; accessed on December 4, 2012.

tential focus was too individualistic, narrowly concerned with the personal piety and salvation of those who performed these penances. Such a tendency could lead to spiritual pride while simultaneously failing to address larger social issues, including the church's and the individual's complicity in social ills.

The chapter will conclude by observing that there was a clear need for reform in regard to penance as it was practiced in the United States. The particularities of that reform would be determined to some extent by the changing notion of sin as described in the previous two chapters. The legalistic tendency of nonsacramental penitential practices had accorded with a legalistic understanding of sin and a focus on the individual identifying personal, actual sin using narrow categories. In order to improve upon this, Catholic leadership would focus upon modifications that seemed to personalize penance, emphasizing freedom and responsibility in order to secure a broader and more profound meaning of sin and penance.

Dispensation and Development of Penitential Practices

Even the practices that were well established in the United States at the time of Vatican II had undergone numerous changes throughout American church history. All of the practices of fast and abstinence by the time of Vatican II were based on the 1917 Code of Canon Law applicable to the whole of the Latin rite church—that is, canons 1250–54. Prior to 1917, the general law required the faithful to fast on all the days of Lent except Sunday, on Wednesdays, Fridays, and Saturdays of the Ember weeks, and on the four vigils of All Saints, Christmas, Assumption, and Pentecost. By custom in many places, such as Rome, the faithful also fasted on Wednesday and Friday during Advent. Fasting according to the general law of the church included only one meal a day, abstinence from meat, abstinence from eggs and milk products during Lent, and abstinence from fish at those meals where meat was eaten on a fast day as well as on Sundays of Lent. Abstinence from meat without fast was observed by the general law on all Fridays and Saturdays throughout the year.[3]

3. "Report of the Bishops' Committee on Fast and Abstinence" (1951), 19, Frederick R. McManus papers from the American Catholic History Research Center and University Ar-

As sometimes happened, however, the Holy See granted dispensations to different episcopal regions on account of their situations and needs that made adhering to these canonical prescriptions difficult. In contrast to canon law, these regulations for fast and abstinence, including various dispensations, were regarded as common law. Before the 1917 Code, the church in the United States determined how best to apply fast and abstinence rules in their jurisdiction. In some cases they requested dispensations. For example, in 1837, the Third Provincial Council of Baltimore asked for and was granted a dispensation from the custom of fasting on Wednesdays and Fridays of Advent and from abstaining on Wednesdays of Advent; in 1840 the Fourth Provincial Council of Baltimore asked for a perpetual renewal of an indult dispensing from abstinence on Saturdays, and this indult was renewed for twenty years by Pope Gregory XVI. In 1866, the Second Plenary Council asked that all dispensations granted to the diocese of Baltimore be extended to other American dioceses, but Pope Pius IX preferred individual requests from each bishop in the United States. In 1884, the U.S. bishops who were meeting at the Third Plenary Council decided it would be difficult to pass uniform legislation on the subject of fast and abstinence and hence left it to the authority of provincial councils to determine what was best for their territories. Leo XIII in 1886 granted U.S. bishops the authority to dispense each year from abstinence on Saturdays. That same year, Cardinal James Gibbons consulted the archbishops in the United States at the request of the Holy See and then sent a petition for a uniform set of fast and abstinence regulations.

This petition was granted by Pope Leo XIII in a document entitled *Indultum quadragesimale*, which permitted the faithful in the United States the use of meat, eggs, and milk products at all meals on Sundays during Lent, and at the principal meal on Monday, Tuesday, Thursday, and Saturdays, excepting Saturday of Ember week and Holy Week. It also allowed

---

chives at the Catholic University of America (hereafter "McManus papers"), box 1, series 2, folder 25. Thanks to Carter Rawson of the Catholic University of America Archives for assisting me with the McManus papers. It would be fascinating to know the extent to which these fasting and abstinence practices were observed by Europeans. The fact that Catholic immigrants to the United States seem to have brought such practices with them as a part of their lives would indicate that adherence to these rules was widespread among the laity in Europe in the twentieth century.

for the use of eggs and milk products at the evening collation daily during Lent and at the principal meal when meat was not allowed. *Indultum quadragesimale* further allowed a small piece of bread in the morning with a beverage, the possibility of taking the principal meal at noon or in the evening, and the use of lard and meat drippings in the preparation of foods. Those exempt from the law of fasting were permitted to eat meat, eggs, and milk more than once a day.[4]

The 1895 so-called workingmen's privilege allowed the bishops in the United States to permit the use of meat in circumstances where there was difficulty in observing the common law of abstinence, excluding Fridays, Ash Wednesday, Holy Week, and the Vigil of Christmas. This workingmen's privilege (or indult) allowed only for meat once a day during Lent, taken at the principal meal, and never taken in conjunction with fish. This particular indult was extended not only to the laborer but to his family, as well.[5] The motivation of such an indult was no doubt to allow for enough sustenance such that the many Catholic immigrants to the United States who worked as manual laborers could perform their difficult, energy-demanding physical work without danger to their health. Moreover, those with little variety in terms of food options would not have it unnecessarily further narrowed.

After the 1917 Code, some additional documents modified fast and abstinence rules, particularly to accommodate difficult wartime conditions that included limitations in food availability. In 1917 Pope Benedict XV granted the faithful of countries in World War I the privilege of transferring Saturday Lenten abstinence to any other day of the week, excepting Friday and Ash Wednesday. In 1919 Cardinal Gibbons was granted his request of transferring Saturday Lenten abstinence to Wednesday for all dioceses in the United States. This permission, as well as the workingmen's privilege, was frequently renewed, but after 1931, this permission was only on the basis of personal requests from individual bishops. During World War II in 1941, Pope Pius XII granted to all bishops the power to dispense entirely from fast and abstinence, excepting Ash Wednesday and Good Friday. He extended this again in 1946. In 1949, several years after the close of World War II, Pius XII placed some

4. "Report on Fast and Abstinence," 21.
5. Ibid., 22.

Penance in a New Land

restrictions on the earlier granted dispensations, once again requiring yearlong Friday abstinence and fast and abstinence on Ash Wednesday, Good Friday, and the Vigils of Assumption and Christmas, but allowing eggs and milk products at collations on days of fast and abstinence.[6]

The "Report of the Bishops' Committee on Fast and Abstinence," prepared in advance of the bishops' annual meeting of 1951, detailed the fast and abstinence regulations for the United States, while also providing commentary on these regulations. The origin and mandate of the committee, which included bishops Leo Binz, William O'Connor, and John Cody, was stated in their preamble: "the bishops generally have desired to clarify, simplify and to unify fast and abstinence practices in the United States."[7] While each of these committee members held doctorates in sacred theology, they consulted both theologians and canonists in preparing tentative regulations on fast and abstinence that were sent to all bishops in the United States with a request for comments. The revised formula, with one modification, was submitted to the bishops at their annual meeting on November 14, 1951, and adopted by the bishops as the uniform penitential norm for the Unites States.[8]

The bishops noted the purpose of fast and abstinence regulations in the first paragraph of the text for the document: "To foster the spirit of penance and of reparation for sin, to encourage self-denial and mortification, and to guide her children in the footsteps of Our Divine Savior, Holy Mother Church proposes by law the observance of fast and abstinence."[9] After detailing the abstinence and fast regulations, including the days and seasons of these fasts as well as defining who was obligated to adhere to the directives, the bishops concluded the regulations by stating:

We earnestly exhort the faithful during the periods of fast and abstinence to attend daily Mass; to receive Holy Communion often; to take part more frequently in exercises of piety; to give generously to works of religion and charity; to perform acts of kindness toward the sick, the aged and the poor; to practice voluntary self-denial especially regarding alcoholic drink and worldly amusements; and to pray more frequently, particularly for the intentions of the Holy Father.[10]

6. Ibid., 22–23.
7. Ibid., 3.
8. Ibid.
9. Ibid., 4.
10. Ibid., 5.

The commentary that followed these regulations gave an account of the special faculties granted by the Holy See to bishops in the United States. Of particular importance was Pius XII's 1949 decree that set forth a minimum of abstinence and fast for the faithful throughout the world, regardless of prior indults; these regulations were abstinence on all Fridays and fast and abstinence on Ash Wednesday, Good Friday, and the vigils of the Assumption and Christmas.[11] However, this decree also allowed local ordinaries the authority to determine when to dispense from fast or abstinence.

Pius XII's decree also gave the bishops the authority to determine how best to apply the workingmen's privilege (or partial abstinence). The U.S. bishops chose to extend this indult to all the faithful in the Unites States in 1951 when they updated the fast and abstinence regulations. The workingmen's privilege was a relative norm wherein a fast day was defined as allowing one full meal and two collations that together did not total a full meal. The relative norm had long been in use in Europe, until the absolute norm of two ounces (first collation) and eight ounces (second collation) was introduced by Alphonsus Liguori to assist the scrupulous in deciding how much food they were allowed on a fast day.[12] The bishops thought that the relative norm allowed for the person to take enough food to do his daily work properly, and hence the relative norm "makes it possible for most persons to fast, whereas ... most persons cannot fast according to the '*absolute norm*.'"[13] In some places, such as Ireland, a modified relative norm allowed for one full meal (the size of which was to be determined by the individual) and two collations totaling no more than twelve ounces, or eighteen total ounces of food for those who needed the sustenance to perform strenuous work.[14] By 1950, however, many other countries had agreed upon uniform fast and abstinence regulations for their regions by also sanctioning the relative norm.[15]

This and the other regulations detailed in the 1951 report were still in

11. Ibid., 7.
12. It would be interesting to know how many people had access to the weight measurement that would be required by this absolute norm and how this amount compared to the amounts consumed by those using the relative norm.
13. "Report on Fast and Abstinence," 10.
14. Ibid., 14.
15. Ibid., 13–19.

effect up until 1966, with a few modifications. One such adjustment was in regard to the end of the Lenten fast. It had formerly ended at noon on Holy Saturday, but in 1956 the fast was extended to the midnight between Holy Saturday and Easter Sunday.[16] A third revision was to transfer the vigil fast and abstinence from the feast of the Assumption (August 15) to that of the Immaculate Conception (December 8), with a decree noting that many ordinaries of various nations informed the Apostolic See of the difficulties, due to circumstances of time and place, "that constantly stand in the way of the complete observance of the law calling for fasting and abstinence on the vigil of the Assumption."[17] A dispensation was also granted from fast and abstinence on the Vigil of All Saints' Day in the United States, and in 1959, Pope John XXIII granted to all the faithful the option of transferring their Christmas vigil fast, normally December 24, to December 23.[18] The following sections provide a more detailed description of each of these penitential practices observed in the United States in the 1950s and until 1966.

Friday Abstinence

Meat abstinence was perhaps the most familiar public marker of Catholic identity; it was a penitential practice noticeable to non-Catholics as well as Catholics in religiously pluralistic America.[19] The church's 1917 Code of Canon Law defined the law of abstinence as forbidding the eating of flesh meat and the juice of meat, but not eggs, dairy, or condiments made of meat fat.[20] Abstinence from meat was to be observed on Fridays

---

16. Archbishop Leo Binz, letter to Edward Cardinal Mooney, dated November 14, 1956, 1; McManus papers, box 1, series 2, folder 25.

17. "Catholics Must Fast, Abstain on Dec. 7 Vatican Officials Rule," NCWC News Service, August 5, 1957; McManus papers, box 1, series 2, folder 25. Though no further explanation is given, one might surmise that this difficulty had to do with summer agricultural work as well as maintaining health in the midst of warm weather.

18. Unfortunately there is no data as to how many Catholics actually observed these fasts. Given the private nature of eating meals in one home, it would probably be difficult to judge. By the popularity of discussions surrounding fasting found in pastoral publications, however, it seems that the clergy took these fasts seriously and likely communicated that to their parishioners.

19. O'Toole, *The Faithful*, 224.

20. Canon 1250, in *Codex iuris canonici* (Rome: Tipografia Poliglotta Vaticana, 1917), 345:

throughout the year, as well as on Ash Wednesday, the Fridays and Saturdays in Lent, Ember Days, and the vigils of Pentecost, Assumption, All Saints' Day, and Christmas Day.[21] In particular, it was the weekly recurrence of the Friday meat abstinence that was a constant reminder that Catholics were different from their compatriots. Though Christians of many denominations used Sunday as a day for rest and worship, Catholics were distinct as the group whose faith required them to do something particular on Friday, as well. This distinctiveness may even have added to the penitential nature of the practice, since Friday meat abstinence sometimes drew criticism and mocking from non-Catholics.

The importance of Friday meat abstinence at this time period was evident in *American Ecclesiastical Review* when Fr. Francis Connell tackled the question as to whether a Catholic who accidentally ordered a meat dish on a Friday could eat it on the grounds that it would be an inconvenience to lose money on it and waste food. Connell stated that there was no categorical answer to the question because of the variety of circumstance, but he believed it best to try to switch out the dish for something without meat. Connell's argument focused on the issue of scandal. A Catholic seen eating meat in public on a Friday would no doubt give rise to scandal, and this was especially true if he were a Catholic priest. In such a case, the priest could appear as a hypocrite, asking that his parishioners do something that he clearly was not doing. Protestants who witnessed the priest eating meat on a Friday might be confused as to the Catholic regulations, thinking perhaps that they had misunderstood the Catholic Friday meat abstinence rule.

Hence Connell suggested that a priest would certainly do his best to find a way to pass up the inadvertently ordered meat.[22] While the basis for this answer may appear to be superficial in nature inasmuch as it is concerned with external appearances rather than the internal signifi-

---

"Abstinentiae lex vetat carne iureque ex carne vesci, non autem ovis, lacticiniis et quibuslibet condimentis etiam ex adipe animalium"; see also T. Lincoln Bouscaren, SJ, and Adam C. Ellis, SJ, *Canon Law: A Text and Commentary* (Milwaukee: Bruce, 1946), 630, as well as Stanislaus Woywod, OFM, *The New Canon Law: A Commentary and Summary of the New Code of Canon Law*, 7th ed. (New York: Joseph F. Wagner, 1929), 256.

21. Canon 1252, §2, Canon 1250, in *Codex iuris canonici*, 346.

22. Connell, "Meat on Friday," in "Answers to Questions," *American Ecclesiastical Review* 129 (1953): 274–75.

cance, it nonetheless captures the prominence accorded to Friday meat abstinence. Friday meat abstinence was supposed to be an act of penance, of course, but it was also an important opportunity to witness to the Catholicism and its distinct penitential view embodied socially through established penitential obligations. A priest publicly ignoring such a well-known rule could cause a misunderstanding of Catholicism as a whole. Or, even worse, it could undermine the faith by making Catholics appear to be ignorant or hypocritical, unable to adhere to their own rules.

The Lenten Fast

The next most recognizable time of penance for Catholics in the United States was the season of Lent. Catholics were obliged to fast on every day of Lent, excluding Sundays. This fast was also one of partial abstinence from meat; one principal meal—normally lunch, but it could be supper instead—was of normal proportions and could include meat, with the exception of Fridays, which were always meatless. The other two meals, named "collations," were not to total a full meal and could not include meat. Whereas the tradition of Friday meat abstinence was more clearly defined, Lenten fasting and partial abstinence were often harder to demarcate. Due to the nature of the relative fast, one man's collation could be another's principal meal. Moreover, dispensations from Lenten fasting were more liberally given in various cases, such as for men who were manual laborers or women who were pregnant. Despite this variation in practice, however, Lenten fasting was a social practice meant to facilitate penance among the faithful. And it was a penitential practice from which the faithful did not easily excuse themselves or even easily seek official dispensation.

Perhaps because of the imprecision of the prescriptions for Lent, these regulations were often the subject of considerable discussion, particularly among the clergy as they strove for clarity in communicating the requirements to the faithful. The canonist John Danagher wrote several articles for *Homiletic and Pastoral Review* (*HPR*) on the subject of Lenten fast and abstinence. In one piece from 1956, Danagher noted that the faithful often had questions in regard to fast and abstinence. He sought to give solutions to these problems: first, the case of someone who inadvertently ate meat at other than the principal meal, and second, the question of whether children should be served meat during lunch at a Catholic school. Danagher explained that the essence of the law of fasting consisted in taking only one full meal; hence the inadvertent eating of meat at other than the principal meal did not violate the essence of the law, nor did it mean that it must be counted as the principal meal, nor that meat must be avoided at the principal meal. Another way of saying this is that partial abstinence from meat was ancillary to the prescriptions for fasting.[23] On the basis of this conviction, Danagher could easily solve the problem as to whether children could be served meat on the weekdays of Lent. Because the children were not obliged to fast, they were not bound by rules of partial abstinence and therefore could be served meat, excepting days of complete abstinence, such as Ash Wednesday and Fridays.[24]

It was not just Danagher and other canon lawyers who were concerned with the legal side of fasting and abstinence. The topic frequently gave rise to questions from readers, most of whom were priests. One inquirer wrote in to ask whether it was a mortal or venial sin to eat meat deliberately at a nonprincipal meal on a day of fast. The canonist responded by saying that anything more than two ounces of meat at a collation was "grave matter."[25] Another person asked whether those who were traveling were bound by the law of fast, and Danagher responded by explaining that traveling did absolve from the laws of both fast and abstinence, but that the journey should be necessary and a dispensation should be sought.[26] Another time, a priest asked whether confessors should freely dispense with fast and abstinence regulations for members of their parish who sought dispensations.[27] An additional frequently asked question concerned whether milk, chocolate milk, milkshakes, or other beverages were permitted between meals on fast days. Fr. Connell answered several questions related to this in *American Ecclesiastical Review*.[28] And

23. John C. Danagher, CM, "Notes on Fasting and Abstinence," *HPR* 56, no. 5 (1956): 398–400.
24. Ibid., 401–2.
25. Cecil L. Parres, "Quality and Grave Matter in Fasting," Questions Answered, *HPR* 59, no. 4 (1959): 379.
26. Danagher, "Journeys and the Law of Fasting," 694.
27. Parres, "In Doubt about Fast and Abstinence," Questions Answered, *HPR* 57, no. 9 (1957): 850 and 852.
28. Connell and Walter J. Schmitz, "A Problem in Fasting," Answers to Questions, *Ameri-*

4-1 "The Time Rich in Grace," P. Karch, illustrator, *Treasure Chest of Fun and Fact* (February 27, 1958), 5.

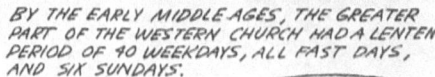

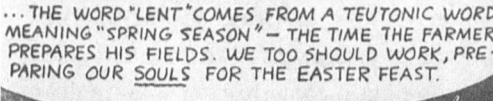

a related question was whether the taking of vitamins violated the fast.[29]

It was clear that at least some Catholic clergy, and perhaps the laity as well, were concerned with getting the fast right. Yet there was meant to be meaning to Lent beyond the attention to fasting regulations, and the faithful also seemed aware of this. In one suggested homily published in 1956, the priest noted the problematic attitude encapsulated by the saying, "I'm just a layman." He pointed out that laymen are "doers" for Christ, witnessing by their actions to people who may never hear a priest speak. Practically speaking, the homilist recommended "penance with a smile," focusing on kindness, cheerfulness, and love, rather than on voluntary penances like giving up cigarettes or moving pictures. He promoted "positive" penitential practices, such as reading the gospels or attending Mass daily as a way to advance in the love of God.[30]

Another homily, a year later in 1957, observed in the same vein that the church is purified by the annual observance of Lent: "we pray that whatever we gain by abstinence we may follow up with good works." The author further explained, "Abstinence ... is a means to an end; that is to say, we abstain from meat in order to obtain something else more desirable."[31] Both fasting and abstinence, the priest suggested, were done for the good of the soul; the dearth left by these practices could be filled to overflowing with the fullness of Christ. The exterior practices of fast and abstinence should rouse the heart and raise the mind to meditate on the supernatural; in this way the external practices of the body could aid the internal efforts of the soul.[32] These homilies imply that at least some people saw the penitential dimension of Christian life as facilitating progress toward a supernatural end. Even with the vigorous attention paid to the legal aspect of the Lenten fast, fasting was also promoted not simply as an obligation but as a spiritual opportunity.

---

can Ecclesiastical Review 136 (1957): 275; see also Connell, "A Nourishing Drink on a Fast Day," *American Ecclesiastical Review* 136 (1957): 364.

29. Parres, "Vitamins and Fasting," Questions Answered, *HPR* 59, no. 7 (1959): 673.

30. Gerard P. Minogue, "First Sunday of Lent: For a More Positive Lent," *HPR* 56, no. 4 (1956): 327–28.

31. William F. Wiebler, "First Sunday of Lent: Exterior and Interior Worship," *HPR* 57, no. 5 (1957): 441–42.

32. Ibid., 442–43. This point is fairly standard in terms of traditional spiritual writings on these topics.

Penance in a New Land

Advent, the "Little Lent"

In many places of the world, such as England, Ireland, and Australia, the church also observed the season of Advent with obligatory and hence communal penitential practices—specifically, abstinence from meat on Wednesdays in addition to Fridays, as well as fasting on Wednesday and Friday.[33] This had its roots in a widespread practice of the early church, and it remained a custom in many Catholic communities in Eastern Europe, no doubt influenced by Eastern Orthodox and Eastern Catholics who practiced a strict forty-day "Philippian fast" during the season of Advent.[34] In 1837, the United States had been granted a dispensation from the custom of fasting on Wednesdays and Fridays during Advent, as well as a dispensation from Wednesday abstinence during Advent. However, as new Catholic immigrants came to the United States, they often brought with them the penitential customs still practiced in their homelands. Hence the tradition of using Wednesdays and Fridays during Advent as particular days for penance continued to be observed by Polish Catholics in the United States, for example. Though that practice of fast and abstinence on Wednesdays and Fridays of Advent was no longer obligatory throughout the United States, Advent nonetheless maintained a penitential nature in virtue of the violet vestments worn by priests, as well as the omission of the "Gloria" at the Mass and the omission of the *Te Deum* in the Divine Office during the season.[35] The 1941 version of *My Sunday Missal* explained, "During Advent Christ lives and works in the soul, imparting joy and urging preparation by penance for His coming."[36]

The penitential nature of Advent was also described by Pope Pius XII in his 1947 encyclical *Mediator Dei*, on the liturgy:

In the period of Advent ... the Church arouses in us the consciousness of the sins we have had the misfortune to commit, and urges us, by restraining our de-

---

33. James David O'Neill, "Abstinence," in *The Catholic Encyclopedia*, vol. 1 (New York: Robert Appleton, 1907). Woywood's *New Canon Law*, 256, seems to indicate that fasting was at one point considered by the faithful to be obligatory on Fridays of Advent.

34. The Philippian fast is so named because it begins following the feast of St. Philip, which, on the Orthodox calendar, is celebrated on November 14.

35. *Divine Office: The Hours of the Divine Office in English and Latin*, vol. 1., prepared by the staff of the Liturgical Press (Collegeville, Minn.: The Liturgical Press, 1963), 1054.

36. Stedman, *My Sunday Missal Explained*, 31.

sires and practicing voluntary mortification of the body, to recollect ourselves in meditation, and experience a longing desire to return to God who alone can free us by His grace from the stain of sin and from its evil consequences.[37]

Priests in the United States ascribed to the traditional penitential understanding of Advent as a season for reform and penance inspired by the expectation of the coming of Christ. For many ethnic groups this was simply a continuation of fast and abstinence practices rooted in the obligatory practices of their home country. But even for those Catholics who had lived in the United States longer, voluntary penance during Advent was highly encouraged, even if that penitential practice did not have the same social element resulting from longstanding practice. The voluntary nature of this penance promoted by priests meant that penance could take on various forms beyond the more traditional fast and abstinence practiced by pockets of particular ethnic groups. In either case, however, the emphasis was on acknowledging sins and preparing for Christmas by penance.

Writing for the liturgical magazine *Worship* in 1951, the Benedictine Basil Stegmann described Advent as the opening scene for the drama of salvation played out liturgically:

The world must realize, first of all, its utter misery brought on by sin. It must recognize the divine power to avenge man's injustice and ingratitude, and that only humble repentance and a renewed faith in God's love will restore peace to the earth, through the merciful intervention of the promised Redeemer.[38]

As the article continues, Stegmann comments upon the Advent reading that features John the Baptist proclaiming the message to "do penance." Stegmann writes, "Every generation must look forward to the coming of the Redeemer, and prepare itself by penance."[39] Homilists in *HPR* likewise suggested numerous voluntary and quite diverse Advent penances throughout the years, such as cheerfulness, almsgiving, and giving up smoking.[40] Homilists also urged the faithful not to neglect their interior

---

37. Pius XII, *Mediator Dei*, Encyclical on the Sacred Liturgy, no. 154, November 20, 1947, http://www.vatican.va/holy_father/pius_xii/encyclicals/documents/hf_p-xii_enc_20111947-mediator-dei_en.html; accessed on November 21, 2012.
38. Basil Stegmann, "The Opening Scene: Advent," *Worship* 26, no. 1 (December 1951): 7.
39. Ibid., 8.
40. John E. Coogan, "Sacrifice in Hope: First Sunday in Advent," Homilies on the Liturgy of Sundays and Feasts, *HPR* 63, no. 2 (1962): 150.

Penance in a New Land

preparation for the holy day of Christmas as they worked upon the external preparations associated with decorations, gift-giving, and feasting.[41] The faithful were encouraged to increase their personal prayer or attendance at parish devotions and daily Mass.[42]

A cartoon in the magazine *Treasure Chest of Fun and Fact* shows how this message of preparation was communicated to Catholic school children. A segment entitled "Advent Action" showed a group of girls discussing what they could do to prepare spiritually for Advent. After some discussion, the girls decide to make a visit to the Blessed Sacrament after school during each day of Advent and to encourage friends to do the same. While many of the students initially agreed to these church visits, by the end of Advent only a few were faithful to the practice. Hence in the last frame of the cartoon, a caption notes that "for some, Advent was a time of giving. For others it was a wasted opportunity," as the various figures' prayer bubbles indicate. Whereas one says, "Baby Jesus, please take my visits and whatever merit I earned as your Christmas gift," another says, "I didn't do much for you this Advent, dear Jesus, but I'll do better next year."[43] A text-dense follow-up to the cartoon ends its explanation with the following: "The main purpose of doing penance in Advent should be to honor God because we love Him, and to lessen the punishment due for our sins. It makes a wonderful birthday present for the Baby King Who came into the world so he could die on the cross to save us all."[44] This cartoon is representational of the common view that Advent was about spiritual preparation that was associated with penance as reparation for sin. This message was instilled in Catholics from a young age, showing that even kids could embrace penitential practices and that partaking in such practices would help prepare them spiritually for a major liturgical celebration such as Christmas.

---

41. John P. Sullivan, "First Sunday of Advent: Just in Time," Homilies on the Liturgy of Sundays and Feasts, *HPR* 57, no. 2 (1956): 157.

42. John J. Cassela, "Prepare!: Second Sunday of Advent," Homilies on the Liturgy of Sundays and Feasts, *HPR* 65, no. 2 (1964): 151.

43. "Advent Action," The Little Things, *Treasure Chest of Fun and Fact*, December 7, 1961, 12; see appendix A for full cartoon/article. This theme also occurs in a 1957 article entitled "The Perfect Christmas Present," You're Important! *Treasure Chest of Fun and Fact*, December 18, 1958, 34.

44. "Advent Action," 14.

4-2 "Advent Action," in *Treasure Chest of Fun and Fact* (December 7, 1961), 9–13, The Little Things series.

Another Advent theme was expressed in several homilies that encouraged the faithful to use the season to make greater effort to fight sin in their lives. One homilist in 1957 addressed the problematic nature of work-sponsored Christmas parties: "What travesty! What a travesty especially for a Catholic who should have some conception of the fact that Advent, the period before Christmas, is supposedly a time of preparation and of penance."[45] This priest advised that Catholics might have to forego their work Christmas parties in order to maintain a clear conscience. Enthusiastic celebration during a penitential season seemed unlikely to foster a spirit of penance, nor would it aid in the struggle against sin. As another priest emphasized, Advent was a season to make efforts to get rid of sin, sometimes by rooting out near occasions of sin and not giving in to selfish desires.[46]

The clergy wanted it to be clear that Advent was a season of longing and desire, contrition and purification, not satisfaction, indulgence, and celebration.[47] One priest author proposed that the penance of Advent would be complemented with the grace of God, especially if the church's members ordered their penance to the proper growth of the soul with regular, well-thought-out penitential acts, rather than performing penitential works haphazardly.[48] Though the message of Advent as penitential seems to have been frequently communicated to American Catholics, for those of the faithful increasingly exposed to religious pluralism in the workplace or in the suburbs, it might have been complicated to implement the advice contained in these homilies, especially if it meant appearing uncharitable or judgmental toward Protestant coworkers or neighbors. The undertaking of voluntary penance for Advent was already a challenge, but the practical situation of American religious pluralism could make it even more difficult, particularly when a Catholic was surrounded by non-Catholics already partaking of Christmas celebrations.

45. Very Rev. Msgr. Edward S. Schwegler, "Christmas Parties: Fourth Sunday of Advent," Homilies on the Liturgy of Sundays and Feasts, *HPR* 58, no. 2 (1957): 189.

46. William B. Faherty, "How Best to Prepare for Christmas?: First Sunday of Advent," Homilies on the Liturgy of Sundays and Feasts, *HPR* 60 (1959): 63.

47. Leslie Rumble, "Redemptive Mission of Christ: First Sunday in Advent," Homilies on the Liturgy of Sundays and Feasts, *HPR* 61, no. 1 (1960): 79.

48. Wiebler, "Christmas Trees Sprung from Decay: Fourth Sunday of Advent,"Homilies on the Liturgy of Sundays and Feasts, *HPR* 59, no. 2 (1958): 173.

Penance in a New Land

No doubt there was some degree of concession as Christmas celebrations slowly crept into the season of Advent.

Also writing in the 1950s, the Benedictine liturgist Ermin Vitry struck a similar theme in his *Worship* article entitled, "Aspirations for Advent." While not speaking of penance per se, Vitry nonetheless warned of the danger of Christian complacency, or what he called "the most insidious sin of the modern Catholic, namely, compromise."[49] Vitry described laziness in the struggle for sanctity, the contemporary self-conceit that he believed would prevent the receptivity to which the Catholic was called, especially highlighted during the season of Advent. Vitry did not think it necessary to forego completely progress and modern comforts, but he saw the spirit of the times as opposed to the living of one's vocation. Advent was a time to try to use the things of the world wisely without being enslaved to the world.[50] It was a time for reflection, prayer, and action— a renewed conversion to the quest for sanctity. Again, such a message could seem inconsistent with life in religiously pluralistic suburbs; it might even appear as mere panegyric. It could inspire and motivate, but it is unlikely that it was embodied by the majority of the faithful. Revitalized attention to the interior life accompanied by greater simplicity in the exterior life could be difficult to enact without the social support characteristic of other American Catholic penitential practices such as Friday meat abstinence and Lenten fasting.

By the late 1960s and early 1970s, priests shifted their focus, minimizing the apparent contradiction of liturgical Advent in the midst of preemptive Christmas celebrations and instead reflecting the reality experienced by American Catholics. The emphases in regard to Advent moved from penitential preparation to a less countercultural notion of joyful expectation. Advent homilies focused on penance and self-denial were few and far between.[51] Even those suggested homilies with penance in their title failed to mention the subject in a substantive manner.[52]

---

49. Ermin Vitry, "Aspirations for Advent," *Worship* 28, no. 1 (1953): 21.

50. Ibid., 25.

51. Albert W. Cylwicki, "Advent Preparation: Second Sunday of Advent," Homilies on the Liturgy of Sundays and Feasts, *HPR* 73, no. 2 (1972): 40.

52. See, for example, Marion J. Sitzmann, "Penance and Joy: Second Sunday of Advent," Homilies on the Liturgy of Sundays and Feasts, *HPR* 75, no. 1 (1974): 39.

The Catholic understanding of Advent as a time for penitential preparation was losing its standing as Catholics in the United States became more like their Protestant compatriots. Proclaiming a message of penance in the weeks before Christmas became a stance more countercultural in nature than most Catholics were willing to adopt. Compared to the 1950s, there was little social support for embracing the penitential nature of Advent, and hence, outside of the prayers of Mass, it was difficult to maintain any sense of Advent as penitential.

Meanwhile, one homilist who brought up the subject of sin during Advent spoke about social sin, minimizing the private and personal nature of sin in order to highlight the role of the community in preparing for confession and in benefiting from confession. This same homily downplayed personal effort in order to accentuate the notions of grace and gift. Using the language of conversion, to speak of penance, the priest notably quoted Bernard Häring.[53] A more lengthy article entitled "Advent Has Its Problems" treated Advent in a more in-depth manner, considering particularly where the emphasis should lie: Christ's birth in Bethlehem or his second coming at the end of time. It made no mention of doing penance or the penitential nature of Advent. Rather, the author suggested that Vatican II had restored Advent as a time of joyful expectation.[54] Sin and penance were no longer a primary focus of Advent as discussed by clergy or laity.

This change in tone for Advent was perhaps captured by the move among some liturgists and clergy to replace the violet vestments common to Advent and Lent with blue vestments that were specific to Advent. Despite the fact that the *General Instruction of the Roman Missal* excluded blue from the list of acceptable main colors for liturgical vestments, many wanted to distinguish Advent from Lent, specifically in order to minimize the association between Advent and Lent, and hence to downplay

---

53. Oscar J. Miller, CM, "I'm an Innovator: Fourth Sunday in Advent," *HPR* 70, no. 2 (1969): 141–42. Miller's quotation of Häring (unspecified text) was as follows: "For sin has offended the Church, marred her harmony and unity; and conversion must lead the sinner back again to the community of love and life in the Church. Conversion—such is the clear meaning of the rites of the Church—is not the result of personal effort, but grace and gift from the sacred community of the kingdom of God, with which the sinner by his own free endeavor must cooperate toward reacceptance" (143).

54. Charles E. Miller, "Advent Has Its Problems," *HPR* 73, no. 2 (1972): 25.

the recognition of Advent as a penitential season.[55] One former seminarian, who had a negative experience of this trend during his time in the seminary in the 1980s, states that blue-focused liturgists strove to rid Advent of its penitential character and the notion that it was the "little Lent."[56] This move may also have been ecumenically motivated or related. The use of a blue called "Sarum blue" for Advent was a norm among other churches, such as the Episcopal Church, which attributes its use to an ancient English custom symbolizing heaven and Mary.[57] It is possible that liturgists wanted to highlight the unique nature of Advent as preparation for Christmas, rather than seeing it as a lesser version of Lent.

Regardless of the exact motivation for changing the liturgical color of Advent, it seems to have been one of the unauthorized implementations of Vatican II that persists in the United States today. In those Catholic parishes that continue to use blue vestments, Advent is visually distinguished from Lent, and this may therefore diminish Advent's penitential character and the association with Lent that signifies both seasons as times of preparation for major liturgical feasts. The difference between penitential preparation and joyful expectation might be best understood in terms of action. The former term implies doing something to get ready for Christmas, whereas the latter phrase is more passive, indicating waiting or anticipating. Advent is a season of both preparation and expectation, but as the liturgical emphasis moved toward expectation, penitential preparation diminished. This change in emphasis followed upon, and was likely related to, the changing demographics of Catholics increasingly integrated with non-Catholics who did not share in a liturgical season that was meant to guide the spiritual preparation for Christmas. Performing penance during Advent in a religiously plural setting would have to be countercultural and primarily driven by the commit-

---

55. *General Instruction of the Roman Missal*, 3rd ed. (Washington, D.C.: United States Catholic Conference of Bishops, 2010), nos. 345–46.

56. Leon Suprenant, "Blue Advent," http://archkckblog.wordpress.com/2011/12/08/blue-advent/; accessed on November 9, 2012.

57. Christopher Webber, *Welcome to Sunday: An Introduction to Worship in the Episcopal Church* (Harrisburg, Pa.: Morehouse, 2003), 44–45. Episcopal churches apparently have the option of using violet, under Roman custom, or "Sarum" blue, under English custom. There is debate about whether Sarum blue is actually blue, however, or actually violet. Some people also suggest that the notion of blue vestments was a marketing scheme of Almy, the Anglican-based vestment makers, who gained business by promoting the need for another color of vestments.

ment of the individual or nuclear family, as there were no significant social structures or obligatory practices in place to support penitential practices during Advent.

Vigil Fasts

Prior to Vatican II, the season of Advent concluded with a fast on December 24 before the feast of Christmas on December 25. Often this vigil fast could be transferred to December 23 without a dispensation. This pattern of fasting before feasting was a longstanding tradition of the church and was prescribed in the United States for several vigils, with the idea that penance served as a preparation and a way to focus prior to a major celebration.

As previously mentioned, there were changes through the years as to which vigils should be observed with fast and abstinence. Per the 1917 Code of Canon Law, the vigils of Pentecost, Assumption, All Saints, and Christmas were to be days of fast and abstinence. Modifications in 1949 reduced these vigil days to two: Assumption and Christmas. Later, in 1957, the December 7 vigil of the Immaculate Conception was substituted for the August 14 vigil of the Assumption.[58] In 1959 Pope John XXIII allowed for December 23 to be substituted for December 24 as a day of fast and abstinence anticipating Christmas.[59] Moreover, the Lenten fast that had formerly ended at noon on Holy Saturday was in 1955 extended until midnight of Easter Sunday by the decree *Maxima redemptionis mysteria*.[60]

In all cases, the fast and abstinence observed on the vigils of feasts were meant to remind people of the upcoming feast. There is little evidence to indicate how well these vigil fasts were kept by religious or laity, so it is not certain how they were experienced by the faithful or what significance they might have held. Perhaps because the feast itself was

---

58. "Fast and Abstinence in the United States," Decrees and Decisions—Canonical, McManus papers, series 2, box 1, folder 25, 117. Also under section (2) in commentary on Canon 1252 of document entitled "Section II of Part II, Book III," in McManus papers, box 1, series 2, folder 25.

59. "Fast and Abstinence on the Vigil of Christmas," Decrees and Decisions—Canonical, December 7, 1959, McManus papers, series 2, box 1, folder 25.

60. Under section (2) in commentary on Canon 1252 of document entitled "Section II of Part II, Book III," in McManus papers, box 1, series 2, folder 25.

Penance in a New Land

the focus of the liturgical celebration, rather than the vigil fast, there is very little discussion as to the meaning or importance of vigil fasts. There were no homilies featured in *HPR* that would indicate any particular emphasis on the importance of fasting prior to that feast. The obligatory nature of these fasts, however, would indicate that this penitential preparation was also practiced socially, as was the liturgical celebration of the feast.

The Ember Days

The Ember Days occurred four times annually, roughly at the beginning of each of the four seasons. The practice of fast and abstinence for the Wednesdays, Fridays, and Saturdays after the Feast of St. Lucy (winter), after Ash Wednesday (spring), after Pentecost (summer), and after the Exaltation of the Holy Cross (fall) were officially prescribed by various ecclesiastical leaders at different times and places. One mnemonic rhyme that helped the faithful to remember when Ember Days occurred was, "Lenty, Penty, Crucy, Lucy." A Latin mnemonic for Ember Days was *Sant Crux, Lucia, Cineres, Charismata Dia / Ut sit in angaria quarta sequens feria*.[61] According to the *Catholic Encyclopedia*, the practice of Ember Days dated from the third century as an effort to sanctify a pagan Roman practice of having religious rites associated with the three times of planting, harvesting, and vintage.[62] The church adopted seasonal religious rites in order to thank God for gifts of nature, make use of them in moderation, and help the needy. At some point in the following centuries a fourth season was added.[63] With Gregory VII (ca. 1085) the Ember Days also became connected with ordinations. The fast and abstinence on Ember Wednesdays, Fridays, and especially Saturdays were to be offered in a particular way for those who would receive the sacrament of Holy Orders on Ember Saturdays.

    61. "Ember Days," http://www.fisheaters.com/emberdays.html.; accessed on April 5, 2013; translation provided on the site: Holy Cross, Lucy, Ash Wednesday, Pentecost, are when the quarter holidays follow.
    62. Francis Mershman, "Ember Days," in *The Catholic Encyclopedia*, vol. 5 (New York: Robert Appleton, 1909), http://www.newadvent.org/cathen/05399b.htm; accessed on April 6, 2013.
    63. Gaspar Lefebvre, *Saint Andrew Daily Missal with Vespers for Sundays and Feasts* (St. Paul, Minn.: E. M. Lohmann, 1952), 30.

The *Saint Andrew Daily Missal* explained that fasting and prayer was a way of consecrating to God a new season and also calling down God's graces on those to be ordained.[64] The penitential nature of the Ember Days was indicated by the priest's vesting in violet, as well as the prayers used for the liturgy on those days:

May our fasts be acceptable to thee, O Lord, we beseech Thee: and by expiating our sins render us worthy of Thy grace, and lead us to Thy everlasting promises.[65]

Graciously look down, O Lord, we beseech Thee, upon the devotion of Thy people, that they who are mortified in body by abstinence, may be refreshed in mind through the fruit of good works.[66]

That our fasts may be acceptable to Thee, O Lord, grant, we beseech Thee, that by the oblation of this sacrifice, we may offer up to Thee a purified heart.[67]

Grant to Thy servants who humbly pray to Thee, O Lord, that while abstaining from food for our bodies we may likewise abstain from sin in our souls.[68]

Almighty and everlasting God, who, by salutary abstinence, dost heal us both in soul and body; we humbly beseech Thy Majesty that appeased by the fervent devotion of those who fast, Thou wouldst grant us help now and in the time to come.[69]

The masses said on these days also featured additional moments of silent penitential prayer done in the kneeling position.[70]

The bishops' report of 1951 noted that some had suggested dropping Ember Days as days of abstinence, a suggestion that likely arose from the

---

64. Ibid., 240.
65. Ibid.; Secret of Ember Wednesday in Advent, 33.
66. Ibid., Collect of Ember Wednesday in Lent, 245.
67. Ibid., Secret of Ember Saturday after Pentecost, 255.
68. Ibid., Collect of Ember Wednesday in September, 821.
69. Ibid., First Collect of Ember Saturday in September, 828. The 1966 interim Sacramentary's prayers for Ember Days were consistent with those previously quoted, with the primary difference being the second-person pronouns used for addressing God in the translation of the prayers from Latin; i.e., *St. Andrew's Missal* uses the English words Thy and Thee, whereas the English translation found in the Sacramentary uses your and you; see, for example, the prayers for Ember Friday of September in *The English-Latin Sacramentary for the United States of America* (New York: Catholic Book Publishing, 1966), 173.

70. *English-Latin Sacramentary*, 174–75. On Ember Wednesdays and Fridays, kneeling prayer was done after the *Kyrie*, whereas on Ember Saturday, particularly when using the long form of the Mass, kneeling was also done after each of the multiple readings. The one exception to this appears to be the Ember Days in the octave of Pentecost, where the prayers were not said in the kneeling position; see 155–60.

fact that most Catholics in the United States were no longer in an agricultural setting, and Ember Days seemed inapplicable to their situation and hence unnecessary.[71] Others insisted that Ember Days traditionally had a very important place in the liturgy, "and fear was emphatically expressed that a complete dispensation would diminish their traditional importance."[72] By 1966, the reverence for Ember Days had apparently weakened to the point that the NCCB's "Pastoral Statement on Penance and Abstinence" removed the fast and abstinence requirement for these days entirely. In 1969, with the implementation of the *Missale romanum* by Pope Paul VI and the subsequent *General Instruction of the Roman Missal*, the celebration of Ember Days was left to the discretion of the local episcopal conferences. In the United States, the observation of Ember Days and the traditions associated with them became optional and hence practically defunct, realizing the bishops' initial fear expressed back in 1951. Following the course of other penances, when the Ember Days ceased to be communally obligatory but rather became individually voluntary in nature, their social practice ceased, with only a small minority choosing to observe Ember Days as days of fast and abstinence, and the liturgical celebration of Ember Days ended.

Bearing the Ills of Life

One other key penitential practice of Catholics in the United States was the practice of offering up suffering as expiation for sin. Unlike the practices previously mentioned, this one has no particular association with liturgical days (Fridays, fasts before feasts) or liturgical seasons (Advent, Lent). Rather, "the patient suffering of the ills of life" was listed by the *Baltimore Catechism* as one of the chief means to satisfy God for temporal punishment due to sin, and this form of penance could be used at any time by those under duress.[73] The *Baltimore Catechism* included a list of the "ills of life," including misfortune, poverty, sickness, trial, and af-

---

71. On the other hand, this distance from the agricultural context could stand as an argument for the necessity of Ember Days, so as to help urban and suburban Catholics recall the source of their food and many other resources, despite their own distance from agriculture.

72. "Report on Fast and Abstinence," 8.

73. *Baltimore Catechism*, Q. 221, http://catholicism.about.com/od/baltimorecatechism/f/Question_221_BC.htm; accessed on November 10, 2012.

fliction. Temporal punishment was to be expected as a consequence of sin, and in some cases this was evident. The man who found himself in poverty as a consequence of excessive gambling, for example, could bear the temporal punishment of poverty, offering it as satisfaction for his sin of gambling.

On the other hand, these ills of life were regarded as particularly valuable penance when they were not brought on by one's own sin but were the result of such events as natural disasters, political conflicts, ordinary sickness, unexpected injury, inadequate employment, or fidelity to the church.[74] The temporal punishment in such a case could be applied to any sin, even that of another person or a social group, such as a country. The difficult life experienced by Catholic immigrants to the United States provided ample opportunity for bearing patiently the ills of life. Families were often crowded together in small, urban spaces, money was frequently short, and food was scarce. Fathers worked hard, mostly at low-paying jobs, and mothers worked hard, too, raising large families in challenging circumstances and sometimes trying to earn a little extra money on the side.

It was in this context that American Catholics heard the message that suffering could be useful as a penance for sin. Comfortable living with no difficulty was not praised or glorified, but rather was frequently criticized and associated with materialistic Protestant values.[75] The demanding situations of life, in contrast, presented a truly valuable opportunity for sanctification. Catholic life in America could be tough, but if Catholics could voluntarily embrace the sufferings thrust on them involuntarily, then they gained an important tool in making satisfaction for sin. The religion scholar Robert Orsi notes that physical distress of all sorts, from chronic, genetic conditions like cerebral palsy to the unexpected illness and injury, was understood as an individual's opportunity for spiritual growth: "Pain purged and disciplined the ego, stripping it of pride and self-love; it disclosed the emptiness of the world."[76]

74. Connell, *Father Connell's Confraternity Edition: New Baltimore Catechism No. 3* (1949; repr. Cincinnati: Benziger Brothers, 1955), Q. 809.

75. Anna-Margaret Record, "This Side of Sainthood," chap. 5, *Ave Maria*, February 12, 1955, 19.

76. Robert Orsi, *Between Heaven and Earth: The Religious Worlds People Make and the Scholars Who Study Them* (Princeton: Princeton University Press, 2005), 21.

Penance in a New Land

Jay Dolan suggests that the Sorrowful Mother Novena, which was the most popular devotion during the late 1930s and early 1940s, was appealing precisely because it focused on sorrow, supporting a sense of sin and guilt among Catholics who were suffering through crisis and hardship and seeking jobs and financial success in the midst of the Great Depression and world wars.[77] This novena provided a social way for Catholics to express their conviction that suffering was meaningful as penance. It helped the faithful to offer up the ills of life as penance for their sins. Orsi argues that the novena also reminded the sick and suffering that Jesus' pain in his passion and death was far greater than theirs; those who maintained the Catholic perspective would therefore minimize their distress.[78]

A fictional series that appeared in the magazine *Ave Maria* in 1955 gives evidence of this Catholic perspective on suffering as penance leading to sanctity. The stories featured Marcy Bailard, a Catholic mother of six children who accepted the church's teaching against artificial birth control and embraced the challenges of raising a large family, finding consolation for her many sacrifices in the support of her husband and joy of her children. From the very first paragraph, Marcy is shown dealing with the difficulties of raising a large family; at the grocery store she is seeking bargains, looking for half-price dented cans, and doing her best to make the money stretch.[79] Throughout the rest of the series, Marcy struggles with disobedient toddlers, a messy house, mountains of laundry and ironing, exhaustion, a lack of opportunity to rest from her childcare and housework despite a physical illness, trying to get her whole family to Sunday Mass, the criticism of non-Catholic in-laws who fail to understand their family life, not being able to afford things that she would like to buy, and extending hospitality to others in the midst of a busy home.

But it is her illness that best illustrates Marcy's embodiment of the Catholic perspective on suffering as penitential. As her pain increases leading up to an eventual operation, Marcy quotes a poem she had once had stuck in the frame of her mirror: "*I do not ask a truce / With life's in-*

---

77. Dolan, *American Catholic Experience*, 385.
78. Orsi, *Between Heaven and Earth*, 27.
79. Margaret Record, "This Side of Sainthood," chap. 1, *Ave Maria*, January 15, 1955, 18.

cessant pain, / But school my lips, Lord, / Not to complain."[80] Marcy finds it harder and harder not to complain in her discomfort, and she reflects on the meaning of suffering:

the days passed, and the value of suffering took on meaning in her mind and soul. The ways it could be fashioned to one's eternal future fascinated her: as expiation for past sin; as an offering for the souls suffering in Purgatory—who would, in turn pray for those who had helped them (how comforting was the doctrine of the Church United!); and as a freely accepted cross, borne with dignity for love of Him Who had said, "If anyone will come after Me, let him take up his cross and follow Me."[81]

As she looks ahead to her surgery, Marcy strives to put her spiritual life in order, reflecting on the meaning of the sacrament of confession in relation to death: "[She] searched her conscience that she might leave nothing out that weighed upon her in the slightest degree as sin."[82]

Though Marcy's hysterectomy procedure goes well, during her recovery she becomes severely ill, and Marcy faces the realization that her death is imminent. Marcy offers her pain, praying, "*Take it, Lord. For my many sins, take it in expiation. And have mercy on me. Have mercy on me when the moment comes.*"[83] When the priest comes to visit her, Marcy tries to concentrate, blotting out all thought but that of penance. Later in her delirium Marcy again prays, "*Lord God on the cross of agony, help me, and for my sins take it in reparation.*"[84] Though fictional, the character of Marcy Bailard seems adequately to represent an embodiment of Catholic teachings, including the *Baltimore Catechism*'s description of bearing patiently the ills of life. Marcy not only bears patiently with the difficulties of raising a large family, she also embraces the pain and suffering of her illness, offering them as penance for her sin.

The religion scholar Robert Orsi views Marcy's story within a particular genre: "the long-suffering, self-sacrificing housewife, silent and cheerful in her pain and humiliation and on her way to sanctity ... had long been a familiar figure in devotional culture."[85] Orsi suggests that Catholic immigrants' daughters in the United States grew up with "these domestic

80. Ibid., chap. 8, March 5, 1955, 20.
81. Ibid.
82. Ibid., 21.
83. Ibid., chap. 9, March 12, 1955, 20.
84. Ibid., 21.
85. Orsi, *Thank You, Saint Jude*, 72.

Penance in a New Land

hagiographies at a time when social and economic circumstances, as well as the extended horizon of their own ambitions and achievements, were making it increasingly unlikely that their lives would (or could) resemble those of the kitchen athletes."[86] They were told to embrace a suburban asceticism, and when they failed to do so, they were condemned for their shortcomings. In particular, women were blamed for embracing American consumerism and for seeking work simply in order to purchase luxuries. Though Orsi's judgment here is evaluative and negative, his portrayal of the culture at this time nonetheless confirms the Catholic emphasis on suffering as penitential and therefore ultimately worthwhile.

Moreover, it is important to note that the author of the "This Side of Sainthood" series was not a preachy priest trying to make women feel bad, but rather a well-educated laywoman named Anna Margaret Record, herself a mother of six children. One can surmise that Marcy's perspective in raising a family of six bears similarity to Record's own views and experience of living out those Catholic values. Hence, rather than seeing such a series as primarily critical, it can be regarded as exhortatory and illustrative of the joy in raising a large family, despite the sacrifices of comfort or pleasure involved. Marcy was happy, despite her difficulties and suffering. In 1955, such views as those expressed in this fictional series would not have seemed out of place. In later years, however, the value of sacrifice and suffering as penitential would wane; figures like Marcy were (and are) used as examples of what was wrong with Catholic views, rather than what was right.

As many Catholics became upwardly mobile and moved from urban to suburban locations, they faced a different set of challenges than those encountered by their parents and grandparents. Joseph Chinnici and Angelyn Dries state, "While the traditional ascetical practice of penance had emphasized the importance of sacrifice, highlighting the wartime values of thrift and rationing, a new era of the disposable and planned obsolescence required a different motivation and more subtle discernment."[87] Dolan emphasizes that the move to suburbia was a major residential shift for the church: "In suburbia the old immigrant organiza-

---

86. Ibid., 73.
87. Chinnici and Dries, eds., *Prayer and Practice in the American Catholic Community*, 182.

tions had disappeared, the closeness of city neighborhoods was gone, and the moral integrity of family life seemed threatened."[88] This new life was fast-paced and mobile, and as Dolan says, "When compared to the city... suburbia seemed to be a pleasant place. The problems of race and poverty were downtown, out of sight and out of mind. That is just where the vast majority of Catholics in the 1950s wanted them: out of sight and out of mind."[89]

As they sought financial stability, moved to the suburbs, and assimilated to the larger American culture, Catholics found new ways to avoid and address some of the sufferings of earlier generations, and suffering was not romanticized to the degree it had been in the past. For those who used it, contraception allowed them to limit their family size. Education led to better jobs and hence better paychecks, and this in turn offered more comfort in less-crowded living spaces. There were new ways to address other ills of life, as well. Counseling and popular psychology provided ways of dealing with personal problems and seeking to change situations, rather than just "bearing the ills of life cheerfully" or "offering them up" as a form of penance. Medicine became increasingly effective in dealing with many illnesses. Domestic chores found assistance in new cleaning tools and convenience foods. In Orsi's words, "The ethos of pain was being elaborated in Catholic magazines alongside tips for arranging new furniture, recipes, beauty hints, and ways to throw successful birthday parties for children, all written in the upbeat prose of women's magazines."[90] An "uneasiness" between material success and the good of suffering characterized American Catholics, who embraced American ambition and material achievement but had been formed in a Catholic culture that advocated self-denial and sacrifice.[91]

The sufferings encountered by American Catholics of this generation were increasingly unrelated to their being poor immigrant Catholics in a wealthy, Protestant society that was hostile to them; rather, Catholics were sharing in the tribulations endured by other Americans.[92] During

---

88. Dolan, *American Catholic Experience*, 381.
89. Ibid., 382. No doubt this was true for non-Catholics, as well.
90. Orsi, *Between Heaven and Earth*, 33.
91. Ibid., 34.
92. Americans everywhere had lost loved ones in war, for example, and dealt with limited

Penance in a New Land

the time of World War II, for example, the pope's dispensation from the usual traditional penitential practices indicated that the war brought difficulties enough that could be offered as penance. And yet these hardships deemed as potentially penitential and affirmed so by the pope's dispensation were hardships endured by Catholics' compatriots, as well; though perhaps only Catholics took a penitential outlook on the ills of life brought on by war, they shared their sacrifices with non-Catholics. These hardships shared by all Americans worked to build up national identity rather than the Catholic identity facilitated by unique penitential practices.

Nonetheless, the importance of bearing the ills of life as a form of penance continued during this time period, and Vatican II did not bring a theological change in this regard. This topic was addressed in the midst of the discussion of the universal call to holiness in chapter 4 of *Lumen gentium*. The council fathers wrote, "For besides intimately linking [the laity] to His life and His mission, [Christ] also gives them a sharing in His priestly function of offering spiritual worship for the glory of God and the salvation of men."[93] Among the ways in which the laity share in the priestly function, *Lumen gentium* described "even the hardships of life, if patiently borne" as a spiritual sacrifice offered by the laity.[94]

Once again, however, the words of Vatican II and their implementa-

---

food resources during wartime. This fact was acknowledged by Pope Pius XII's suspension of fast and abstinence regulations for the faithful whose countries were engaged in World War II. The implication was that daily life already provided sufficient opportunity for bearing suffering; the church would not impose anything significant in addition to this. On the other hand, this kind of suffering could be narrated as assisting primarily in building up national identity, rather than a specifically Catholic identity, and those second- and third-generation American Catholics who soon moved to the suburbs may thus have felt more American than their parents and grandparents.

93. *Lumen gentium*, no. 34.

94. Ibid.: "For besides intimately linking them to His life and His mission, He also gives them a sharing in His priestly function of offering spiritual worship for the glory of God and the salvation of men. For this reason the laity, dedicated to Christ and anointed by the Holy Spirit, are marvelously called and wonderfully prepared so that ever more abundant fruits of the Spirit may be produced in them. For all their works, prayers and apostolic endeavors, their ordinary married and family life, their daily occupations, their physical and mental relaxation, if carried out in the Spirit, and even the hardships of life, if patiently borne—all these become "spiritual sacrifices acceptable to God through Jesus Christ." Together with the offering of the Lord's body, they are most fittingly offered in the celebration of the Eucharist. Thus, as those everywhere who adore in holy activity, the laity consecrate the world itself to God."

tion took place in a different culture than the one in which they had been written. The ensuing popularity of "the universal call to holiness" chose to highlight other aspects than the notion of bearing the ills of life as a sharing in offering spiritual worship. With an increasing focus on the freedom and responsibility of the laity, the emphasis turned more toward action in society and participation in the liturgy. The notion of "offering it up" became less appealing to American Catholics, perhaps viewed as a quaint way that naïve, uneducated, and poor Catholics had used to endure problems rather than to solve them.[95] The supposed supernatural value of suffering may have been comforting to some in the past whose lives presented substantial challenges, especially financial. For younger American Catholics in more comfortable situations and with fewer of the other socially practiced penances, this language was not as compelling. The importance of the penitential dimension of the Christian life, emphasizing the opportunity presented by suffering, continued to diminish in the decades following the 1960s. The changing perspective on bearing the ills of life was a part of the overall decline of the penitential practice of American Catholicism. The benefit of this particular kind of penance was not as apparent to the faithful without the presence of a variety of other penances—such as Friday meat abstinence—that had permeated Catholic life.

Perceived Problems with Penitential Practices

The penitential practices previously described had numerous natural benefits, such as promoting social cohesion among American Catholics and providing a communal context for the individuals who participated in what might otherwise have seemed to be difficult practices. Moreover, these practices marked Catholics as unique in a religiously pluralistic culture. They assisted in the maintenance and strengthening of Catho-

---

95. An even stronger version of this claim seems to be Robert Orsi's position in his chapter "Imagining Women," in *Thank You, Saint Jude*, 70–94. Orsi indicates that the exhortation to "offer it up" served primarily as a way of disciplining women: "Suffering was not only the central social fact of women's lives, in this imagining, but their spiritual destiny and vocation," 87; "The path marked out for women was clear: rebellion, autonomy, ambition brought terrible punishment, while suffering and pain made women beloved, graceful, capable of healing and helping. All women had to do is keep silent"; 88.

lic identity in a primarily Protestant country. These obligatory and hence socially practiced penances fostered a habit, sometimes identified as the virtue of penance. On the other hand, these penitential practices often came under criticism similar to that applied to the sacrament of penance as it was practiced among American Catholics. The sacrament of penance was criticized for having a perfunctory nature, tending toward legalism, detracting from the sense of the relational nature of sin, failing to cultivate a suitable interior sentiment, fostering scrupulosity, not adequately addressing spiritual and personal problems, and neglecting social sins, such as racism, while also emphasizing rules, such as Friday meat abstinence, that seemed trivial in comparison.

Fast and abstinence were likewise criticized for seeming perfunctory and tending toward legalism. Many felt that these habits had become so much a part of the routine of Catholic life in America that they failed to reflect a corresponding interior sentiment of sorrow for sins. Catholics appeared to participate in penitential practices because they were obliged, because they just always had, and because everyone did it. There was little examination about the meaning of these practices, but much focus as to how to interpret canon law in regard to these practices. This tendency toward legalism was signified by the many questions and articles among the clergy as to the finer points of fast and abstinence regulations. Within the long tradition of casuistry, the interpretation of this law was crucial to clergy because of their duty to inform the faithful of their obligations. Especially because the trespassing of these ecclesiastical laws was regarded as sin, priests felt a need to "get it right" when it came to penance.[96] There even seems to have been an "*ad cautelam*" rule for bishops advising caution and perhaps best translated in this case as, "when in doubt, dispense." This would best protect the faithful from

---

96. Frederick McManus, in a three-page letter, reviewed the policy for addressing the vigil fast when the Immaculate Conception fell on a Sunday in 1957, noting that December 7 remained a day of fast and abstinence, although liturgically the feast would be celebrated on Monday, December 9, since the Second Sunday of Advent eclipsed the actual feast date. McManus observed the confusion about the feast and vigil fast, writing, "In our diocese the mistake was made of giving an elaborate explanation of the whole business, which only confused the priests." McManus also advised obtaining a Roman Ordo from Vatican Press, since it "is rather authoritative ... unlike the American publishers of Ordos, they simply question the Congregation if any question or doubt arises"; McManus, letter addressed to "Dave," October 29, 1957, 2; McManus papers, box 1, series 2, folder 25.

falling into confusion or—even worse—falling into sin, in failing to observe penitential practices.[97]

The faithful imbibed the message regarding the importance of penance, especially pertaining to Friday abstinence. Often those Catholics who failed in many other aspects of Christian life, including failing to attend Mass on Sunday, were unswerving in their Friday meat abstinence. One reason for this may be that the Friday abstinence was a fairly straightforward rule, easy to understand and not too difficult to observe, in contrast with determining the collation amount for each meal during Lenten fasting or bearing patiently the ills of life. Additionally, there was strong community and even commercial support for Friday abstinence, including Friday fish specials and parish fish fry events. Such fun social events may have made the penitential element less evident, but it also increased the visibility of Catholic identity and made it simple to adhere to this penitential practice. The Friday meat abstinence was inherently social in nature.

Because of the perfunctory nature of fast and abstinence and the tendency toward legalism and obligation, fast and abstinence regulations could be seen as impersonal and unreflective. When it came to these practices, there did not appear to be any personal examination as to how to make these practices more authentically penitential. There was little thought as to what might be the most meaningful penance for an individual. It did not seem as though the faithful reflected on the interior conversion that ought to accompany penance. Rather, fast and abstinence as prescribed by church law appeared to be "one size fits all," without regard for a person's unique challenges and strengths. In this sense, penance was not individualized enough and might appear as restrictive of the person's freedom, which could be better addressed by identifying the most appropriate penance for the person—that is, a penance that would produce the intended effect of making satisfaction for sin.

The concern was that penance might lose its effectiveness when it became routine; individually selected penances could counter this ten-

---

97. Binz, letter addressed to Edward Cardinal Mooney, dated November 14, 1956, 2, from the McManus papers, box 1, series 2, folder 25. Discussing the Vigil of All Saints, Binz writes, "After much discussion we have agreed to recommend "ad cautelam" a complete dispensation from fast and abstinence for the Vigil of All Saints." Ad cautelam could be translated here as "to be on the safe side" or, more literally, "for caution."

Penance in a New Land

dency. But rather than relying on the person's maturity and responsibility to perform penance without strict prescriptions, the church had traditionally imposed it upon everyone who did not qualify for a dispensation. The weakness of such a habit was its potential to be disconnected from contrition, with an emphasis on exterior performance of the act in accordance with social expectations rather than exterior act serving as an expression of the interior contrition. The obligatory and communal practices could potentially cease to be truly penitential—that is, accompanied by contrition.

Another criticism of these practices was related to the social or relational nature of sin. The *Baltimore Catechism* had also listed almsgiving, as well as spiritual and corporal works of mercy, as ways of expiating for the temporal effects of sin. These works were focused on others, fostering reconciliation through service to others and helping those who were in need. Penance performed in these acts clearly benefited others in a natural way and was other-centered, whereas it was harder to narrate how fast and abstinence provided natural and spiritual benefits. In this assessment, penance was again too individualized, focused on a couple of narrow practices done by individuals without any apparent benefit to the larger society that was so obviously in need. It seemed that people chose to observe obligatory practices only because they were concerned for their own salvation and not for the overall well-being of others; this was implicitly the criticism the bishops would address when they emphasized the great potential for witness in performing corporal works of mercy. Hence there was a push to affirm positive acts—"doing something"—rather than negative acts, such as abstaining from meat or eating less food.

One instance where penance seemed harmfully individualistic in the context of social difficulty and need was the issue of racism. A young Michael Novak worried that fasting, voluntary sacrifices, and extra masses or devotions would not be enough. After describing in detail the variety of Lenten sacrifices, Novak, writing in *Christian Century*, voiced his concern:

But will these millions of Catholics be led by their sincere efforts to a new concern for their Negro brothers, the poor in whom Christ especially lives, the millions of hungry children of this world? It is to be feared that many retain too individualistic a piety to understand that the liturgy speaks always of a "we," always of an entire people and always of a whole and entire, not merely ecclesiastical or devotional, life. Social life, civic life, political life—these, too, need to be revivified by new awareness and new earnestness. One of the major concerns of Roman Catholics in Lent 1965, blessed as they are with a liturgy now partly in their native tongue and plainly inviting their active participation as a priestly people, is to forge a more conscious bond between liturgy and life, between the church and the world in which it is buried as yeast in heavy dough.[98]

Novak's critique was one also applied to Catholics who regularly partook of the sacrament of penance. Penance, whether it was the sacrament or Lenten fasting, seemed of little value if these practices only made the penitents more self-focused without challenging their overall vision. The faithful might fail to acknowledge their participation in social sins like racism. Despite their good intentions to avoid sin, and despite their practice of Lenten penances, the faithful could persist unreflectively in these social sins.

Like the sacrament of penance, these other practices of penance were firmly entrenched among Catholics in the United States. They were a part of the culture and a habit of the people. Although partaking of the sacrament was in a sense more voluntary—that is, the individual chose when to go and what to say—whether it was the sacrament of penance or other nonsacramental penitential practices, Catholics understood penance as a normal part of everyday Catholic life. Sin was a reality, and these penitential practices were the counterpart to sin. That most Catholics would abstain from meat on Fridays, fast daily during Lent, and show up for confession frequently was expected at a time when the status quo was close-knit Catholic communities. Catholics saw themselves as distinct from other non-Catholic Americans and often lived in cohesive Catholic communities centered in the parish and the parish school. These penitential practices were at home in such a context; there were social structures in place to facilitate the penitential dimension of Catholic life.

The move of Catholics away from urban Catholic settings to more religiously pluralistic suburbs in the 1950s and 1960s brought change in many respects. But what officially changed the way penance was practiced in the United States was not a matter of geographic location or an altera-

---

98. Michael Novak, "Catholics and Lent," *Christian Century* (March 17, 1965): 323.

Penance in a New Land

tion in Catholic identity. Rather, changes to fast and abstinence regulations in the United States came from the decision of the U.S. bishops as a response to and implementation of Pope Paul VI's call for a renewal of penance in the wake of Vatican II. The changing culture of Catholicism in the United States did, however, condition Catholics to receive these alterations to penance in a particular way. Without strong Catholic culture and the cohesive community of the past, individualized, voluntary penance was difficult to sustain. The bishops' decision ultimately, though inadvertently, minimized penitential practice as expressed through fast and abstinence while failing to replace these with other more meaningful, socially enacted, penitential practices as had been hoped.

5   To Eat Meat or Not?

Paenitemini, The NCCB's Pastoral Statement, and the Decline of Penance

The penitential dimension of American Catholicism was firmly established by the mid-twentieth century. Though there was a unique history regarding the development of fast and abstinence as practiced in the United States from the colonial period through World War II, the faithful in America largely observed the traditional Catholic penitential practices that were common elsewhere. Recent Catholic immigrants to the United States sometimes even maintained a more rigorous penitential practice akin to that of their homelands.

The traditional penitential acts of fast and abstinence could, however, be criticized. For while Catholics were largely faithful to the outward expressions of such penance, it seemed there was often little reflection as to the meaning of penance accompanying their actions; these practices could appear to the outside observer as simply unthinking routine rather than a sign of genuine repentance. Moreover, conversation about fast and abstinence tended to have a legalistic focus rather than a spiritual one, hence reinforcing the lack of attention to the interior dimension of penance. Though the faithful were clearly fulfilling an obligation to penance, it was not certain that they were really living the penitential dimension as the faith required. Hence at the close of Vatican II, Pope Paul VI issued the apostolic constitution *Paenitemini* in an attempt to bring about the renewal of penance throughout the Catholic Church.

Paenitemini was a groundbreaking document, not because of Paul's perspective on the importance of penance, which was very much in keeping with the Catholic tradition, but rather because *Paenitemini* sought the renewal of penance by relying on the authority of local episcopal conferences. Paul VI apparently thought that penitential regulations were best decided regionally rather than defined generally for the entire church. The practical import of this was substantial, bringing about dramatic change in the lives of the ordinary lay faithful. In the United States, the National Catholic Conference of Bishops' implementation of *Paenitemini* was found in the "Pastoral Statement on Penance and Abstinence," released, like *Paenitemini*, in 1966.

An examination of the NCCB document reveals the underlying theology of the time, which favored individual choice with the belief that freely chosen penance would be more meaningful, indicating "inward penitence and conversion."[1] This document also demonstrated great confidence in the liturgical changes for reinvigorating a meaningful penance. The changes implemented by this letter greatly reduced the obligatory days of penance practiced in the United States, and the emphasis on individual choice unwittingly led to the decline in such longstanding penitential practices as the Friday meat abstinence and Lenten fasting. The move from socially instituted, communally practiced penance to individually chosen penances was a response to recognizable problems in penitential practice; nonetheless, the attempt at reform ultimately destabilized the established structures of penance without replacing them with social structures that would better facilitate nonsacramental penitential practice.

While this chapter acknowledges that there was a need for reform

1. "Pastoral Statement on Penance and Abstinence: A Statement Issued by the National Conference of Catholic Bishops," November 18, 1966, no. 2.

in regard to penitential practices, it argues that those changes to penance implemented by the NCCB did not ultimately lead to the renewal of penitential practices in the United States. The emphasis on individually, voluntarily chosen penance weakened the social structures that were in place to facilitate the practice of penance among the faithful. While the intended objective was to renew penance in the faithful, the modification of the practices away from the obligatory and communal toward the voluntary and individual undermined the beneficial social support that accompanied regulations shared by the faithful. This emendation to penitential regulations corresponded with a decline in the nonsacramental external practices associated with penance, such as fasting and abstinence from meat.

The chapter begins with an examination of *Paenitemini*, particularly noting the paragraphs where Paul VI granted authority to local episcopal conferences to determine penitential practices for their regions. The next section discusses the American implementation of *Paenitemini* found in the NCCB's "Pastoral Statement on Penance and Abstinence," placing it within the context of the changing conception of sin at both the popular and academic level. This assists in the concluding observations as to the ultimate failure of a renewal of penance among Catholics in the United States.

Paul VI's *Paenitemini*

Three months after the close of the Second Vatican Council, Pope Paul VI released his apostolic constitution *Paenitemini*, in English entitled "On Fast and Abstinence." This brief document consisted of an introduction and three chapters, with the purpose of emphasizing the importance of penance and calling for renewed penitential practices, possibly in updated forms more suited for the times. At the beginning of the statement, the pope identified as a grave and urgent problem the necessity of reminding the church "of the significance and importance of the divine precept of penitence."[2] He explained that the church "has gained a clearer awareness that, while it is by divine vocation holy and without blem-

---

2. Paul VI, *Paenitemini*, introduction.

ish, it is defective in its members and in continuous need of conversion and renewal, a renewal which must be implemented not only interiorly and individually but also externally and socially."³ Paul VI noted that the council had reflected upon its role in the earthly city, and he asserted that the church values abstinence in order to prevent the faithful from being delayed in their pilgrimage by things of the world.⁴

In chapter I, Paul VI reminded the reader that "external penitential practices are accompanied by an inner attitude of 'conversion,' that is to say of condemnation of and detachment from sin and of striving toward God." Beginning with a consideration of the Old Testament, Paul VI stated that the aim of penance is love and surrender to God and that it is both a personal and religious act. He noted, moreover, that in the Old Testament, the social aspect of penitence was important; penitential liturgies were a condition for belonging to the people of God. Additionally, individuals like Moses often suffered through penance on behalf of the whole people. The Old Testament picture provided by Paul VI hence emphasized penance as both individual and communal, both external and interior. Penance in the Old Testament, however, was only a foreshadowing of what was to come.⁵

The pope continued to explain that penitence "assumes 'in Christ and the Church' new dimensions infinitely broader and more profound." Penitence is linked to the sufferings of Christ and the call to *metanoia*, or conversion and the imitation of Christ. Within this context, Paul VI highlighted the importance of the sacrament of penance, noting that the penitence of the individual Christian has an intimate relationship with the whole ecclesial community because the gift of *metanoia* is restored and reinvigorated in those who seek the sacrament of penance in order to address their sin. The sacrament also reconciles penitents with the church that they have wounded by their sins, and the acts of penance imposed in the sacrament "become a form of participation in a special way in the infinite expiation of Christ to join the sacramental satisfaction itself every other action he performs, his every suffering and sorrow."⁶

Following this narrative of penance in the Old Testament and in Christ and the church, Paul VI continued to consider particular expres-

3. Ibid.
5. Ibid., chap. I.
4. Ibid.
6. Ibid.

sions of penance. In the first paragraph of chapter II, therefore, he reaffirmed the necessity of the external practice of the virtue of penance and suggested that the church, "always attentive to the signs of the times," might "seek beyond fast and abstinence, new expressions more suitable for the realization ... of the precise goal of penance."[7] He emphasized that physical asceticism must be a part of this, as bodily mortification aims at the liberation of man, who can become a slave to his senses. But the pope also emphasized that penitence cannot simply be external; it must be accompanied by inner conversion.

In chapter III, Paul VI began with an invitation for everyone "to accompany the inner conversion of the spirit with the voluntary exercise of external acts of penitence." The apostolic constitution first highlighted what was discussed in chapter 4 of this volume as "bearing patiently the ills of life"—that is, involuntary penitence, including the patient bearing of trials in one's work or community life, faithfulness to the duties of one's state of life, infirmities, illnesses, poverty, misfortunes, and persecution for the love of justice. All of these provide an opportunity to satisfy as penitence and can lead to beatitude. The pope also noted that more was expected of priests in regard to penance, and he subsequently emphasized the need for voluntary acts of penance apart from the difficulties imposed by everyday life.[8]

Paul VI suggested that there may be penitential practices more suited to the times, and he invited the bishops to discern in their episcopal conferences norms that might be more suitable to the local conditions. He noted the traditional triad of prayer, fasting, and charity and exhibited enthusiasm at the powerful witness of asceticism for those in situations of economic well-being. But perhaps the most important paragraph of *Paenitemini* is the following:

Therefore, the Church, while preserving—where it can be more readily observed—the custom (observed for many centuries with canonical norms) of practicing penitence also through abstinence from meat and fasting, intends to ratify with its prescriptions other forms of penitence as well, provided that it seems opportune to episcopal conferences to replace the observance of fast and abstinence with exercises of prayer and works of charity.[9]

7. Ibid., chap. II. 8. Ibid., chap. III.
9. Ibid., chap. III, VI. B.

To Eat Meat or Not

The responsibility placed on the episcopal conferences was to discern whether "other forms of penitence" were more appropriate than fast and abstinence. Each episcopal conference could determine to maintain the same prescriptions if they discerned them to be opportune, but they were also permitted to choose other forms of penance. It was this paragraph that put responsibility upon the episcopal conferences to select penitential norms other than the traditional fast and abstinence. Paul VI seemed to imply that such changes would be advantageous and that the Vatican would willingly accept the modifications to penance determined by local episcopal conferences, even if they replaced fast and abstinence with prayer and works of charity.

Despite these suggested changes in penitential practice, however, Paul VI reaffirmed that certain days and liturgical seasons were designated for penitence. His declarations followed this observation, duly emphasizing the penitential character of Lent and all Fridays and describing the fast and abstinence rules in place. While the local conferences were tasked with deciding when there might be a need to substitute abstinence and fast with other forms of penitence, they were not given the liberty to change the days and seasons of penance.

At the close of Vatican II, the pope's *Paenitemini* made it clear that Paul VI had not moved away from the importance of penitential practices. Vatican II had in no way diminished or eliminated the traditional emphasis on the penitential dimension of Christian life. Rather, Paul VI's apostolic constitution aimed at the renewal of penance in the church, which he saw as crucial for a church taking a new, more open stance to the world. Penance was to be essential for the successful implementation of the Second Vatican Council. For those in wealthier countries, the witness of asceticism could be a powerful reminder of heaven; those in poorer countries could promote social justice while also offering their suffering in prayer.[10]

By leaving the implementation of *Paenitemini* up to the local episcopal conferences, Paul may have hoped that regionalized penitential practices would take on greater significance, much in the way that hearing the Mass in one's own language allowed for fuller participation, consequently making the Mass more personal and meaningful. Significantly, although

10. Ibid., chap. III, C.

he emphasized the role of the social in penance, Paul VI was ambiguous as to whether the changes in specific penitential practices should be imposed on whole communities by local episcopal conferences, as fast and abstinence had traditionally been uniformly regulated, prescribed in standard form for all the faithful.

One interpretation of *Paenitemini* would be precisely this—namely, that local episcopal conferences knew best what penances were suited to their populations—and they could choose something specific and clearly defined and impose this on the local church in the place of fast and abstinence. For example, they could decide to retain the Friday meat abstinence for their jurisdiction or impose an abstinence from something else that was more appropriate. A second interpretation of *Paenitemini* would be that the choice of penitential practice was not merely in the hands of the episcopal conferences, but actually in the hands of the individual Catholic, who could best discern what penance would be most meaningful to himself or herself. This latter option was the American interpretation of the apostolic constitution; the NCCB decided to maintain only two days of fast and abstinence (Ash Wednesday and Good Friday) and Friday abstinence solely during Lent, but for all the Fridays throughout the year and for the whole season of Lent, the choice of penance was left to the decision of the individual. This lack of clearly defined and obligatory penitential practice resulted in a multitude of different Friday and Lenten sacrifices, as well as an overall diminishment in the practice of these once-communal penances during designated penitential days and seasons.

The NCCB's Pastoral Statement on Penance and Abstinence

In the same year that Paul VI penned *Paenitemini*, the National Catholic Conference of Bishops in the United States released its "Pastoral Statement on Penance and Abstinence," which was the American implementation of the apostolic constitution. More than just an implementation, however, it indicates an interpretation of *Paenitemini* influenced by the popular currents in theology and the bishops' understanding of Catholicism in the United States. An examination of this twenty-eight-paragraph document reveals its historical context, including the time period's prevailing theological convictions about morality, as suggested by its approach to penance. It is evident that the bishops wrote from a standpoint of great confidence in their congregations' penitential ability and commitment to penance. In the close-knit Catholic communities the penitential dimension of Catholic life was firmly established, as indicated by the previous chapter's description of many of the nonsacramental penitential practices that characterized American Catholicism up until 1966.

Yet the bishops also affirmed the importance of freedom, in accord with newer trends in theology like that of Bernard Häring; hence they thought that the faithful's penitential actions would be more effective as penance if freely chosen rather than imposed. They looked for the responsibility of the laity and a willingness freely to embrace penance, rather than relying upon obedience to obligations. Moreover, given the simultaneous changes to the liturgy, including use of the vernacular, the bishops greatly trusted in the liturgical renewal as a way of reinvigorating a sense of penance even without the traditional penitential practices of fast and abstinence.[11] Hence the NCCB letter provides both a window

11. There is some indication that a canonist turned liturgist, Frederick R. McManus, was influential in the writing of the NCCB letter; Thomas Krosnicki, SVD, email to Morrow, February 11, 2013. Fr. Krosnicki expressed confidence in McManus's authorship but did not have documentation to prove it. The suggestion of McManus as ghostwriter of this letter makes sense not only because he was the executive director of the Secretariat of the Bishops' Committee on the Liturgy for the National Conference of Catholic Bishops at that time period, but also because of the numerous references to liturgy and the liturgical renewal that appear in that letter, as well as his experience with penance regulations in the United States and their relationship to canon law. Unfortunately, however, I have not found significant evidence to conclude definitively McManus's role. Notably, in his edited book *Thirty Years of Liturgical Renewal*, McManus did not include the Pastoral Statement on Penance and Abstinence, indicating perhaps that he did not think of this as part of the liturgical renewal; see McManus, ed., *Thirty Years of Liturgical Renewal: Statements of the Bishops' Committee on the Liturgy* (Washington, D.C.: United States Catholic Conference, 1987). Moreover, in undated typewritten notes from his personal papers held at the Catholic University of America Archives, that which seems to be a commentary on the Code of Canon Law regarding the fast and abstinence regulations observes that these regulations fall under the virtues of religion and temperance. It is noteworthy that the author of these notes, likely though not certainly McManus, did not mention the virtue of penance because neither the virtue of religion nor that of temperance depends upon the notion of sin as matter. This perception of fast and abstinence seems to circumvent sin and penance, depending instead upon religion (or piety) and temperance; notes entitled "Introductory Canons (not listed under any title)," found in the McManus papers, box 1, series 2, folder 25. This

into the theological currents popular at the time and a sense of the culture of Catholicism in America.

The NCCB letter consists of a little over two thousand words, containing an introduction followed by four sections covering the following topics: (1) Advent; (2) Lent; (3) Vigils and Ember Days; and (4) Fridays. It had great practical import, exhibited perhaps most significantly with the changes to the practices of daily Lenten fasting and year-round Friday abstinence. Though the necessity of performing penance during Lent and on Fridays did not cease, the form of that penance became a choice of the individual; the bishops determined that each member of the faithful could choose the penance appropriate for his or her situation. Whereas the previous practices had been clearly defined and obligatory and hence communal, the new penitential practices were undetermined and therefore could be quite diverse. Penitential practices in the past were done by all the faithful together, but the NCCB letter altered this so that the penances became inherently individualistic, relying not so much on the support offered by Catholic subculture as on the willpower of the individual person.

As with *Paenitemini*, the bishops began the NCCB letter by insisting upon the obligation to repentance, required by divine law. They proceeded to explain that forms and seasons of penance vary from time to time and people to people, but that personal and communal acts of penance are a pledge of inward conversion.[12] "For these reasons, Christian peoples, members of the church that is at once holy, penitent, and always in the process of renewal, have from the beginning observed seasons and days of penance."[13] The bishops noted that penance had been done communally or individually, in imitation of Christ who went into the desert to fast and pray for forty days; Paul appealed to this example in instructing Christians to "come to the mature measures of the fullness of

---

was the only place where I encountered fast and abstinence being associated primarily with the virtue of religion and the virtue of temperance.

It would be interesting to note the similarities and convergences of moral theology and liturgical renewal during this time period, particularly as regards the quest for greater meaning and freedom, especially as the NCCB letter seems to reflect the currents of thought in both areas. That, however, is not beyond the scope of this particular project.

12. NCCB, "Pastoral Statement on Penance and Abstinence," no. 2.
13. Ibid., no. 3.

To Eat Meat or Not

Christ."[14] Such an introduction did little to indicate the practical import of the changes contained in the rest of the document.

The first section in the NCCB letter concerned Advent. As described in the previous chapter, Advent has traditionally been considered a penitential season, "a little Lent" in preparation for the great feast of Christmas. Due to dispensations granted early on to dioceses in the United States, there were no communal, obligatory penances in place concerning Advent in 1966 when the statement was released. There were, however, some ethnic groups that continued to practice the Wednesday and Friday fast and abstinence penances still in place in their home countries. Moreover, the lay faithful were often encouraged to take on voluntary penances during Advent, such as the daily visit to the tabernacle featured in the "Advent Action" comic. Catholics were also often instructed to avoid parties and Christmas celebrations during the season of Advent.

In the "Pastoral Statement on Penance and Abstinence," the bishops acknowledged that Advent had "unfortunately lost in great measure the role of penitential preparation for Christmas that it once had."[15] Yet the bishops did not suggest a return to the traditional fast and abstinence practices associated with Advent. Rather, they wrote the following:

Zealous Christians have striven to keep alive or to restore the spirit of Advent by resisting the trend away from the disciplines and austerities that once characterized the season among us. Perhaps their devout purpose will be better accomplished, and the point of Advent will be better fostered if we rely on the liturgical renewal and the new emphasis on the liturgy to restore its deeper understanding as a season of effective preparation for the mystery of the Nativity.

This implied reference to the longstanding custom of Wednesday and Friday abstinence during Advent at once minimized the value of such fast and abstinence while emphasizing the importance of the liturgy. Though the enthusiasm for the liturgy can be found elsewhere in this document, the NCCB's confidence in the liturgical renewal for reinvigorating the church was nowhere more apparent than in this section on Advent. In a mere five paragraphs on Advent, the liturgy and liturgical renewal were mentioned a combined eight times.

14. Ibid.
15. Ibid., no. 5.

Nor did "liturgical" seem an adjective limited to the Eucharistic liturgy of the church: "If in all Christian homes, churches, schools, retreats, and other religious houses, liturgical observances are practiced with fresh fervor and fidelity to the penitential spirit of the liturgy, then Advent will again come into its own."[16] The bishops noted in this vein the development of a rich literature concerning family and community Advent liturgical observances. They did not specify anything, but stated that they urged instruction based upon this literature and were "counting on the liturgical renewal of ourselves and our people to provide for our spiritual obligations with respect to this season."[17]

The newness of hearing the penitential prayers of the Advent season in English for the first time may have added profundity to the recognition of Advent as a penitential season in 1966. However, as noted earlier in this chapter, Advent's penitential character was already waning and seemed to do so more rapidly in the following years as the anticipation of Christmas became more and more a preemptive celebration of Christmas. The faithful were no longer encouraged to embrace customary penances like fast and abstinence or to undertake voluntary penances such as a daily visit to a church, nor were they reminded to forego early and perhaps immoral Christmas parties. Perhaps some of the faithful immersed themselves in the penitential spirit communicated in the Advent liturgy. For many, however, the penitential prayers of the Sunday Advent liturgy served as one brief, weekly message of penance to Catholics immersed earlier and earlier each year in Christmas joy, especially given the ever-increasing American focus on gift giving.

In the second section of the "Pastoral Statement on Penance and Abstinence," the bishops addressed the season of Lent. The bishops wrote that they hoped to intensify the penitential observance of Lent. While they maintained the fast of Ash Wednesday and Good Friday, the bishops eliminated the longstanding traditional daily fasting (excepting Sundays) that had characterized the season of Lent in the United States. The NCCB did preserve Friday abstinence from meat during the season of Lent, as well, and this soon became a trademark of Lent as Friday abstinence ceased to be obligatory on other Fridays throughout the year.

16. Ibid., no. 8.
17. Ibid., no. 9.

To Eat Meat or Not

In place of daily fasting, the bishops promoted individually chosen and self-imposed penances, with some particular recommendations:

For all other weekdays of Lent, we strongly recommend participation in daily Mass and a self-imposed observance of fasting. In the light of grave human needs which weigh on the Christian conscience in all seasons, we urge, particularly during Lent, generosity to local, national, and world programs of sharing of all things needed to translate our duty to penance into a means of implementing the right of the poor to their part in our abundance. We also recommend spiritual studies, beginning with the Scriptures as well as the traditional Lenten Devotions (sermons, Stations of the Cross, and the rosary), and all the self-denial summed up in the Christian concept of "mortification."[18]

In the penultimate paragraph of the section concerning Lent, the bishops emphasized the importance of witness that could be exhibited by the corporal works of mercy. In particular, the NCCB drew attention to "the poor, the underprivileged, the imprisoned, the bedridden, the discouraged, the stranger, the lonely, and persons of other color, nationalities, or backgrounds than our own," indicating important social issues of the time.[19] The major practical effect of this change was a rapid decrease in daily Lenten fasting, as few chose to continue this practice self-imposed when it was no longer obligatory.

The third section of the NCCB letter was entitled "Vigils and Ember Days," and it required only one paragraph to reaffirm that vigils and Ember Days no longer required fast and abstinence. The popularity of Ember Days had already begun decreasing, particularly because the emphasis on agriculture with the change of the seasons seemed increasingly unsuitable for urban and suburban Catholics who had little regular contact with the rhythms of planting and harvesting. The liturgical observance of Ember Days seems to have diminished in accord with the end of the fasting and abstinence associated with Ember Days.

When it came to the longstanding tradition of fasting before a feast that had once been obliged by the prescribed vigil fasts, the bishops once again suggested that the liturgical renewal would bring deeper appreciation of the joy of holy days during the year. They suggested that the anticipation of such great feasts would inspire self-imposed fast-

18. Ibid., no. 14.
19. Ibid., no. 15.

ing before a feast. Thus, like Advent, there was an emphasis on the liturgy and confidence in the liturgy that made the past obligatory rules seem unnecessary. The bishops thought that some of the devout would "freely bind themselves, for their own motives and in their own spirit of piety, to prepare for each Church festival by a day of particular self-denial, penitential prayer and fasting."[20] This demonstrated the aforementioned confidence that the bishops had in regard to the faithful's penitential commitment, in this case as it pertained to preparing for great feasts. It seems, however, that the bishops' expectations for self-imposed fasting were not realized significantly in the long term, aside from perhaps some religious communities. There is no evidence that the laity embraced self-imposed fasting before a feast when the obligation to fast ceased; perhaps the faithful were so attuned to paying attention to the rules that they failed to recognize the interior dimension of penance that would have led to them to want to fast freely, without obligation. Or perhaps their pastors did not encourage them to continue to embrace vigil fasts. And it is also possible that without the consciousness of the need to fast, the laity might have failed to recognize and appreciate major feast days on the horizon, especially since the social and cultural context in suburban America did not clearly demarcate these holy days, such as the Solemnity of the Immaculate Conception, as particularly festive.[21]

The bishops' words on self-imposed fasting on the occasion of vigils to major feasts also pointed to an underlying theological claim—namely, that penance freely chosen is of greater merit and meaning than penance that is imposed. This theme was expressed again and perhaps most explicitly in the final section of their letter, which was entitled "Christ Died for Our Salvation on Friday." Unlike Advent or Lent, Fridays were not linked to a particular liturgical season but rather a specific day; hence the meaning of Fridays would not be easily reinvigorated through liturgical renewal. Rather, the premises of this section expressed in the first few paragraphs indicated that Friday had long been a day of Christian penance and that changing circumstances made it seem that meat

20. Ibid., no. 17.
21. It would be interesting to have some data about how many Catholics actually practiced vigil fasts prior to 1966, especially given the American context wherein certain holy days were often celebrated only by Catholics.

To Eat Meat or Not

abstinence is "not always and for everyone the most effective means of practicing penance."[22]

The NCCB noted that meat had ceased being an exceptional form of food and was now commonplace. Though perhaps counterintuitive, this statement seems to imply a celebratory or special-occasion association with the eating of meat that no longer held true. Since it was commonplace, rather than indulgent or celebratory, abstinence from meat was no longer as effective as a penance. The bishops hence suggested other sacrifices, with the intention of giving the spirit of penance "greater vitality, especially on Fridays."[23] Though they continued to recommend meat abstinence, they also mentioned the potential penitential witness in regard to sacrifices of alcohol and "stimulants," as they call them—likely a reference to caffeine and nicotine. Additionally, the bishops echoed the pope's suggestion of replacing fast and abstinence with prayer and works of charity.[24] Giving a concrete example of the works of charity that Paul VI suggested in his letter, the bishops recommended volunteering in hospitals on Fridays in lieu of abstaining from meat.[25]

The bishops' conviction in favor of individually freely chosen penance over communal obligatory, socially practiced penance is particularly interesting when one considers the words of the *Baltimore Catechism*, which expressed the popular theological understanding of the faithful prior to Vatican II. The *Baltimore Catechism* insisted that the fasting with the greatest merit was not that which was voluntarily chosen but rather that "imposed by the church on certain days of the year, and particularly during Lent."[26] Granted that this is more a reference to the appropriate days and seasons of penance than form of penance, there is nonetheless an assumption contained therein that it is better to do the obligatory than the supererogatory. Obligatory penance is at once traditional, communal, and ecclesial; required participation assures that penance is social inasmuch as it is something the church does together at the same time.

There is nothing wrong with fasting on a random Wednesday in the middle of summer, but given the choice between that fast and the re-

22. NCCB, "Pastoral Statement on Penance and Abstinence," no. 19.
23. Ibid., no. 21.
24. Paul VI, *Paenitemini*, chap. III.
25. NCCB, "Pastoral Statement on Penance and Abstinence," no. 27.
26. Connell, *Father Connell's Confraternity Edition*, Q. 806.

quired fast of Ash Wednesday, the latter is of greater merit according to this understanding precisely because it is imposed, and it is imposed by the church with good reason, as it is the beginning of the Lenten season. Hence the person who observes the Ash Wednesday fast accomplishes two objectives: (1) to do penance and (2) to adhere to church law prescribed for this day. It is both an act of penance and of obedience. The random Wednesday fast during summer, meanwhile, only fulfills the first objective and hence is not worth as much as a penance. The NCCB letter, however, did not employ the language of merit, but rather appealed to "effectiveness," implying that freely choosing one's penance is more effective than doing a specific penance obliged by canon law. While this would not be identical to selecting one's personal days of penance, there is, nonetheless, an affinity in the privileging of choice over obligation, hence the bishops' frequent use of the word "freely" when discussing penance.

On the other hand, it is possible to interpret in their statement a response to the criticism that the faithful are more concerned with following church rules than cultivating genuine penance and acting upon true contrition. The bishops' explanation as to their hopes that Catholics would continue to abstain from meat is paradigmatic as regards this theological position: "We [give first place to abstinence from flesh meat] in the hope that the Catholic community will ordinarily continue to abstain from meat by free choice as formerly we did in obedience to Church law."[27] This expectation was based on two considerations, one of tradition and one of witness. First, meat abstinence would "freely and out of love for Christ Crucified" show solidarity with past generations of believers, for whom it was evidence of fidelity to Christ and the church. Second, it would show a difference from the spirit of the world and hence witness to penance: "Our deliberate, personal abstinence from meat, more especially because no longer required by law, will be an outward sign of the inward spiritual values that we cherish."[28]

While the pope had suggested that "new expressions" of penance might be preferable, he had not explicitly advised leaving the choice of the penitential practice to the preference of the individual, nor had he

27. NCCB, "Pastoral Statement on Penance and Abstinence," no. 24.
28. Ibid., no. 24, a., b.

To Eat Meat or Not

prioritized choice over specifically imposed obligations practiced socially. The NCCB's decision to prioritize individual preference or "freedom" is an interpretation of *Paenitemini* that hence reflects the theological currents of the time. The bishops' implementation of *Paenitemini* was an attempt to revitalize sluggish, routine penance in the spirit of renewal after Vatican II. They felt called upon to make some kind of change to penitential practice, and perhaps they suspected that people would not respond well to replacing the communal meat abstinence with a communal Friday alcohol abstinence or communal coffee abstinence. It was not clear what penitential practice would have national appeal and significance; the former regional variations in penitential practices were to some extent an expression of the benefit in making such regulations local. In places such as New Orleans, for example, a more penitential sacrifice might be to abstain from seafood on Fridays, rather than meat.

Rather than reestablish penance that was dictated by the local ordinary, however, the bishops looked to individually imposed Friday sacrifice. This indicated trust in the Catholic commitment to Friday penance and would involve advising Catholics to discern a sacrifice that would be meaningful for them as individuals. In this sense, it was the counterpart to the liturgical renewal's answer to the routinization of the liturgy. Just as speaking the prayers in one's own language would allow for fuller, more meaningful participation, so also performing a freely chosen penance would allow for fuller interior participation and hence more meaningful penance. Moreover, this penance would seem to be more effective precisely because it was elective, and penance would therefore be associated with the maturity to know one's sins and embrace the responsibility to repent rather than simply following the crowd and sticking with a long-ingrained habit.

This view was in keeping with trends exhibited in theologians such as Häring, and it was in contrast to the likes of Ford and Kelly. As mentioned in chapter 3 of this volume, Ford and Kelly believed that adherence to obligations was meant to facilitate freedom. Ford and Kelly recognized that Catholic morality was often lived out minimalistically, but the solution to this was not to abolish the law or external adherence to it, nor was it to diminish the specificity of that law or leave it to the preference of the individual. Had the bishops taken this perspective of obligations as facilitating freedom, they would not have addressed the renewal of penance through granting fewer obligations and more choices in regard to penance. Rather, the bishops might have emphasized catechesis, formation, and the interior dispositions of the faithful, striving for the faithful's intentions to match their actions. This position would have regarded external action as a baseline, and the significance of these actions could be improved by a rectifying of intention in respect to the imposed obligation. The communal practice of specific penitential actions could even aid in the meaning of these actions, while also providing support for those who were trying to perform their penance well, both interiorly and exteriorly.

Ford and Kelly never took up the cause of penance, however, and the bishops did not base their implementation of *Paenitemini* on the understanding of obedience to obligations facilitating freedom. But even if the Jesuits' position on obedience and obligation had been assumed by the bishops, it would have been insufficient to address the issues of the time. Ford and Kelly lacked the language to express the important context of the penitential dimension of Catholic life and the conviction that social structures could facilitate the exercise and growth of penance in order to advance the faithful to their telos of supernatural beatitude. Their account of obligation and obedience would not have been compelling, removed as it was from the interior dimension of the spiritual life. The focus on obedience and obligation was increasingly less effective as motivation for embracing penance.

That the bishops did not presume this relationship between obligation and freedom as described by Ford and Kelly is an indication of the turn taken in theology by this time. The bishops' response to the perceived legalism and minimalism of Catholic morality bore similarity to Häring's assessment of the situation discussed in chapter 3 of this volume. The bishops seemed to agree that Catholics were more concerned with merely fulfilling the law in the easiest way possible than they were with seeking holiness. The concern with following church rules detracted from a genuine Christian love, which, as Häring emphasized, ought to be the motivation for all Christian action. Moreover, Häring thought that this legalism did not adequately serve the individual, catering rather to routine and social conformity. One can observe similar concerns in the bishops' statement, as though they realized that for many Catholics, Friday meat abstinence and Lenten fasting were perfunctory rather than motivated by love. They recognized the need for a more personal and profound penance, both for the benefit of Catholics and for the power of Catholic witness in a changing world and country.

Like Häring, the bishops wanted to call the faithful beyond the bare minimum of simply doing what they were obligated to do. They were looking for and counting on the responsibility of the laity. Instead of making decisions for the laity, they wanted the laity to utilize their freedom, motivated by love, and be responsible for choosing their own penance as opposed to participating in a herd mentality that crushed independence and individuality. In Häring's estimation, this would involve the ability to respond to God's call for penance and an interior motivation for practicing penance, rather than a motivation imposed by an external authoritarian structure that regulated the how of penance. The renewal of the church in the modern world seemed to call for this kind of maturity of the faithful. The notion of the universal call to holiness indicated a kind of responsibility placed on the shoulders of the laity; they were called to be holy, and hence they must respond to God's call lovingly, rising to the penitential obligation through acts of their own choice. They could use their freedom to commit to a penance that would be meaningful for them, knowing that their interior sentiment would match the exterior act of penance, and the performing of this penance would be an expression of their responsibility as a mature Catholic.

This interpretation of the bishops' decision was expressed in *America* magazine by a Jesuit priest, who wrote:

"Paenitemini" and the Bishops intended to reaffirm the primacy of the religious and supernatural values of penance as opposed to the pharisaic formalistic reification of a penitential practice. According to this new spirit, the matter is no longer the primary determinant of the obligatory observance, but rather the sincere and serious will to observe ... laws. Hence the new spirit stresses not the exteriority of the matter of the law, but the interiority of personal responsibility before the obligation incumbent upon all to do penance in common with the Church at certain hallowed times specified by the law.[29]

29. Vincent M. Burns, SJ, "More than Exhortation," Letters to the Editor, *America* 116, no. 1 (January 7, 1967): 3.

In case someone might misunderstand the bishops' intention, the writer continued to note that the reduction in the specified number of days of obligatory penance was not because less penance was needed, but rather because more penance was needed—that is, true spiritual penance and not merely the form or external appearance of penance. The emphasis was on effective and genuine penance rather than a multiplicity of penitential acts that were lacking the interior dimension and therefore not really penitential. Hence, "personal responsibility is made the norm of following the obligation of law."[30] Rather than relying on the faithful's fear of committing mortal sin in breaking a church law, the emphasis was on the person choosing to do penance out of genuine desire to make reparation. To many it seemed that the added reflection necessary would make for better penance.

And perhaps the bishops' optimism and confidence in the penitential commitment of the laity likewise led them to believe that Catholic enthusiasm for penance would be greater if the faithful had the opportunity to choose their own reparation for their sins. In a time when the laity were being represented as embracing their freedom and responsibility within the church, choosing a Friday penance would seem a relatively small task. What the bishops failed to anticipate, however, was the demographic change underway and how that would influence the reception of the changes to penitential practices. The bishops might also have been overly optimistic as to the faithful's willingness to continue an act of penance that had not been specifically required. Chapter 2 mentioned Peter Steinfels's observation that the context in which Vatican II occurred was different from the context in which it was received. So also, the assumed context from which the U.S. bishops implemented *Paenitemini* was much different from the context in which it was received and subsequently lived out.

Friday meat abstinence was an ingrained habit of American Catholicism; it was one practice that most of the faithful seemed to do and do consistently. Being Catholic meant not eating meat on Friday, as one author in *America* magazine wrote: "in this country at least, meatless Fridays had seemed the shibboleth of Catholicism. Everyone has heard of people, with little other attachment to religious practice, who steadfastly

30. Ibid.

To Eat Meat or Not

resisted any temptation to eat meat on Friday. This, they seemed to feel, was some kind of ultimate and easy passport to heaven."[31] The bishops seemed to express confidence in their congregations' commitment to Friday penance in their decision to introduce an element of choice to the Friday sacrifice. This new and diversified penance would become a point of renewal for the church as the faithful became more individually proactive in regard to their penance. The bishops apparently believed that Catholics would understand that Friday penance had not been dropped, but rather modified. The Friday meat abstinence was increasingly criticized as not suitably penitential; granting flexibility to the penance was one way of addressing the perceived weakness.

For many of the laity, however, this change in Catholic practice was not a point of renewal; for many it was not even understandable. Just one week before November 27, 1966, eating meat on a Friday was commonly understood to be a mortal sin. Suddenly, eating meat on Friday was not any kind of sin, much less a mortal sin. For years, Catholics had been haunted by the phrase "binding under pain of mortal sin." Now even that phrase became a source of controversy when the NCCB letter went into effect. *America* magazine explained to its readers that meat abstinence even during Fridays of Lent was no longer binding under pain of mortal sin: "The Bishops state, however, that Catholics will not lightly excuse themselves from the custom of abstinence on Fridays in Lent. Thus, unless the Bishops direct otherwise before Lent, we are clearly exhorted—but not strictly obliged—to observe meatless Fridays during that penitential season."[32] In the next issue of *America*, an adamant letter to the editor contested this interpretation of the NCCB letter. The protesting author noted that the bishops' legislation on the matter of Friday abstinence during Lent was not original, but rather applying universal penitential law to their jurisdiction: "Hence to the extent that the traditional abstinence is maintained, its obligation must be judged in the light of the universal legislation, which states that 'their substantial observance binds gravely.'"[33]

If even the clergy, with better access to relevant documents, were

---

31. "Friday Laws Modified," Current Comment, *America* 115, no. 23 (December 3, 1966): 727.
32. "Meatless Fridays in Lent," Current Comment, *America* 115, no. 24 (December 10, 1966): 765.
33. Burns, "More than Exhortation," 3.

confused about the new changes, it is unsurprising that the laity were also perplexed. Despite the NCCB's insistence in their statement that "every Catholic Christian understands that the fast and abstinence regulations admit of change," this was not evident as the changes to fast and abstinence played out among American Catholics.[34] In Lent of 1966, *Ave Maria* published a brief conversation between a mother and her eleven-year-old daughter wherein the daughter was informing her mother that Sister had taken the salami out of her sandwich at lunch time, saying, "I don't care what the Pope said. We're not going to eat meat here on Friday."[35] Perhaps this was meant to be humorous, a not-so-subtle jab at those Catholics who held on rigidly to Friday meat abstinence, even, in this case, for children not bound by that canon. But although *Ave Maria*'s anecdote may have been intended for a laugh, what had served as a punch line there was an actual direct quotation from an Irish waitress in Chicago. Quoted in *America* magazine in November of 1966, the waitress said, "I don't care what the Holy Father says, I wouldn't eat meat on Friday."[36] This waitress had not only a misunderstanding of papal authority and what the pope had said regarding penance, but also a strong conviction that Friday abstinence was an unalterable part of the Catholic faith. Having lived Friday abstinence for her whole life, she would not consider abandoning this penance that was so ingrained in her. Likewise, an article in the Kansas City diocesan newspaper recounted a telephone conversation that took place shortly after the Friday meat abstinence regulation was changed. A staffer's wife called to ask what he wanted for dinner. He responded that, same as always, he would eat whatever she put on the table. "'It's a good thing you said that,' she said, 'because if you want meat, you can stay downtown and eat.'"[37]

Anecdotes such as these seemed to confirm the reluctance of Catholics to embrace change to this longstanding rule of American Catholicism. The author of the article in *America*, however, was certain that the waitress quoted would be in the minority of Catholics who would react in such a way to a change in penitential practices. He noted in an approving

---

34. NCCB, *Paenitemini*, 25.
35. "No Salami on Friday," *Ave Maria*, April 16, 1966, 5.
36. "Meat on Friday," Current Comment, *America* 115, no. 20 (November 12, 1966): 575.
37. Albert de Zutter, "No Kettle of Fish Anyway," *Catholic Reporter*, December 9, 1966, 9.

To Eat Meat or Not

tone that, "in keeping with the post–Vatican II Church's desire for greater freedom, doing penance will be left more and more to the discretion of individuals." The author observed, moreover, that such changes to penitential practices had already been made in other countries such as Italy, Canada, and France.[38]

In the months prior to the change in penitential practice, the popular Catholic periodical *Our Sunday Visitor* published a piece with the headline "Fish or Hamburgers on Friday?" The author, Dale Francis, began by mentioning a national survey wherein Catholics responded that "they considered the rule that they not eat meat on Friday more important than the law of love for neighbor."[39] Francis was critical of the implications drawn from this survey, insisting that Catholics did not think they could go to heaven by abstaining from meat while not loving their neighbors. Francis suggested rather that it had to do with the Catholic understanding of the church as Christ's own church, and therefore church laws were accepted as what Christ asks of them: "You ask them which is the more important, obeying what Christ asks of them or having love for neighbor, they answer obeying Christ. It wasn't an abandonment of neighbor they were affirming but an obedience to Christ in the Church."[40]

Francis conceded that perhaps love for neighbor had not been adequately emphasized, but he still indicated some ambiguity about the potential alteration to Friday meat abstinence:

The law of abstinence on Friday has always been just a rule of the Church. It hasn't even been universal. But even those who have understood it to be just a law of the Church will have some tug of regret at its passing.

You see, it has become other things for us. In a way it has been a kind of badge of our faith. Here in the United States it has set us apart—Catholics are people who eat fish on Friday, it has become a kind of a symbol of our faith, something that shows us to the world as believers.

You don't give up that kind of a symbol without a little wrenching. Even if it was a rule that didn't go back into antiquity, it was a rule that belonged to our own past and the past of our parents, and whatever tears us from the past leaves us a little wounded.

38. Ibid.
39. Dale Francis, "Fish or Hamburgers on Friday?" *Our Sunday Visitor*, October 16, 1966, 9.
40. Ibid.

But the real reason we abstained was often lost. Friday was the day Our Lord died to redeem us. The Church asked the people to commemorate that day by a sacrifice of our own.

But not having meat on Friday never was much of a sacrifice. For me it certainly never was—I prefer seafood to steak. But even people who don't care much for seafood never really had to sacrifice much.

Friday for many was not in any way a sacrifice. You could have lobster on Friday and make it the most expensive meal for the week, and ingenious housewives found ways of preparing dishes without meat that were delicious.

So finally abstinence from meat on Friday became just a kind of badge of the fact we were Catholics, and the spirit of abstinence was really lost.[41]

Having acknowledged the failure of Catholics to live up to the spirit of abstinence, Francis encouraged the faithful not to mourn this potential change to Friday penance but rather to "accept it as a challenge to change yourself and to renew the spirit of sacrifice in your own lives."[42]

Francis also observed that the current age was one wherein the church was asking for more individual responsibility. "If the law of abstinence is changed, then it doesn't mean the Church is asking you to make less sacrifice; it will mean only that the Church is asking for more individual responsibility. Don't accept any change as an invitation to laxity; accept it as a challenge to your own maturity."[43] Francis perceived an opportunity to make personal sacrifices more meaningful, and he suggested that such a possibility for making sacrifices on account of love of Christ should bring joy.

After the penitential alterations were announced, the Brooklyn Catholic weekly the *Tablet* ran this front-page headline: "'If Eating Fish Fooled You, Eat Meat and Get About Your Father's Business.'" Author Don Zirkel pithily summarized the NCCB statement thus: "If American Catholics have fooled themselves into believing that they are fulfilling a major part of their responsibilities by eating fish on Fridays, then it's time to let them eat meat. And get on with the real job."[44] Zirkel paired his account of the "Pastoral Statement on Penance and Abstinence" with the NCCB's statement on "Race Relations and Poverty." Zirkel observed:

41. Ibid. 42. Ibid.
43. Ibid.
44. Don Zirkel, "'If Eating Fish Fooled You, Eat Meat and Get about Your Father's Business,'" Brooklyn *Tablet*, November 24, 1966, 1.

To Eat Meat or Not

Today the world sees poverty in an affluent society, and can say: "Look at these Christians, how they eat fish on Fridays."

For tomorrow, the bishops have asked "other forms of penitential witness." The world may one day say again, "Look at these Christians, how they love one another," especially how they love the poor and the victims of racial discrimination!"[45]

Zirkel concluded his front-page piece by stating that the bishops had asked for an end to the era where Catholics were identified by abstinence from meat rather than love for one another. Whereas abstinence from meat was still recommended, it was now voluntary; opposition to racial discrimination, on the other hand, was not voluntary, but rather, a clear duty.[46]

The *Tablet* complemented its front-page coverage of the pastoral statement with the text of the NCCB statement in its entirety, as well as a substantial piece detailing the history of abstinence through the years.[47] The following issue of the periodical brought two letters to the editor with contrasting opinions. The first read:

> The abolition of Friday abstinence is another mile-stone in the steady and insidious erosion of Catholicism in this Nation.
>
> It is not the dietary issue which matters, nothing could be per se more trivial. What does matter is the increasing relaxation of every discipline, the constant catering to the preferences of a naturally hedonistic human nature, the abandonment of cherished traditions, the defiance of constituted authority even by the clergy, the scarcely veiled questioning of basic dogma, and the headlong rush to do away with any external sign which might still distinguish the People of God from the outside world.
>
> Our bishops are indeed naïve if they think that abstinence or any other penance will be practiced voluntarily by the great majority, or even by an appreciable number. Let them make Sunday Mass also voluntary, and they will have solved their problem of overcrowding![48]

The second letter highlighted the hypocrisy of "fish eaters" who continued racial discrimination and lauded the change in penitential practice:

45. Ibid.
46. Ibid.
47. "Abstinence over the Years," Brooklyn *Tablet*, November 24, 1966, 4.
48. Eugene J. Doyle, "End of Abstinence: A Sign of Naivete or Mark of Trust," Brooklyn *Tablet*, December 1, 1966, 14.

The change in emphasis for Friday penance is a wonderful mark of trust in the laity by the American bishops. That the laity will be treated as mature Christians capable of making their own sacrifices, is a step forward in letting us develop in spiritual as well as physical and mental affairs.

In the past, Friday abstinence seemed to mark the man who was a "good" Catholic. Now, it looks like we will really have to start living the life of Christ if we are to be recognized as Christians.[49]

An additional letter to the editor proposed volunteer work in New York City Catholic hospitals as a wonderful work of charity in lieu of Friday meat abstinence.[50] Only time would tell whether the bishops' alterations to penitential practices in favor of trust in the laity and more meaningful sacrifices would lead to a penitential renewal and more authentic morality or to a decline in penitential practice.

It appears that many diocesan newspapers printed the full text of the NCCB statement, or at least summarized it, and included various articles on the topic as had *Our Sunday Visitor* and the *Tablet*.[51] An article in *America* likewise covered the change, making it clear that the church had not abolished penance, but rather thrown light on the truth that being a Christian "demands charity, dedication, social responsibility and other much more important matters than merely giving up meat on Fridays."[52] Catholic periodical readers were hence aware of the changes and the varying perspectives that accompanied them.

But while Catholics clearly got the message that they were no longer bound to Friday meat abstinence, they did not internalize the message that they were supposed to continue practicing penance on Fridays. Catholics did not embrace other forms of penance as substitutes for Friday meat abstinence. That the custom of Friday penance did not endure in long-term practice may be the result of poor catechesis in the implementation of these penitential changes. Another contributing factor may involve the simplicity of Friday meat abstinence in contrast with other suggested penances, such as volunteering in a hospital. Not eating meat

49. William Reilly, "End of Abstinence: A Sign of Naivete or Mark of Trust," Brooklyn *Tablet*, December 1, 1966, 14.

50. "Work of Charity for 'Meat-Eating' Men," Brooklyn *Tablet*, December 1, 1966, 14.

51. Other examples of diocesan newspapers that reported on the change were Kansas City's *Catholic Reporter* and the *Denver Catholic Register*.

52. "Friday Laws Modified," 728.

To Eat Meat or Not

did not take any extra time; it was a rule that was easy to understand and to follow, especially with the support of other Catholics making the same sacrifice. As Francis had indicated in the *Our Sunday Visitor* piece, Friday abstinence was not even a sacrifice at all for many Catholics. It was, however, a tradition and a discipline, however mild, and as Eugene Doyle had predicted in his letter to the editor of the *Tablet*, voluntary penance did lead to a decline of penitential practice among American Catholics. If the bishops believed that their congregations were overly legalistic and minimalistic, then it is curious that they did not consider that such a change to penance—one that was not fixed, defined, or measurable—might be setting up the faithful for failure.[53]

What happened as a consequence of this change was that the freely chosen individual Friday sacrifice waned until it was no longer noticeable as a Catholic identity marker, motivating Catholic sociologist Andrew Greeley, writing in 2004, to suggest that among the implementations of Vatican II in the United States, it "may have been the most unnecessary and the most devastating."[54] Catholics were already losing much of their distinctive identity, as they assimilated to the national culture and found themselves immersed in religious pluralism. Greeley asserted that the alteration to Friday penance was not needed as were other changes following Vatican II. Greeley's quotation highlights how the diminishment of penitential practices, especially the Friday meat abstinence, furthered this loss of Catholic identity and hence was devastating to Catholicism as a whole. Perhaps more consistent catechesis would have prevented the decline of penance, but the manner in which the changes to penance were communicated failed to foster more effective penance.

Additionally, given the context of the dissolution of the Catholic subculture, it is not surprising that when Catholics were given the opportunity to choose their own penance, they chose, like most other Americans, not to do penance at all. Catholics in past years may not have done penance as well as they could have; perhaps only a small percentage engaged in penance out of genuine contrition and a desire to make satisfaction for sins. But at least they made some effort and knew that the meat abstinence was supposed to be a sacrifice, part of the penitential dimen-

53. My thanks to an anonymous reviewer for this insight and this particular phrasing.
54. Greeley, *Catholic Revolution*, 54.

sion of the Christian life. The social structures were present to facilitate penitential practices, even if these structures were poorly used in terms of interior commitment to penance. Without communal support and a sense of Catholic solidarity in these penitential practices, penance became increasingly countercultural, hence more difficult to do. No doubt to some it appeared as a quaint practice of an overly controlled religious past. The individually chosen Lenten sacrifice, though not as easily lost as the Friday sacrifice, nonetheless also became more dependent upon individual willpower than on a shared communal sacrifice.[55]

Nor was Greeley the only person to note the adverse consequences of these changes to penitential practices. One author asked the question, "Has the Church Gone Permissive?" in titling his 1973 article in *HPR* seven years after the change. The article suggested that the church's permissiveness in regard to penance had taken a toll on the church, unintentionally giving an image of approving a decrease in penitential observances: "I maintain that the former strict observance of laws concerning fast and abstinence … had a healthy effect on the lives of the Catholic people. It was an inspiration to fellow Christians."[56] The author wondered what had become of penance: "What happened to Friday as a day of penance when the laws of abstinence were changed? Did the change in the laws result in greater union with God through better Friday observances? I hardly think so. The same could be said with regard to Lent. For the vast majority, Friday and Lent are no longer days of special penance."[57] His solution was for the faithful to re-embrace the Friday meat abstinence. By this time, however, it seemed there was no going back for the majority of the faithful; the habit of Friday abstinence had disappeared among the laity, and it seemed unlikely that the majority would now take it up again by free choice. Future generations of American Catholics would have no idea that such a regulation had ever even existed.

---

55. In some ways the family was the locus for the communal nature of Lenten fasting prior to 1966. This is indicated by the fact that the workingman's indult extended to his family. Given that many Catholic immigrants lived in intergenerational homes and ate their meals together throughout Lent, the fast was something done by the family. In the case of diverse individually chosen sacrifices, however, the family can make adhering to those sacrifices more challenging.

56. Robert J. Fox, "Has the Church Gone Permissive?" *HPR* 73, no. 5 (1973): 62.

57. Ibid., 62–63.

To Eat Meat or Not

Meaningful Penance Is Hard

The U.S. bishops' alteration of penitential practices for American Catholics was an instance of acknowledging problems in practices and seeking to reform them accordingly. The faithful seemed to be too focused on their legal obligation and too worried about avoiding sin. The penitential practices in place left little room for consideration of individual preferences with respect to the person's freedom; at the same time, they did not illuminate adequately the social and relational nature of sin and penance as did almsgiving or the corporal or spiritual works of mercy. For years the emphasis in "doing penance" had been on the doing, rather than on the penance. Whereas one interpretation stresses the external action, the other highlights that these actions are the expression of an interior sentiment of sorrow for sin, which moves the person to do penance as tangible counterpart to her contrition.

Encouraged by the pope's *Paenitemini*, the American bishops sought to make penance more meaningful to American Catholics, and they hoped to make their penance "more effective." Each of the changes they made was meant to address the problems already identified. With the guidance of the prevailing theology of the time, the bishops believed that penance would be more meaningful if freely chosen. They hoped to call their faithful beyond the legalism and minimalistic morality of the past to a more mature practice of the faith, motivated by love rather than law. There are echoes of Häring's work in the bishops' statement and a clear bias in favor of personal choice, contra the worth of specific imposed obligations like those valued by Ford and Kelly.

Here, however, the bishops may have failed to read the signs of the times. This change in penance was implemented in the midst of both a decline in the notion of sin understood in terms of one's personal, actual sin and the dissolution of Catholic subculture.[58] The close-knit urban Catholic communities where practices of penance had been sustained were no longer the primary location of American Catholics. Friday sacrifice soon faded away, as did communal Lenten fasting. The American Catholic culture into which these changes were received was different

---

58. According to one account, Catholics celebrated the first Friday of Advent in 1966 by having steak dinners.

than the one where abstinence and fast—and the sacrament of penance, for that matter—had been practiced so faithfully.

One can imagine a counterfactual situation wherein passionate, educated Catholics continued to live in close-knit communities and to choose their own Friday penances in a context of strong support with the knowledge that the continued obligation of penance was meant to facilitate growth in the virtue of penance. Had this been the case, the bishops' statement might not have hastened the diminishment of penance, but rather genuinely been a cause for a renewal of penance. Individually chosen penances, if universally adopted by Catholics, may have provided adequate social support to help increase the culture of meaningful penance.

On the other hand, though penance for sins may not have always been foremost in the minds of those who abstained from meat on Friday in accordance with church regulations, there were at least social structures in place that provided an opportunity to be reminded of their faith and the Catholic conviction in the penitential dimension of Christian life. Even minimal effort at penance enabled an opportunity for an exercise in discipline and mindfulness of the faith exhibited in church law, whereas the complete omission of external penitential actions did not.

There may also be other explanations in regard to the rapid decline of penitential practices. For example, it may be that the bishops not only (or primarily) misread the signs of the times, but also that they, like Häring, realized the problematic nature of a morality driven by legalism; such a morality could easily tend toward minimalism and fail to foster an adequate interior attitude of penitence. In assessing the nonsacramental penitential practices of their faithful, they may have detected a routine element that fostered minimalism and legalism. To counter this, they turned to the concepts of freedom, responsibility, and maturity; they wanted the laity to do penance on their own, from their own volition and not a sense of obligation. Indeed, the Catholic concept of penance, as discussed in chapter 1, is not merely about following church regulations, but rather is about contrition for sins and a desire to make reparation for them. The interior dimension of penance is crucial for understanding an act or habit to be penitential.

But selecting and remaining committed to a person's own unique penance without adequate social support can be quite difficult. Though the theory behind it indicates an important point as to the significance of the interior life of the person, in practical terms it is difficult to assure that individual penance happens. Without law, there is encouragement and exhortation, and this can be effective as motivation. However, in this particular context of great demographic change for Catholics and major ecclesiastical changes regarding the celebration of the Mass, penance was likely unappealing, seen more as a throwback to before Vatican II in the Catholic ghetto than as a crucial part of the future of Catholicism in the United States.

The move to make penance depend upon the choice of the individual diminished the context of community solidarity and social support, hence relying upon a person's intention and willpower to execute on the intention of making satisfaction for sin. Furthermore, the reduction of penitential days lessened the habitual nature of fast and abstinence. Penance like that associated with Ash Wednesday or Good Friday now stood out as unusual, rather than as one of many penitential days of the Catholic year. Many of those who no longer felt compelled by an obligation to perform penances delineated by the church simply ceased to do penance in any kind of regular and consistent manner.

Rather than going beyond the minimum prescriptions for penance and embracing more effective penance, American Catholics began to do even less than that which had been standard. Ironically, the attempt to move beyond minimalism by lessening the minimum brought the level and quality of penance even below what had been the bare minimum. When not borne out in any particular form of laws adhered to by a community practicing them together, "the law of love," as promoted by Bernard Häring, failed to take root as was hoped. Despite the problematic legalistic tendency of obligations, the penitential regulations had provided an impetus that both reminded the faithful of the need to do penance and provided them with a community in which to do that penance.

Penance in the past had been criticized for consisting primarily of external actions, rather than interior sentiments in accord with authentic penance. The emphasis on the new maturity and autonomy of the laity supported the notion that penance should be freely chosen, a responsibility taken upon oneself rather than required by obedience to obligatory laws. These alterations to penitential regulations in the United States, combined with a diminished notion of sin as a reality, did not revitalize the practice of penance for the majority of American Catholics. Instead, the percentage who observed regular penitential practices, especially abstinence from meat on Friday, greatly declined, coincident with a decline in the sacrament of penance. The result of these changes was not a renewal of penance like that had originally been sought by the Second Vatican Council, the pope, the American bishops, or even by Bernard Häring.

6   Thinking outside the Box

The Decline of Sacramental Confession

Many have noted the rapid decline of the sacrament of confession in the late 1960s, and the question of how to restore the sacrament to its former popularity is often proposed. I have reserved the subject of the sacrament of penance for the final chapter in order to place it in a larger context than is often presumed. While some would consider the decline of the sacrament of confession in isolation from nonsacramental penitential practices and fail to note the coincident rapid decline of nonsacramental penances such as Friday abstinence and Lenten fasting, I propose that these histories are not only mutually enriching but also closely related, sharing a common root in the change of the conception of sin as described in chapters 2 and 3.

The committed practice of both the sacrament of penance and nonsacramental penance depended upon the notion of one's personal, actual sin and the knowledge that it could be addressed through penance. If such a connection between sacramental and nonsacramental penance seems tenuous, it is interesting to note that similar criticisms were leveled at both forms during the same time period. Apparently both sacramental penance and nonsacramental penance were often perceived as legalistic, minimalistic, and tending toward mindless routine. The various solutions proposed to address the perceived weaknesses in both depended upon the faithful's maturity in exercising freedom and responsibility in such a way as to bring greater meaning and less routine to penance. As was seen in chapter 5, the bishops' changes to penitential practice made in their 1966 "Pastoral Statement on Penance and Abstinence" relied upon the individual Catholic's initiative and commitment to penance rather than habitual obedience to an obligation. However, the implementations were followed by a widespread rapid decline of penitential practice such as the Friday sacrifice, which had once been observed as meat abstinence by American Catholics. The decline of the sacrament of penance occurred in the midst of the decline in nonsacramental penitential practices, and it is the task of this chapter to consider the sacrament in such a context.

When Dorothy Day wrote her autobiography in 1952, she began with a description of her experience of the sacrament of confession:

When you go to confession on a Saturday night, you go into a warm, dimly lit vastness, with the smell of wax and incense in the air, the smell of burning candles, and if it is a hot summer night there is the sound of a great electric fan, and the noise of the streets coming in to emphasize the stillness. There is another sound too, besides that of the quiet movements of the people from pew to confession to altar rail; there is the sliding of the shutters of the little window between you and the priest in his "box."

Some confessionals are large and roomy—plenty of space for the knees, and breathing space in the thick darkness that seems to pulse with your own heart. In some poor churches, many of the ledges are narrow and worn, so your knees almost slip off the kneeling bench, and your feet protrude outside the curtain which shields you from the others who are waiting....

Going to confession is hard—hard when you have sins to confess, hard when you haven't, and you rack your brain for even the beginnings of sins against charity, chastity, sins of detraction, sloth or gluttony. You do not want to make too much of your constant imperfections and venial sins, but you want to drag them out to the light of day as the first step in getting rid of them. The just man falls seven times daily....

Outside the Box

"I have sinned. These are my sins." That is all you are supposed to tell; not the sins of others, or your own virtues, but only your ugly gray, drab, monotonous sins.[1]

Like many Catholics of her time period, Day frequented the confessional often, a practice known as "devotional confession." This practice of devotional confession was apparently the fruition of much positive promotion of the sacrament. The sacrament of penance was central to Catholic practice in the United States as early as the beginning of the nineteenth century.[2] By the Civil War, efforts were made to regularize confession, and the promotion of frequent confession seemed to be effective. O'Toole notes that "long hours in the box were the norm for the clergy in the face of steadily increasing demand from the laity." This extensive time in the confessional for priests gave rise to a new rule in 1855 wherein Rome exempted American priests from reading the prayers of their breviary on any day when they spent more than five hours hearing confessions.[3]

The popularity of the sacrament of confession continued throughout the first two-thirds of the twentieth century and showed no signs of abating. The sacrament was connected to other popular religious practices, such as the "First Friday" devotions to the Sacred Heart, where Catholics received communion at Mass on the first Friday of the month for nine consecutive months. Parishes accordingly added confession times on the preceding Thursday to supplement their usual Saturday schedule.[4] Parish missions, where guest preachers gave inspiring spiritual talks to parishioners, and the Forty Hours devotions, when parishioners took part in forty hours of Eucharistic devotion, also were associated with participation in the sacrament of confession.[5] By the mid-1950s, however, Catholics—both lay and clergy—were beginning to voice concerns about

---

1. Day, *The Long Loneliness* (New York: Harper and Row, 1952), 9–10.
2. O'Toole, "In the Court of Conscience," 131.
3. Ibid., 133.
4. Ibid., 134–35. O'Toole notes that "precise measurements are hard to come by" and "broad-based statistics are few," but examples such as parishes in Milwaukee, Wisconsin, indicate that even with growing parishes, the number of penitents declined; see 169 for O'Toole's discussion.
5. Ibid., 136–37. O'Toole's detailed chapter provides a valuable and interesting discussion in different rates of confession based on gender and ethnicity, which are somewhat tangential for the purposes of this chapter.

how the sacrament of confession was practiced in the United States. The expression of these concerns indicated the beginning of its decline.

By the 1960s, the sacrament of penance in the United States was openly criticized by some clergy and laity as an unthinking habit, lacking in meaning and overly focused on law. Though routine can, indeed, become an obstacle to meaning if a practice goes unexamined, it was not merely the repetition of the sacrament that was identified as a problem. Instead, the routine nature of the sacrament led to an interrogation of the motivation for receiving the sacrament. Some critics regarded those making frequent use of the sacrament of penance to be insufficiently disposed and overly concerned with minor sins while overlooking more important ones; penitents could mistakenly look upon the sacrament of penance mechanistically, as an easy fix to wipe out sins with minimal effort on their own part. Though the external actions of penance were evident in the person who knelt down in the confessional, the interior penance was not apparent, and some doubted it was adequately present.

This concern reflected, to some extent, the theological understanding that in order for the sacrament to be efficacious, the person must have contrition. This requires a strong conviction in the presence of sin as a reality and a reaction to sin exhibited in contrition, based on a relationship with God—that is, sorrow for doing injustice to God. The interior act of contrition is then expressed exteriorly in penitential acts, such as the verbal confession and satisfaction associated with the sacrament. Some critics during the time period at hand judged that those making frequent use of the sacrament of penance were simply subject to routine and therefore not properly motivated by a desire for authentic and profound conversion. Even those with a strong sense of sin and desire for the sacrament of penance could struggle with identifying sins fit for the confessional, as evidenced by Day's words previously cited. It would not be surprising if those less well-formed than Day in the faith would easily fall into routine reception of the sacrament with a narrow and insufficient examination of conscience that did not include suitable contrition.

If this were the case, then it would become possible to imagine that the frequent use of the sacrament of penance was really a form of hypocrisy, used by Catholics to distract and excuse themselves from waging important battles against social sins like racism while they were busy fighting insignificant skirmishes with observing the Sunday Mass obligation. To many critics during the time period, Catholics seemed obsessed with sins, but only those of a ritual nature (eating meat on Friday, going to Mass on Sunday) or sexual nature (using contraception). Those who sought the renewal of the sacrament of penance hoped for a more personal and profound conversion, seeking authenticity to counter hypocrisy, while also expanding the conception of sin beyond the personal, actual sins many were apt to identify and confess. Critics questioned the emphases in the conventional lists of sins and the routine and individualistic nature of the sacrament.

This chapter will first address the recognized problems in the practice of confession during this time period. Next, it will describe the theological responses to these problems, as well as how these theological responses were expressed practically and pastorally. By minimizing the value of repeated confession—especially for venial sins—and by emphasizing freedom of conscience instead of a multiplicity of laws with corresponding sins, priest-theologians hoped to inspire a more genuine use and positive view of the sacrament, focused on relationships and communal reconciliation with the larger church. Ultimately, however, these responses undermined penance by minimizing the reality of actual sin and the value of the sacrament of penance to counter sin in everyday life. Hence these attempts at reforming the sacrament of penance also unwittingly contributed to its decline.

The Practice of Confession and Its Problems

In the 1960s many troubling issues arose as to how the sacrament of confession was practiced in the United States, and, according to O'Toole, "all the accumulated dissatisfactions with confession among the laity were the starting point" for explaining the rapid decline in practice of the sacrament.[6] O'Toole's claims are supported by the writings of clergy and laity from the time period, as indicated in the available primary source information. Those that practiced the sacrament of confession generally fell into two categories. First, there were those who partook frequently of the sacrament (monthly or even weekly) in a practice that was known as de-

---

6. Ibid., 171.

votional confession. The second group of penitents could be considered "special occasion" penitents. The confessions of these penitents were of a more annual nature; they confessed during the Lenten season in order to prepare for their Easter obligation of receiving communion. This annual group might also be moved to confess at another time during the year on the occasion of a parish mission, where exhortations to confession and opportunities for the sacrament were common. Or they might confess in association with their parish's Forty Hours devotion or even confess monthly for a time in association with the Sacred Heart "First Friday" plenary indulgence. And of course, when death seemed imminent, many of the faithful desired to receive the sacrament one last time.[7]

Even in the 1950s, when the sacrament was at the height of its popularity, clergy and laity were acknowledging problems in how the sacrament of confession was practiced. But as the 1960s progressed, these criticisms became more pronounced. The list of concerns was extensive, including the following: the void in meaning associated with the routine nature of the sacrament; the legalistic tendency of the sacrament, detracting from the sense of the relational nature of sin and suitable interior sentiment; scrupulosity and issues of conscience formation; the failure adequately to address spiritual and personal problems; and a lack of attention to the communal nature of the sacrament, including the neglect of recognizing social sins, such as racism. The panegyric accorded to the sacrament in the 1950s was replaced in the 1960s with this list of a range of failures. The sacrament of confession as practiced was no longer lauded for its benefit; the faithful had little inspiration for rallying behind it in the midst of the implementations of Vatican II. The discussion of these problems will serve as preparation for the explanation of the ensuing theological, pastoral, and practical expressions that were responses to these problems.

Devotional Confession

In the practice of devotional confession the faithful— clergy, religious, or lay—sought the sacrament of confession frequently, even if only for

---

7. Ibid., 136.

venial sins. In his 1943 encyclical *Mystici corporis Christi*, Pope Pius XII articulated the esteem for devotional confession, which he deemed to be in peril due to contemporary criticisms of the practice by younger clergy:

> It is true that venial sins may be expiated in many ways which are to be highly commended. But to ensure more rapid progress day by day in the path of virtue, we will that the pious practice of frequent confession, which was introduced into the Church by the inspiration of the Holy spirit [sic], should be earnestly advocated. By it genuine self-knowledge is increased, Christian humility grows, bad habits are corrected, spiritual neglect and tepidity are resisted, the conscience is purified, the will strengthened, a salutary self-control is attained, and grace is increased in virtue of the Sacrament itself.[8]

It would seem that many Catholics in the United States shared the pope's sanguine view as to the benefit of frequent confession, as they sought the sacrament of penance regularly, whether monthly, biweekly, or weekly.

Many priests, likewise, continued to exhort the laity to partake frequently of the sacrament of penance. The topic was raised regularly, for example, in the sermons provided by *HPR*, which was a popular publication for priests and likely served as the basis for homilies heard by many American Catholics each Sunday. In 1956, one priest entitled his homily for the Third Sunday after Pentecost "Unpublished Miracles of the Confessional." After a rousing description of sin attacking the soul, the priest urged those hearing the homily to seek confession in order to address this sin: "The soul has ... recourse to the confessional where the priest is really a doctor. Let the sinner but declare his weakness frankly; let him regret his faults; let him be disposed to take the means to fall no more, and there will take place in the confessional a cure. There will take place the most marvelous of resurrections."[9]

Such glowing portrayals of the sacrament were common, as were the admonitions in regard to the risk of disregarding the sacrament. In 1958, Fr. Lincoln Whelan reminded the faithful in his suggested homily that temptations easily turned into sin, and hence he warned against neglect-

---

8. Pius XII, *Mystici corporis Christi*, no. 88, June 29, 1943, http://www.vatican.va/holy_father/pius_xii/encyclicals/documents/hf_p-xii_enc_29061943_mystici-corporis-christi_en.html; accessed on September 24, 2012.

9. Jerome Dukette, OFM Conv., "Third Sunday after Pentecost: Unpublished Miracles of the Confessional," *HPR* 56, no. 8 (1956): 680.

ing the sacrament of confession: "Catholics cannot afford the luxury of indifference and neither can we afford to follow the crowd along the path of least resistance, because that is always a down-hill deal. We are destined by the sacraments to go up. But one of the cold facts that we must consider on this warm day is the evidence that too many parishioners neglect the sacrament of Penance during the summer season."[10] Missing out on the sacrament meant foregoing its valuable assistance.

And it was not just the people in the pew who were exhorted to regular confession year round, either. In 1960, Fr. Winifrid Herbst wrote an article for *HPR* entitled "The Priest's Confession," wherein he encouraged his fellow priests to have frequent recourse to the sacrament. Herbst noted early on that Canon 125 prescribes frequent confession for clergy, and though the law did not delineate "frequent" in relation to clergy's confession, Canons 1367 and 595 stipulate weekly confession for seminarians and religious respectively. Herbst continued by observing that there are some priests who find devotional confession to be a heavy burden and thus postpone it, even avoiding the sacrament despite the numerous benefits and sanctifying grace associated with the practice of devotional confession. Seeking to inspire his confreres, Herbst drew from the example of the saints:

Weekly confession would not seem to be so superfluous if one were to think of the great saints who went every day, e.g., St. Charles Borromeo, St. Catherine of Siena, St. Bridget, St. Ignatius of Loyola. St. Francis Borgian went to confession even thrice a day. In this, of course, the saints are to be admired, not necessarily imitated; but their example should spur on the priest to penitential regularity in receiving this great sacrament.[11]

Herbst ended his piece with some practical advice for the priest about finding a good confessor for weekly confession, advising which venial sins the priest should confess, and providing instruction on contrition and firm purpose of amendment. Herbst's accolades as regards the happiness of beginning again after each weekly confession affords a panegyric that may have gained the attention of at least some priests reading it

---

10. Lincoln F. Whelan, "Sorrow for Ourselves—or for Our Sins?" Homily for 12th Sunday after Pentecost, *HPR* 58, no. 10 (1958): 981.
11. Winifrid Herbst, SDS, "The Priest's Confession," *HPR* 61, no. 3 (1960): 264.

Outside the Box

in *HPR*, while also perhaps feeding an expectation for relief and joy that the sacrament did not always meet in the person's experience.

Likewise, for the young girl who might be considering a vocation to the convent, devotional confession was of tantamount importance. Such was the subject of Fr. Joseph Champlin's 1962 article entitled, "Father Confessor and Future Sister." Here Champlin described how best to advise a young female penitent who was interested in becoming a nun, with his proposed objective to discuss *"frequent confession* to a *regular* confessor as a means of preserving and fostering the germ of a religious vocation already present in a young lady's soul."[12] This regular interaction through the confessional, Champlin argued, could provide adequate spiritual direction to foster the young girl's discernment of religious life. It would allow the confessor to suggest spiritual practices common in religious life. And finally, Champlin noted, spiritual direction through the confessional would require the young lady to come frequently and regularly to the sacrament, which would require effort on her part. Endurance of such a practice as devotional confession for six months would indicate a stability suitable to the religious life, and the reward for the confessor's effort was likely to be prayers from the convent![13]

In *HPR*'s suggested homily for Low Sunday (the Sunday after Easter) in 1963, Fr. Joseph Beckman chose "Frequent Confession" as the title and subject of his sermon. No doubt with objections to devotional confession or even the Easter duty confession in the front of his mind, Beckman proceeded to explain how frequent confession helps people to give up habitual sin, to become more perfect, and to increase grace in order to fight against future sins. Beckman even drew upon the example of religious sisters, who "don't rob many banks or commit many murders" yet seek the sacrament weekly. "If they need confession so often to remain close to God, what about us who do commit more serious and varied sins?"[14] Beckman described the confessional as one of God's greatest gifts, but with a value dependent on how well and often the penitent uses it. He ended his homily with the exhortation, "Receive penance often and

---

12. Joseph M. Champlin, "Father Confessor and Future Sister," *HPR* 63, no. 2 (1962): 125.
13. Ibid., 128.
14. Joseph F. Beckman, "Frequent Confession: Homily for Low Sunday," *HPR* 63, no. 6 (1963): 318.

6-1 "Sacraments: Penance," Lloyd Ostendorf, illustrator, *Treasure Chest of Fun and Fact* (January 3, 1957), 17–22, Passports to Paradise series.

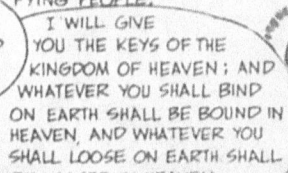

your life will be revolutionized in a wonderful way for the good."[15] Such panegyric exhortation to frequent use of the sacrament of penance was not unusual at the time, but rather supported the view that the sacrament of confession was of inestimable value to living a good Catholic life.

The Meaning Void in the Assembly Line of Penance

By the mid-1960s, however, misgivings regarding the practice of devotional confession were being voiced more and more frequently. To some, it seemed that the sacrament should have more meaning, be more significant as an encounter with Christ and experience of God's forgiveness; the sacrament of penance did not seem always to live up to its more positive portrayals. The clergy expressed reservations about how the sacrament was practiced. One priest, suggesting that devotional confession seemed more like passing through an automat than a personal encounter with Christ, summed up the criticism in this way:

> The penitent enters a small box-like structure, often situated in one of the darkest and most undecorated corners of the church, marks his sins on an invisible scoreboard, and slides them impersonally through the confessional grill. Bad marks erased, rapidly he recites a formula of contrition precisely while the priest recites, perhaps with greater rapidity, a formula of absolution.[16]

This criticism pointed to a concern that the sacrament was so quick, routine, and impersonal that it diminished its meaning.

In accord with this concern, the Benedictine author worried that the personal element of confession was absent in the perfunctory manner in which the sacrament was normally practiced. Resonating with the popular contemporary notion of personalism, the priest noted that Christian sorrow is deeply personal, bespeaking an intimacy with Christ and a conversion back to the Father. With hope for changes in the sacrament at the conclusion of Vatican II, the author recommended an anticipation of these changes by a recollection of the true meaning of the sacrament: "As priest and penitent become aware that they are engaged not in an impersonal inquisition, administration, or treatment, but that together and

15. Ibid., 318.
16. Roderick Hindery, "Penance, Sacrament of Conversion," *HPR* 65, no. 3 (1964): 203.

Outside the Box

personally they celebrate the conversion of the sinner and the mercies of God, they will seek to express themselves like human persons."[17] This new dynamic that he imagined would be different than past expectations for the brief and anonymous sacrament, and he recognized that such an acknowledgment of the personal meaning of confession might require some architectural and liturgical changes—better soundproofing, for example, brighter lighting, and perhaps the use of a candle representing Christ's presence in the confessional.

Another critique of the sacrament based on the concept of personalism addressed the issue previously mentioned in regard to spiritual direction; some critics believed that the sacrament was not used enough to offer spiritual direction for those who needed or desired it. In the rush to get penitents through the line, priests could not often listen well or offer adequate spiritual guidance. In this analysis, the priest was losing an important opportunity for helping the faithful really to advance in their faith. Spiritual direction had long been valued in the church, but the contemporary focus was merely to judge sins, assure adequate contrition, and absolve so the line could move on. Some thought that the sacrament ought to have a more casual and conversational form, which would be better suited for spiritual direction. Although one author insisted that the confessional must not become a psychiatrist's couch, he nonetheless hoped for an experience of the sacrament that would not require the penitent's anonymity or kneeling posture, but rather a face-to-face, personal discussion with the priest-confessor taking on the role of "soul-friend" or "*anamchara*," an Irish term drawn from that penitential tradition.[18] Such a view assumed that the confessional setup did not best facilitate conversation.

An old concern for confessors had been the importance of assessing the penitent's contrition. This was based on the Thomistic understanding, described in chapter 1 of this volume, that contrition, confession, and satisfaction constituted the matter of the sacrament of confession. While the priest heard the penitent's confession and assigned the pen-

---

17. Ibid., 205.
18. James Leehan, OSC, "Penance and Its Social Dimension," *HPR* 68, no. 6 (1968): 500–501. For more on "soul-friends" in the Irish traditions, see Hugh Connolly, *The Irish Penitentials: And Their Significance for Penance Today* (Dublin: Four Courts Press, 1995), 14.

ance that would make up the satisfaction part of the sacrament, he could not always be certain as to the penitent's sorrow for her sins. Fr. John Danagher, a canon lawyer writing in 1956, entitled his *HPR* article "Was the Penitent Sorry or Not?" And indeed, Danagher's article went through various scenarios of penitent's contrition or lack thereof, and the appropriate responses of the confessor who must be able to judge both the sins and the contrition of the penitent. The very title of Danagher's article implies a relationship between the confessor and penitent akin to an impersonal courtroom, rather than the more affective concerns previously mentioned.

Homilies in the 1950s, meanwhile, supported the emphasis on the penitent's contrition. In one such homily, for example, a description of the benefits of the sacrament was followed by the warning that "no sin can be forgiven unless a man is sorry for it. If he is not sorry, he does not turn away from sin; he does not turn back to God."[19] Similarly, another homily from the same year of 1956 informed the faithful as follows: "[The Confessor] is a father, a judge, a doctor. He makes the decisions, gives the advice—and it is your duty to obey. Remember, too, that the most important part of Confession is sorrow for sin, a sorrow that includes a firm purpose of amendment."[20] To some, it may have been an inspiring homily, but to others this description may have been off-putting.[21] The phrase "duty to obey" may have seemed a bit audacious for some adults to accept fully in addition to the pompous portrayal of the priest's role. By 1969, for example, a man wrote in a letter to *Sign* magazine: "I and countless other middle-class thinking Catholics are no longer willing to submit to confessors' warnings and judgments."[22]

During the 1960s, the concern for contrition shifted to an appraisal

19. "Twenty-first Sunday after Pentecost: Freedom and True Contrition," *HPR* 56, no. 12 (1956): 1030.

20. "Eighteenth Sunday after Pentecost: The Confessional 'Bogey,'" *HPR* 61, no. 11 (1956): 944.

21. It would be interesting to know the reception to this and other homilies with a similar message during the 1950s. While there are no such records in this case, secondary sources indicate that laity were beginning at this time to object to such messages.

22. Quoted in O'Toole, "In the Court of Conscience," 173. O'Toole has many other similar quotations where the laity asserted their ability to make mature decisions as capable adults without the input of a confessor. O'Toole notes that "the flat assertion that lay people must 'accept exactly what God has decreed' from the lips of the confessor was no longer convincing."

Outside the Box

as to the possibility of genuine conversion of heart in the context of devotional confession. The common denominator for both contrition and conversion was a conviction that there must be an interior sentiment of sorrow to match the exterior actions of confession and satisfaction in the exercise of the sacrament. Thomas Aquinas had made a distinction between two notions of penance: first, penance as sorrow, which is a "passion of the sensitive appetite"; and second, sorrow as "an act of the will."[23] During the 1960s, the focus turned toward this first more emotional and experiential understanding of sorrow, rather than sorrow as an act of the will expressed by the acts constituting the matter of the sacrament.

The habitual, seemingly perfunctory practice of the sacrament caused a reevaluation of the interiority that was based on a more dramatic conversion of the heart, rather than contrition, which was understood as an act of the will not necessarily requiring an emotional outpouring of sorrow. This critique was evident in Fr. Ronald Modras's *HPR* article entitled, "Frequent Devotional Confession: How Often a Change in Heart?," wherein Modras suggested that some adult confessions sounded like kid confessions, reducing confessors to bite their lips to stay awake or to wring their hands in anguish during their Saturday afternoon of hearing confessions. Such devotional confession, he said, was simply "the sacrament of reconciliation, reduced to a routine comparable to brushing one's teeth in order to get that nice, clean feeling."[24]

This priest's main concern was that devotional confession seemed to undermine a sense of penance as a conversion of heart: "Penance is a change of heart. Besides a person with a habit of mortal sin, how many people are capable of having a change of heart or of intensifying such a change once a week? Or even once a month?"[25] He suggested that a person's recourse to the sacrament should not be based on the calendar, but rather on the penitent's desire for reaffirming her conversion. Modras believed that the sacrament had been reduced to a mere formality, with

---

23. *ST* III, q. 85, a. 1.
24. Ronald Modras, "Frequent Devotional Confession: How Often a Change in Heart?" *HPR* 66, no. 8 (1966): 650. Of course, given the consensus as to the value of regular toothbrushing, this is an interesting criticism. What if people only brushed their teeth when they felt them to be particularly dirty and really had a desire to have clean teeth?
25. Ibid., 658.

an underlying misunderstanding as to sacramental causality. The laity seemed to think that they received grace simply by receiving the sacrament, when in fact a conversion of heart was necessary for the actions of the penitent to constitute the matter of the sacrament. Devotional confession was not necessarily an easy ticket to an increase in grace, according to Modras: "And in the case of devotional confession of venial sins, without this intensification of conversion, of sorrow and intention of amendment, there is no actual increase of sanctifying grace."[26]

Again, the implied criticism was that such a habitual practice of devotional confession was too routine to allow for genuine interior conversion or, to use Modras's phrase, "change of heart." Modras did not think a suitable change of heart was occurring weekly for those seeking the sacrament that frequently. Modras's emphasis on conversion brings to the forefront the problem of differentiating between contrition and conversion. Thomas and the Tridentine church teaching that had adopted his sacramental theology stated that contrition was quasi-matter for the sacrament of penance. For Thomas, even the interior act of contrition was an act of the virtue of penance, and in fact, these two were often closely identified. Although priests in the 1950s worried about the penitent's contrition, their solution was to exhort a greater commitment to detestation of sin expressed in a corresponding vow of purposeful amendment (for instance, avoiding the near occasion of sin). This commitment was a sign of contrition, which was regarded as an act of the will, not a feeling of the heart. In the 1960s the solution tended toward a more intentional and purposeful seeking of the sacrament, motivated by individual instances of desire for the sacrament and change of heart that effected amendment. Both contrition and conversion were interior, but whereas the former implied specific effort and action of the will, conversion indicated something personal, somehow more meaningful and profound because it was rare and perhaps spontaneous, rather than frequent and planned.

Special-Occasion Confessions

This preoccupation with conversion in regard to the sacrament of confession was a replacement for the more traditional concern about contri-

---

26. Ibid., 653.

Outside the Box

tion. As noted previously, contrition had long been a worry for confessors inasmuch as they needed to judge whether a penitent's contrition was sufficient to merit absolution. This was a particular concern for confessors when it came to evaluating those penitents who only sought confession once a year, in preparation for their "Easter duty," based on Lateran IV's prescription that the faithful should receive communion at least once a year.

For some ethnic groups—such as the Lithuanians and Polish, for example—there was a tradition of the confessor handing out "confession cards" or "Easter tickets," signifying that the parishioner had been to confession and communion during the Easter season. These cards were then required in order to join parish societies or enroll their children in the parish school.[27] Especially when associated with the paying of a nominal fee, as it often was, such a practice was problematic in the eyes of many church officials. A requirement for confession on these terms seemed to undermine the penitent's desire for the sacrament and call into question the penitent's contrition. It was likely that the faithful had other objects to their actions, such as enrolling their children in the parish school, rather than simply receiving God's forgiveness and grace in the sacrament. It was not clear that their actions were really penitential. They may have confessed sins and received absolution, but lacked the adequate contrition to constitute as the matter for the sacrament. A genuine "conversion" seemed even less likely in such cases.

One subgroup of annual penitents whose contrition and purpose of amendment were often doubted was those whose yearly confession included the sin of contraception. Leslie Woodcock Tentler, in her book *Catholics and Contraception*, describes confessors as "bedeviled" by the problem of birth control, especially when it was confessed prior to major feasts, as it was in association with Easter. Confessors felt the need to question penitents, who often used unclear language in their confession.[28] Many confessors had a difficult time determining the penitent's firm purpose of amendment as indication of contrition when it came to this sin. As the phrase "Easter duty" implies, it seemed that many of the

---

27. O'Toole, "In the Court of Conscience," 141.
28. Tentler, *Catholics and Contraception*, 146–47.

faithful came to the sacrament merely out of a sense of duty—the necessary preparation for their Easter reception of the Eucharist. As in the case of devotional confession, this practice of annual confession again raised the question of the interior contrition accompanying the exterior practice of the sacrament. If the faithful approached the sacrament primarily out of a sense of duty and habit acquired during childhood, they might be lacking in adequate contrition, including the firm purpose of amendment and commitment to avoid sin in the future. In such a case, penitents might not have the necessary contrition; their use of the sacrament then would not truly be penitential or efficacious, since the end of their acts was not to make satisfaction for sins against God. Moreover, priests had been taught in the seminary that contraception was always understood to be a mortal sin, and this rigidity could make it difficult for confessors to be pastoral in the way they would have liked.[29]

Tentler quotes the postwar judgment of Francis Connell to the effect that the sin of contraception was the most difficult and trying problem that confessors were encountering in the United States. In the following decades, the issue of contraception became even more complicated for confessors to address due to their increasing lack of conviction on the topic. There was a diversity of opinions among the clergy, and, despite earlier statements condemning contraception, such as Pius XI's *Casti connubii*, it was not clear to the faithful that the church had spoken authoritatively once and for all on the use of artificial birth control. The knowledge that a papal commission had been formed to investigate the issue was reason enough to make confessors in the mid-1960s lenient with those who did confess it and to make the laity doubt whether they needed to confess it.[30]

---

29. Ibid., 150.

30. According to one priest's anecdotal account, confessors' leniency on the issue of contraception often varied with their nationality. All the Catholics in one region of New Jersey knew that if you wanted to be absolved from the sin of birth control without interrogation, you went to the Italian national parish, not the neighboring parishes pastored by the Irish. The long lines of penitents at this parish testified to the confessors' optimism in giving the benefit of the doubt to the penitents on the issue of contraception; Morrow conversation with Fr. James Spera, pastor of Assumption parish, June 2012. This description accords nicely with Tentler's account of penitents seeking leniency from their confessors in regard to confessing birth control. Tentler describes Catholics prior to the mid-1960s as accepting church teaching on birth control, even if they found it difficult to adhere to it; see Tentler, *Catholics and Contraception*, 148.

Another significant criticism of the sacrament of penance as practiced annually or on special occasions was that it did not adequately address spiritual or personal problems. This sentiment could also be associated with the practice of devotional confession, but it was more evident among those who only sought confession when they felt compelled to do so by external pressures. Historians such as O'Toole suggest that if the faithful had found the sacrament to be more valuable in terms of responding to their problems, they would have been more eager to receive it.[31] Hence the narrow conception of the sins constituting the matter of the sacrament might also have contributed to the decline of the sacrament. One homilist in 1963 proposed using an Easter homily to address "Once-A-Year Catholics" on the topic of confession. After explaining contrition and a resolution to avoid future sin, the priest further explicated what he had in mind by listing the sins: "This means that we are not willingly going to miss Mass again—on any Sunday—during the coming year, that we will not commit another sin of impurity, practice birth control, eat meat on Friday, or drink to excess."[32]

Such a list indicates what was thought to be the primary subject matter for confession—namely, sins against church law (missing Mass, eating meat on Friday) and sexual sins (impurity, birth control), in addition to the ever-popular sin of drunkenness. But this list of sins did not always seem relevant to the spiritual and personal sin struggles of the people in the pew, and this was particularly the case as they moved out of close-knit urban Catholic communities to more religiously pluralistic neighborhoods where they had increased contact with Protestants. Amidst Protestant neighbors, partaking of meat on Friday did not seem so sinful, and when most of the population was turning to artificial birth control, that also did not seem to be a big issue. The church was emphasizing sins that most Americans did not even categorize as sin.

Moreover, what was missing, again, from this list of sins was a focus on relationships. Suburban Catholics struggled to maintain their Catholic identity in their personal dealings with family and friends, Protestants and Catholics alike. A two-minute trip to the confessional, even on a regular basis, did not seem adequate to address the issues of life, given

---

31. O'Toole, "In the Court of Conscience," 168.
32. Beckman, "To Once-a-Year Catholics: Easter Sunday," *HPR* 63, no. 6 (1963): 316.

the narrowness of sins highlighted in the confessional. More than just resolutions, Catholics sought solutions. Something else was needed as a way of dealing with personal and relational problems. Perhaps this is why some turned to psychology and counseling rather than confession and why so many seminaries in the early 1960s began offering courses in pastoral counseling.[33]

The Demise of Devotional Confession

The perception of a problematic overuse of the sacrament of confession contributed to the decline of devotional confession and even special-occasion confession. As previously mentioned, critics often saw this practice of regular confession as perfunctory and legalistic, judging its practitioners to be lacking adequate interior conversion and a sense of sin as relational. Another common concern was the phenomenon of "Catholic guilt" or, in its more severe form, scrupulosity. In 1959, a Jesuit priest addressed the issue of scrupulosity in *HPR*, advising confessors to be empathetic and understanding of the scrupulous. He noted that for many people, scrupulosity is just a phase, but for others it may be an indication of personality disorders, such as obsessive compulsive behavior.[34] The existence of scrupulosity as a problem in the confessional is also indicated by its occasional mention in homilies to the faithful. One priest advised the scrupulous to choose just a few sins to confess, knowing that all other venial sins would also be forgiven. He criticized the scrupulous for making the confessional a "torture chamber" rather than a "tribunal of mercy."[35] And a canon lawyer counseled fellow confessors not to let

---

33. Gillespie, *Psychology and American Catholicism*, 61. Gillespie states that in 1957 only a few seminaries had classes in pastoral counseling, but by 1962 over a hundred seminaries were offering such courses. Gillespie also describes three psychological studies performed on seminarians (1956), priests (1967), and bishops (1970s), respectively. The study of bishops found that they were "less self-actualized" than the priests in the other study. O'Toole does not provide numbers supporting this claim, nor does he provide an approximate date where more Catholics turned to professional counseling. He suggests that the laity began to see priests as poorly prepared to advise them on the problems that were troubling them; O'Toole, "In the Court of Conscience," 177.

34. Richard P. Vaughan, SJ, "Personal Approach to the Scrupulous," *HPR* 60, no. 7 (1959): 632–34.

35. John J. Fisher, CM, "The Confessional Bogey," *HPR* 57, no. 11 (1956): 943.

the scrupulous delve into the past unnecessarily, unless they thought it would be beneficial for the penitents to make a general confession of all past sins.[36]

This issue of scrupulosity, or sin-obsession, was a particularly important concern when it came to the subject of children. It had been a common practice for Catholic schoolchildren to be taken to confession regularly during their normal school hours at their parish school. It was thought that this recurrent opportunity for confession would help children to form the habit of devotional confession. By the mid-1960s, however, this custom was disparaged for a number of reasons, not the least of which was that forcing children to think about their sins and go to confession would cause scrupulosity or a Catholic guilt complex. In an age of celebration of freedom, moreover, some critics, like Fr. Andrew Greeley, writing in 1965, found it reprehensible that schoolchildren seemed coerced into partaking of the sacrament of confession—for example, before First Fridays.[37] The sacrament should be voluntarily sought out, he argued, not forced upon children.

There is seemingly no documentation as to how detrimental (or if it was indeed detrimental) regular confession was to Catholic schoolchildren, nor did the harmful effects of the early and frequent practice of confession make their way into the debates about children and the sacrament. Rather, the debate about children's confession quickly became a theological discussion of a theoretical nature, rather than an evaluation of pastoral practice on this front. The theological debate involved the relationship between the sacraments of penance and Eucharist and the appropriate age for children to receive each of these. The sacraments of penance and Eucharist had long been linked together, and, since Pius X's lowering of the age of first communion from twelve to seven with the decree *Quam singulari* in 1910, children had been allowed to confess at that early age, as well.

Now, however, theologians were quick to point out that, strictly speaking, the sacrament of penance was only necessary in cases of mortal sin, and, since children before the age of reason are ordinarily viewed as

---

36. Danagher, "Was the Penitent Sorry or Not?" *HPR* 56, no. 12 (1956): 1009.
37. Greeley, "Authority and Freedom," *HPR* 65, no. 12 (1965): 1002.

incapable of mortal sin, there was no need for them to receive the sacrament of penance. Thus many liturgical reformers were eager to separate the two sacraments in the case of children, delaying first reception of the sacrament of penance until the children were more mature and capable of committing mortal sin. One advocate of this position explained it thus: "More maturity is required for confession than mere devotion as is the case with communion. No priest can validly administer a sacrament without a sufficient matter. There must be a well founded presumption that the child to whom a priest gives absolution is really capable of guile or sin."[38] While there were some on the other side who argued for the importance of keeping penance and Eucharist together, gradually this theological position that the sacrament of penance was unnecessary for children led to the pastoral practice of delaying the first reception of the sacrament of penance until several years after the children's first communion.

Even by 1970, when the sacrament of penance had begun its rapid decline, one author was continuing to harp on the problems of legalism in the confessional: "Both children and adults are actually led to an attitude of pharisaical legalism precisely through our confession practice."[39] This priest worried that children get the wrong idea of the Gospel and end up seeking the sacrament of penance in order to circumvent the true penance that is a genuine conversion. Such an understanding implies that the sacrament, especially when routine, is an easy way out of penance and conversion—a manner of excusing oneself from the more difficult work of true conversion and penance. The result was to emphasize penance as something that is a rarer change of the heart coming about gradually and finding expression in significantly changed behavior. The mere repetition of acts of the will such as contrition, confession, and satisfaction did not seem sufficient. This contrasted with the 1950s frequent exhortation to contrition. Frequent efforts at contrition now seemed inadequate; something more profound was needed, and kids, it seemed, were not capable of it because of the inherently venial nature of their sin.

38. Francis Drouin, OP, "The Awakening of Moral Conscience in Children," *HPR* 66, no. 1 (1965): 43.

39. James D. Shaughnessy, "Spotlight on the Liturgy: First Communion before First Penance," *HPR* 70, no. 4 (1970): 300.

Outside the Box

Meanwhile, the Vatican responded negatively to the trend in delaying confession in an addendum to the 1971 "General Catechetical Directory" put forth by the Sacred Congregation for the Clergy. This document emphasized the moral formation of children and the usefulness of confession, even in the case only of venial sin. Specifically, the document noted the importance of confession for the development of the virtue of penance in children and said that the practice of putting confession ahead of communion should be retained. Moreover, it asked that regions that want to change this practice seek approval from the Vatican.[40] The addendum of this document is an indication of how widespread the practice of changing the order of these two sacraments had become. Recognizing this practice, and seeing it as problematic, the Sacred Congregation for the Clergy saw a reason to address the issue formally and affirm the traditional order of penance before Eucharist.

While children were the acknowledged subject on this debate of regular confession at a young age, the theological arguments in support of putting communion ahead of penance were easily applied to the subject of adult devotional confession, as well. Given that confession was only strictly necessary in the case of mortal sin, why celebrate or encourage the practice of frequent confession merely for venial sins? It was not uncommon in the 1960s for priests to advise their parishioners to make less use of the confessional. A Redemptorist priest acknowledged this fact: "Some priests have been discouraging the practice of frequent confession. The aim of these priests, as I understand it, is to offset a routine and mechanical approach to this sacrament."[41] Those practicing devotional confession seemed to be unnecessarily making excessive use of the sacrament; they needed more moderation. In the context of well-established weekly confessions, no doubt few priests expected the nearly complete disappearance of the sacrament in the time period to follow.

Another important factor in this discussion was the distinction between mortal and venial sin. Delineating sins into these two categories had long been the mainstay of manualist moral theology, and the laity

40. Sacred Congregation for the Clergy, "General Catechetical Directory," 1971, http://www.vatican.va/roman_curia/congregations/cclergy/documents/rc_con_cclergy_doc_11041971_gcat_en.html; accessed on October 12, 2012.

41. Daniel L. Lowery, CSsR, "A 'Piety Void'?" *American Ecclesiastic Review* 154, no. 1 (January 1966): 35.

were taught to think in these terms. As time went on, however, mortal sin came to seem more like a myth than a reality—or at least, most people believed that mortal sin must be a very rare occasion and extremely difficult to verify.[42] Here the psychological influences came into play, as discussed in chapter 2; those capable of committing what would categorically be labeled as "mortal" sins most likely suffered a diminished culpability. This meant that they were not as "free," as the manuals might have assumed they were in years past; they lacked full consent of the will. Rather, these sinners were captive to their own past and unknown psychological influences that had taken root in their behavior. Under such circumstances, many sins considered mortal in years past were now relabeled as venial. And many venial sins, such as washing one's car on a Sunday, were no longer regarded as sins at all.

Accompanying this modification in the understanding of mortal and venial sin was a seeming revision in the understanding of sinful matter. The violation of the Friday meat abstinence had long been preached as a mortal sin and hence was conventionally understood to be so by the faithful. When the American bishops altered this penitential practice in 1966, eating meat on Fridays ceased to be considered sinful. For the laity not schooled in the changes of Catholic cultic practices through the years, it was an abrupt alteration that seemed to indicate that other longstanding "sins" might soon no longer be considered sins, either. In particular, there was high hope that the ban on contraception might go the way of Friday meat abstinence. Both Friday abstinence and the stance against birth control were trademarks of American Catholicism. If one could cease overnight to be a sin, why not the other? Though there is obviously a difference between relaxing a discipline and changing moral theology, the laity were not sufficiently aware of this distinction.

And if this list of sins was so easy for the hierarchy to amend, how was the laity to know with confidence which acts that they had been told were sins were really sins? Another possibility was that there was no objective list of sins contrary to God's law; rather, whether an act was a sin or not might depend upon the individual and her circumstances. The

---

42. See Bernard Häring's comment mentioned in chap. 3: "My conviction is that an objective border-line, valid for all, between mortal and venial sin can never be determined"; Häring, *Free and Faithful*, 213.

Outside the Box

notion of sin as one's own personal, actual sin was not as emphasized, and the prioritized list of sins frequently named by priests was not as clear or as important as it had been in the past. The newfound emphasis on conscience led many of the faithful to believe that they were the best judges as to what constituted sin on their part; they were no longer willing to accept the delineation of sins as was communicated to them. The confessor, long recognized as "judge" and even inquisitor in the confessional, now no longer seemed as stable in that role.

Hence the Redemptorist priest previously mentioned agreed that the mechanical approach to the sacrament ought to be countered but suggested that a better response than discouraging penitents from approaching the sacrament would be to provide more adequate spiritual direction in the context of confession while eagerly anticipating the changes to the rite that were no doubt forthcoming in the wake of Vatican II. It was hoped that these changes to the rite of the sacrament would make confession meaningful and desirable.

Thinking outside the Box

The commendation of spiritual direction was an obvious attempt to make the sacrament of confession feel more personal and more focused on relationships. In response to the pastoral and theological problems recognized in the practice of a perfunctory devotional confession and an obligatory annual confession, many priests began to reconsider whether the confessional was even a good place for guiding their flock. In the past, numerous priests had argued that adequate spiritual direction could be delivered to anonymous penitents through the sacrament of confession. In supporting this, confessors were often exhorted to listen well and give the penitents time to ask questions and to seek advice on particular problems.

Another solution to the perfunctory feel of confession was for confessors to make penances more personally suited to the penitent. One priest, writing in the *American Ecclesiastical Review*, suggested:

Surely, the people would appreciate a pastoral updating in the practice of giving penances. There are countless devout Catholics who long for a more imaginative and meaningful approach to sacramental penances. They are devoutly hoping that confessors will soon get over the "three Hail Marys" syndrome. Suiting the penance to the sin and to the real life of the penitent would do much to offset the problem of routine and formalism.[43]

In fact, this change in penance was a constant refrain when it came to trying to improve upon the sacrament of confession. Fr. Gerald Ruano suggested that priests had made confession boring for penitents: "We may have been the reason why good wholesome Catholics have tagged the 'it's a Bore' label on confession or at least on our confessional."[44] Ruano's solution was much like that previously suggested—namely, tailoring the penance to the penitent's needs and personality, not just his sins. In practical terms, Ruano warned against penances that were hard to remember, long in duration, or unusual; they should be able to be completed prior to leaving the church. Penances should be simple but with an edge. Ruano also wanted confessors to get over the obsession with the quantity of prayers assigned in penance and instead to urge quality or intensity of prayer so that it would be more meaningful to penitents.[45]

But while more personal, tailored penances could help to make the sacrament more meaningful, this approach did not seem likely to solve all the perceived problems with the practice of the sacrament. Hence priests also thought there were some things that penitents could do in order to improve upon the practice of the sacrament of confession. In 1967, Fr. John Corrigan published an instructional pamphlet intended as a guide to the sacrament of confession for the laity. Corrigan noted that devotional confession was not an abuse, but he insisted that it presented a challenge for the penitent in terms of making devotional confession valuable for spiritual growth.[46] Corrigan noted that the sacrament of penance is not just a "God and me" affair; rather, every sin is an offense to God and the church. Corrigan saw the typical, impersonal confession as problematic:

If the penitent kneeling for absolution and guidance is merely a voice with two sins of uncharitbaleness [sic] and four sins of impatience, he has confessed

---

43. Lowery, "A 'Piety Void'?," 35.
44. Gerald P. Ruano, "Imaginative Penances," *HPR* 66, no. 10 (July 1966): 837.
45. Ibid., 841.
46. John E. Corrigan, "'Bless Me, Father': A Guide to Confession for Men and Women of Today, with Advice on the Examination of Conscience and Practical Examples" (Chicago: Claretian, 1967), 3.

things and not revealed a person. He has brought his laundry list of sins to the confessional, but not his authentic Christian life. It would require a Cure d'Ars, with power to read the heart to react to such a bloodless avowal of faults with anything more than the most banal considerations.[47]

Corrigan then provided numerous examples of good confessions, emphasizing the importance of the penitent identifying himself according to state in life, profession, and circumstances.

Corrigan also suggested that the penitent provide the context of sins, include significant temptations to sin, and conclude with a specific resolution.[48] Corrigan commented on his example confessions by noting that "they are free of any narrow, legalistic view of sin, and surely the penitents see that minimum requirements of morality are far from the call of Christ, who invites all to perfection."[49] Corrigan exhorted the laity to seek regular confessors, rather than making their decision of a confessor each Saturday based on which line was shorter.[50] Penitents were also advised by priests to ask questions when necessary or seek advice on particular problems. And, most importantly, penitents were to come to confession intentionally and purposefully, when they sincerely desired a conversion of the heart, and not just out of habit.

Although the confessional may not have been the place for protracted discussion of problems, a priest also did not realistically have time for extended spiritual direction *outside* the confessional for every member of his parish, either. The same John Corrigan, now addressing his fellow priests, rather than laity, wrote in *HPR* that, "as a practical approach, one of the pastoral facts of life is that only a few persons come to a priest for regular spiritual direction.... If the great majority of Christians are to receive any person-to-person word of encouragement of counsel, it is going to be heard in the confessional."[51] Hence the confessor had to strive to make God's forgiveness more real and personal for the penitent even in such limited circumstances.

This solution, however, was deemed inadequate for many who perceived the primary problem with confession as related to the box itself.

47. Ibid., 9.
48. Ibid., 11–12.
49. Ibid., 18.
50. Ibid., 24.
51. Corrigan, "The Priest as Confessor and Spiritual Director," *HPR* 67, no. 3 (December 1966): 220.

A darkened, cramped space where the penitent was forced to kneel in an uncomfortable position, unable to see the person with whom she was talking, seemed unlikely to convey the message of God's mercy and forgiveness. If confession were to take on a more personal feeling, it would require more than just effort on the part of the confessor to be Christ-like and come up with imaginative penances. Hence suggestions for face-to-face confession, more in the style of psychological counseling, became popular.[52] Classes on pastoral counseling taught at Loyola of Chicago by Catholic priest, psychologist, and Vatican II *peritus* Charles A. Curran became tremendously popular as priests strove to prepare themselves for a modified role.[53] Some people felt the solution to the impersonal nature of the sacrament of penance would require a new sort of liturgical space:

> The dark confessional should be replaced with a setting more suited to proclaim the joy and warmth of a real "con-celebration" of God's merciful love by penitent and minister. A large, beautifully decorated confessional room should replace the "Box." Such rooms could be built into every new church. In other situations, the sacristy or parlor could be adapted to this use. The penitent then would be able to speak or whisper and have the option to sit or kneel. Anonymity could be preserved or dispensed with by having the confessor seated with his back toward the penitent as he enters or by arranging a sliding veil or curtain between the minister and penitent.[54]

This Paulist priest found that the new theology of the sacrament was inadequately put into practice, and hence the sacrament was remaining individualistic, monotonous, and juridical.

The observation that the practice of the sacrament of confession was limited in its perception of the church and society was another major theological criticism of the box and the traditional "assembly line" of penance. This evaluation was made inasmuch as penitents appeared

---

52. O'Toole, "In the Court of Conscience," 182.

53. Gillespie, *Psychology and American Catholicism*, 122. The change in Charles A. Curran's thought is in some ways indicative of the overall change in attitude regarding psychology and counseling among American Catholics. While Curran's 1952 book *Counseling in Catholic Life and Education* emphasized consonance with a Thomistic model and an emphasis on virtue, his 1969 book *Religious Values in Counseling and Psychotherapy* "shows a clear contrast ... with a shift in emphasis from virtue to value."

54. David F. Gomez, CSP, "The Sacrament of Penance Today," *HPR* 70, no. 9 (June 1970): 682.

Outside the Box

unjustifiably to focus on a narrow list of sins, confessing primarily sins against church ritual practices, sexual sins, and sins in relation to their immediate family members. Some priests noted that even those who practiced devotional confession failed to confess social sins, such as racism. One priest stringently observed:

> Quite often adult Catholics prepare for confession with the same examination of conscience they used as children, with the one exception of their expanded appreciation of the sixth commandment. As a result, their self-knowledge is often little more than preadolescent. The rarity with which sins of racial prejudice are confessed and the almost utter oblivion of Catholics to their unchristian lack of involvement with the needs and problems of their environment point to a deficiency in their appreciation of sin and those responsibilities that go beyond the commandments. These are problems that obviously the mere frequenting of penance will not solve. Indeed, habitual, mechanical confessions serve only to perpetuate them.[55]

Moreover, the conventional list of sins that were identified and brought to the confessional seemed to reinforce a benighted perception of the beneficial effect of penance on the larger community. Penitents appeared unaware of the important theological point that the sacrament signified reconciliation with the larger church, and not just with God. There was a move to call the penitent out of his own little world to a bigger and more complete picture of sin and reconciliation that would prioritize an awareness of social sins and the need for social change.

Fr. James Leehan made just this point in his *HPR* article entitled "Penance and Its Social Dimension":

> Because of this profound unity among men and among Christians, it is becoming increasingly clear that we do not sin alone; there is a deep and definite solidarity in sin. Any sin, whether a proud reaction to the will of God or an apathetic abdication of responsibility, is not only an offense against God but is contrary to the love which builds unity; it destroys or hinders the building of the community of man and is contrary to God's plan for mankind. Every sin is a refusal to love, or at best a lack of love; it is a refusal to be concerned, to open oneself to others and to communicate with them and through them with God. It is a spurious affirmation of one's autonomy and independence from other men and from

---

55. Modras, "Frequent Devotional Confession," 653.

the community. This reaction and resistance to interpersonal relationships is, therefore, a refusal to fulfill oneself as a person.[56]

Drawing on the language and theology of Vatican II's phrase "the People of God," many theologians criticized the penitents who practiced devotional confession as being concerned primarily with their own salvation and sanctity, perhaps even self-obsessed in the case of those who were deemed scrupulous. But where was the sense that penance was something to be performed by the People of God, as a community?

The theological critique had its pastoral application in the move toward communal penance services. Seeking a return to the sources in arguing for an updating of the confessional practice, many theologians turned to early Christian history and the practice of public and communal penance, in contrast to the Irish monastery–influenced, manual-based practice of private confession. They hoped that this early practice of the sacrament would renew and update the current practice of the sacrament.[57] Leehan noted that "these [communal] celebrations are highly effective means for teaching the communal nature of sin and of confession. They also satisfy the need of many for a clearer sign of the communal reconciliation and joy connected with the forgiveness of sin."[58]

Suggestions for the newly described sacrament of reconciliation came in various forms. Among liturgists and others with a post–Vatican II excitement for all things liturgical, the sacrament was now identified as being, properly speaking, "a liturgy" or "a liturgical celebration." In the past, the understanding was that "sacrament" was the umbrella category and the liturgies, rites, or ceremonies that accompanied the sacraments were there to serve the sacraments by making the significance of the sacrament's form and matter more apparent to participants. The sacraments themselves were not considered as instances of enacting the liturgy.[59]

---

56. Leehan, "Penance and Its Social Dimension," 495.
57. For a more recent example of this, see Favazza, *Order of Penitents*.
58. Ibid., 501.
59. Cessario, "The Sacraments of the Church," in *Vatican II: Renewal within Tradition*, ed. Matthew L. Lamb and Matthew Levering (New York: Oxford University Press, 2008), 138–39. Though he does not provide examples, Cessario claims that presently "the study of sacramental theology remains almost exclusively subordinated to the programs in liturgical studies ... students, especially in the United States, who express an interest in studying the sacraments are confided to the care of professional liturgists"; see 140.

But as "liturgy" became the umbrella category, with sacraments serving as instances of liturgies, there was a push to make it more apparent that the sacrament of penance was, in fact, a liturgy. In order to capture reconciliation as both sacrament and liturgy, one priest, inspired by Edward Schillebeeckx's and Bernard Häring's theologies, described a communal penance service that would feature a liturgy of the Word, including a Gospel reading and homily, accompanied by appropriate hymns and prayers. In this format, the group would be kept to thirty or forty of the faithful, who would then have the opportunity for private individual confessions with the two or more priests concelebrating the liturgy.[60]

A Paulist priest, Fr. David Gomez, meanwhile suggested three proposed forms of the sacrament of reconciliation: (1) communal celebration with a general and public confession of sins; (2) communal celebration with the private confession of sins; and (3) celebration by the priest with the individual penitent. In regard to the first option, there would be a general absolution, with the faithful advised to confess their sins in their next private confession. The second option was like that previously suggested, requiring more than one priest and including a Liturgy of the Word. While the first would clearly express the sacrament's communal nature, the second would still emphasize confession as a public act of worship.[61] In the case of the third practice, already in use, there would need to be changes to update the sacrament, in particular communicating to the penitent that sin is not simply an offense against God, but a renunciation of one's identity in Christ that diminishes "the social achievement of reconciliation."[62]

When it came to children, communal penance services appeared to provide an excellent way to communicate the social nature of sin. These services might alert children to the presence of sin without requiring them to undergo private sacramental confession that was deemed theologically unnecessary because they were not able to commit mortal sin. One diocese suggested having second-graders participate in a nonsacramental communal celebration of penance as a way of introducing them into the concept of reconciliation. This same diocese then proposed that

60. Oscar J. Miller, CM, "Confession," 406.
61. David F. Gomez, CSP, "The Sacrament of Penance Today," *HPR* 70, no. 9 (1970): 680–81.
62. Ibid., 683.

the children's first sacramental reception of penance occur in fourth grade in a communal setting (it is unclear whether this service would include private auricular confession). From fifth grade on, students would be able to partake of the sacrament in both communal and private settings.[63]

This seemed to some people an appropriate and gradual outline for initiating children into the sacrament of reconciliation, especially since they would presumably be ready for their first communion prior to the maturity needed for their first confession. Moreover, communal penance was the older form of the sacrament, and public penance had been recognized as a valid and licit form of the sacrament in the past. The only concern expressed in relation to this was that it might seem to be "an easy way," since there was no individual confession involved.[64] This was countered by the plan's supposed merit of not forming children in the habit of routine, mechanistic, and individualistic devotional confession habit, but rather rightly inculcating a sense of the social nature of sin and penance. When children did seek individual confession later in life, it would be with the knowledge that their sins had social impact on the church as a whole and that their reconciliation was not just with God, but with the church, as well. This procedure for introducing children to penance was theoretically put to an end with the previously mentioned "General Catechetical Directory" of 1971.

As related to adults, however, the experimentation with the sacrament of penance continued. In some cases, proposals removed the sacrament of penance from the form of the sacrament altogether—that is, the suggestions for reform actually made penance nonsacramental. In the aforementioned plan for introducing children to the sacrament, for example, several of the steps included nonsacramental penance. This push for nonsacramental penitential liturgies was not restricted only to children. While in 1950s, the confessional had been presented as the quintessential place for receiving God's forgiveness and the best method of seeking God's forgiveness, theologians of the 1960s sought to broaden that understanding. Theologically, many were quick to point out the

---

63. Aidan M. Carr, "Questions Answered: Guidelines for Children's First Reception of Holy Eucharist and Penance from an Unknown Diocese," *HPR* 70, no. 4 (1970): 309–10.

64. Ibid., 312.

church's understanding that numerous penitential actions could bring about a forgiveness of sins, particularly the forgiveness of venial sins. An emphasis on sacramental confession seemed to limit God's power to forgive while also detracting from these other penitential acts.

Crucial to such a theological argument for nonsacramental penance was the understanding of contrition as the most important act of penance and isolatable from the other two. As was evident in the *Baltimore Catechism*'s explanation, the church had taught that perfect contrition could obtain pardon even for mortal sin without the sacrament of confession: "Perfect contrition will obtain pardon for mortal sin without the Sacrament of Penance when we cannot go to confession, but with the perfect contrition we must have the intention of going to confession as soon as possible, if we again have the opportunity."[65] Hence the context for understanding the forgiveness associated with perfect contrition was that of an emergency, say, in the case of impending death without access to a confessor. But it was not an unreasonable conclusion to think that if a perfect act of contrition in emergency circumstances was sufficient for obtaining forgiveness of mortal sin that it might also be sufficient in other (non-emergency) circumstances, including if the person did not have the intention of seeking the sacrament at the first opportunity.

This supposition was expressed in a question posed in the *American Ecclesiastical Review* and answered by Francis Connell. The questioner wondered if a person who had made a perfect act of contrition could receive the Eucharist prior to receiving the sacrament of penance, and Connell replied by asserting that this would be a grave violation of the law and a sacrilege against the Eucharist.[66] Thomas Hanrahan's article in *HPR* at about the same time period alluded to the perfect contrition debate, this time in regard to Protestants receiving the Eucharist without having been formally received into the church. He noted that some people suggest that a non-Catholic could just make a perfect act of contrition prior to receiving the Eucharist, but this position fails to take into account Canon 807, which stipulates that the person must then have recourse to the sacrament of confession within three days. Moreover, ac-

---

65. *Baltimore Catechism*, Answer to Question, 766.
66. Connell, "Some Recent Statements on the Sacrament of Penance," *American Ecclesiastical Review* 155 (1966): 278–79.

cepting such a position would in fact be affirming the Protestant position against the need for the sacrament of confession while also profaning the Eucharist.[67]

As noted in chapter 1, theologians from the time of Thomas Aquinas and even earlier had thought contrition to be an act of the virtue of penance that also constituted the matter of the sacrament of confession. While contrition was not restricted to the confessional, its primary identification was with the sacrament. Both Connell and Hanrahan held fast to this postulation, objecting to circumventing the sacrament of confession through perfect acts of contrition, but not all theologians chose to emphasize this traditional understanding. Many theologians rather sought to emphasize the numerous other ways that sins were forgiven, such as saying acts of contrition, and these theologians thereby minimized the sacrament of confession, especially the practice of devotional confession.[68]

One priest wondered why frequent confession had ever become popular, given that it was out of line with the bulk of Christian history. This author sought to emphasize the efficacious value of various nonsacramental works of satisfaction, suggesting that "perhaps what is now called for is a re-appreciation of personal works of penance, themselves signs of God's salvation operative in the lives of his people, rather than a frantic effort to 'save the sacrament.'"[69] The use of the phrase "personal works of penance" seemed to emphasize the voluntary nature of penance, freely undertaken by the responsible and mature Catholic; the author did not propose a recovery of communal penitential practices such as the Friday meat abstinence but rather undermined the value of the sacrament by promoting unspecified nonsacramental substitutions left to the choice of the individual. This suggestion played down the benefit of sacramental penance involving contrition, confession, and satisfaction.

Others took an opposite, but related approach, seeking to extend the sacramental aspect of penance beyond the confessional ... and without

---

67. Thomas S. Hanrahan, "Whither Confession?" *HPR* 67, no. 4 (1967): 309.
68. Lawrence Landini, OFM, "Drop-Off in Confession: The Epistles of St. Cyprian of Carthage," *American Ecclesiastical Review* 169, no. 2 (1975): 133–34.
69. Ibid.

Outside the Box

the act of individual verbal confession. This was the case in the proposed communal penance services where there was a general absolution without individual confession of sins. Writing in 1970, still in the early stages of responses to Vatican II, author Peter Riga made a suggestion for delivering the grace of the sacrament without requiring the faithful to show up to confession hours: the penitential rite at the beginning of Mass could be made sacramental. The prayers of this rite included the *Confiteor*, where the faithful made a statement confessing that they had sinned, as well as the *Kyrie eleison*, wherein the faithful prayed for God to have mercy. Riga observed that the penitential rite at the beginning of Mass had not reached its full development, but could conceivably become fully sacramental, including a general absolution at the beginning of every Mass. Riga thought that this would be a powerful way of linking reconciliation and the Eucharist, as they had always been linked in the tradition of the church. Moreover, it would communicate more adequately to the faithful that penance is an act of the whole church.

Riga did not think such a change to the penitential rite would negate the practice of private confession, but rather that the two could coexist. Riga then took the separation of absolution and confession a step further by suggesting that confession/spiritual direction become nonsacramental. He suggested that such a format might be more joyful for the faithful and more meaningful because they would then seek confession/spiritual direction out of a desire to do penance rather than to receive absolution. While the latter—that is, approaching the sacrament for absolution—fostered a mechanistic understanding of penance and an unthinking habit of confessing, this new form would result in greater satisfaction.[70] Once again, sacramental penance was undercut in such a solution; the form and the matter of the sacrament would be separated. The absolution constituting the form of the sacrament would be applied to all, even without the faithful's acts of contrition, confession, and satisfaction. Meanwhile, those who expressed contrition in verbal confession and satisfaction would not receive absolution. The penitential rite at Mass would become sacramental penance, while the sacrament would become nonsacramen-

70. Peter Riga, "Liturgy Today: Penance; A New Orientation," *American Ecclesiastic Review* 163, no. 5 (November 1970): 409–10, 413.

tal penance. In short, Riga, and many who wanted to change how the sacrament was practiced, hoped that penance would become more meaningful and hence more penitential without the pressure of penance as a sacrament requiring certain acts of the penitent.

The Liturgical Reform and More Frequent Communion

The criticisms applied to the sacrament of penance during this time were not unlike some of the criticisms of the Tridentine liturgy; like the sacrament of penance, the Mass seemed to be less meaningful than it could be or should be. The regular attendance at Mass seemed more a testament to the faithful's sense of duty in fulfilling an obligation than an instance of enthusiasm and love for God. The rote actions of the Mass bore affinity with the acts of the confessional; the repetition seemed for some to indicate unreflective routine. The perceived problems in the practice of Tridentine liturgy occasioned a move for reform of the Mass. In one of his last public addresses as pope, Benedict XVI noted the need for this and the growth of the liturgical movement after World War I, which he described as follows:

a rediscovery of the richness and depth of the liturgy, which, until then had remained, as it were, locked within the priest's Roman Missal, while the people prayed with their own prayer books ... it was as though there were two parallel liturgies: the priest with the altar-servers, who celebrated Mass according to the Missal, and the laity, who prayed during Mass using their own prayer books, at the same time, while knowing substantially what was happening on the altar.[71]

Benedict spoke of two principles in Vatican II's reflection on the liturgy in preparing *Sacrosanctam concilium*: active participation and intelligibility, which he contrasted with "being locked up in an unknown language that is no longer spoken."[72]

In the United States there were similar concerns about the liturgy prior to Vatican II. The priest's prayers and the people's prayers did not

---

71. Benedict XVI, "Meeting with the Parish Priests and the Clergy of Rome: Address of His Holiness Pope Benedict XVI," February 14, 2013, http://www.vatican.va/holy_father/benedict_xvi/speeches/2013/february/documents/hf_ben-xvi_spe_20130214_clero-roma_en.html; accessed on April 9, 2013.

72. Ibid.

Outside the Box

seem to correspond as they should, and the use of Latin meant that most could not understand what was being prayed. The combined effect was a dearth in meaning; the liturgy was experienced by many as routine and impersonal. Hence one approach by the liturgical movement in the United States was to promote a dialogue Mass wherein the entire congregation said the Latin responses to the priest's prayers aloud.[73] Such active response meant more involvement in the Mass and more attention to the meaning of the liturgy.

Another concern regarding the Mass was the infrequency with which the faithful received communion. In January of 1953, Pope Pius XII released an apostolic constitution reducing the Eucharistic fast to three hours, with even further exemptions for the sick, travelers, those performing tiring work, and priests saying Mass at late hours.[74] Four years later, in 1957, Pius XII's *motu proprio*, entitled *Sacram communionem*, further reduced the fasting obligations.[75] The intent of both of these changes, as well as the new option of celebrating evening Masses, was to encourage and facilitate more frequent communion by the faithful, and, as one priest explained, "Like all the other liturgical changes of Pope Pius XII, this serves the spiritual welfare and greater holiness of the people. The old fast law was for many an obstacle, a hindrance, and an excuse. The new law makes frequent Communion a practical possibility for all."[76]

These changes, combined with the liturgical movement and the implementation of Vatican II's *Sacrosanctum concilium*, opened new possibilities for the faithful in regard to their experience of Mass. They participated in a new, more externally active way and could perceive more clearly what was happening at the Mass. O'Toole suggests two ways the changes to the Mass affected the sacrament of confession. First, the use

---

73. O'Toole, *The Faithful*, 203.

74. Pius XII, "Christus Dominus: Concerning the Discipline to be Observed with Respect to the Eucharistic Fast," January 6, 1953, http://www.ewtn.com/library/papaldoc/p12chdom.htm; accessed on April 12, 2013.

75. Pius XII, *Sacram communionem: On Laws of Fasting and the Evening Mass*, motu proprio issued March 19, 1957, http://www.papalencyclicals.net/Pius12/P12FAST.HTM; accessed on April 12, 2013.

76. McManus, "Principle of Reverence Retained in Revised Fasting Regulations," *Boston Pilot*, March 30, 1957, unnumbered page as found in the McManus files, Catholic University of America Archives, box 2, folder 19.

of anticipation or vigil masses on Saturday evening quickly became popular, but they could conflict with conventional confession times, which had often been on Saturday afternoon or evening: "While some parishioners perhaps continued the old practice of doubling up, most of those in church on Saturday afternoon gave their attention to the Mass rather than to confession, and they would probably have been encouraged by their pastors to do exactly that."[77] O'Toole further observes that the use of the vernacular meant that the faithful now recited the *Confiteor* aloud in English and heard the priest grant them a kind of pardon following it. Moreover, right before receiving communion, the faithful also stated, "Lord, I am not worthy to receive you, but only say the word and I shall be healed." O'Toole states that this also played a role in displacing confession.[78]

More opportunities to attend Mass, encouragement for frequent communion, and hearing and participating in the Mass in English may have turned the attention of clergy and laity to the Eucharist at the expense of the sacrament of penance. The newfound intelligibility of the Mass perhaps made it seem exciting and interesting, whereas confession continued on in its preconciliar form, which now might seem outdated. Those who sought to reform the sacrament of penance could take a cue from the changes to the Mass, hoping to make the sacrament more meaningful and less routine. But while American Catholics were thrust into the liturgical changes, the changes to the sacrament of penance were slow in coming, and its popularity had already diminished by the time the new rite was released a decade after many of the Mass changes took effect.

The New Rite of Penance

When the new *Rite of Penance* was promulgated in the United States in 1976, it turned what had been a two-minute process, with a simple for-

---

77. O'Toole, "In the Court of Conscience," 174. Though O'Toole links anticipation masses with the Vatican II liturgical changes, as previously noted, the evening masses were made possible by Pius XII in 1953, well before Vatican II. I could not, however, find any kind of data as to when evening masses became prevalent or popular in the United States. An earlier date of the presence of vigil masses would indicate that there was actually little correlation between this practice and the decrease of confession that occurred in the late 1960s.

78. Ibid., 174–75.

Outside the Box

mat for the penitent that was easily taught to children, into a much more complex matter.[79] The book had 228 pages containing new prayers and procedures, including those tailored to particular situations—that is, penance services for children or for the season of Advent. This book included three different forms of the rite of penance: the Rite for Reconciliation of Individual Penitents; the Rite for Reconciliation of Several Penitents with Individual Confession and Absolution (what became known as communal penance services); and the Rite for Reconciliation of Several Penitents with General Confession and Absolution.[80] Even for the standard individual confession, the priest had a choice of five introductory statements, including three biblical prayers. The outline of the rite was supposed to include a greeting, the sign of the cross, invitation to trust in God, reading of the word of God, confession of sins and acceptance of satisfaction, prayer of the penitent and absolution, and the proclamation of praise of God and dismissal.[81] The priest was now presented with numerous choices to make when hearing confessions, and the delay in the penitent's confession (after prayer, greeting, and reading) could make it challenging for him to remember his sins, particularly if nervous. The new, longer form of this rite was impractical for both priest and penitent. The rich representation of the significance of penance could not make up for the lack of brevity and simplicity that had long characterized the sacrament as practiced by American Catholics.

The communal penance service was also quite involved, including an introductory rite with song, greeting, introduction, and opening prayer; a liturgy of the word with two readings, responsorial psalm, Gospel, homily, and examination of conscience; a rite of reconciliation including a general confession of sins, a litany, the Lord's Prayer, individual confession and absolution, proclamation of praise for God's mercy, and prayer of thanksgiving; and a concluding rite with blessing and dismiss-

---

79. This is O'Toole's description regarding the old form of confession; ibid., 152, 182 on the new rite.

80. Bishops' Committee on the Liturgy, National Conference of Catholic Bishops, *Rite of Penance* (New York: Catholic Book Publishing, 1975), 6. The third form of the rite was meant to be used only in exceptional cases, and the Vatican soon made it clear that they would not approve of general absolution employed simply by the personal judgment of a bishop, as Bishop Carroll Dozier had done in Memphis; see ibid., 184.

81. Bishops' Committee on the Liturgy, *Rite of Penance*, 32.

al.[82] There is evidence that communal penance services under this form initially enjoyed some success, with 63 percent of parishes in the United States having at least one within a year of their authorization.[83]

In theory communal penance services would be more meaningful because they better emphasized the social nature of the sacrament and were more reflective as to the significance of sin and penance for the church as a whole. The nonsacramental penitential practices such as Friday meat abstinence had long exhibited the social aspect of penance as individuals identified with the Catholic community and relied upon it for support in living out these practices. Perhaps it was the sudden absence of such socially embodied penitential practices that led to a desire to emphasize the communal nature of penance in the sacrament of confession. Penance should have a communal nature; without the obviously communal nonsacramental penances like Lenten fasting and Friday meat abstinence, there was a desire to emphasize the communal nature of the sacrament of penance. But while theologically the person's use of the sacrament was explained as benefiting the whole church, the traditional practice of individual confession appeared to be quite individualistic. As practiced, it seemed the sacrament of confession could do little to communicate to the faithful the important social aspect of penance as reconciliation within the body of Christ.

In some sense, communal penance services filled in the dearth left by the 1966 changes to nonsacramental penances in the United States. But while they admirably communicated the social aspect of penance, in practice communal penance services were inconvenient because they required additional time and effort in comparison with individual confession. The hybrid of a public service with private confession led to impatience on the part of some laity, and ultimately these services did not maintain the popularity that the traditional private confession had for so many years. Additionally, such services were infrequent in comparison with the regular and extensive confessional schedules of earlier years. Hence O'Toole states that "the laity's response was positive, but hardly enthusiastic."[84] In the end, "communal penance services were

---

82. Ibid., 44.
83. O'Toole, "In the Court of Conscience," 183.
84. Ibid.

Outside the Box

not the occasion for widespread return to penance and reconciliation by American Catholics."[85] In the quest to make the sacrament of penance more personal and meaningful, the new rite had also made it much longer and more demanding for the increasingly busy laity who lived in an ever more religiously pluralistic society.

Minimizing the Sacrament of Penance, Undermining Penance as a Whole

It was not common, but also not unheard of during the late 1960s and early 1970s for someone to reference the virtue of penance as a supporting point for changes to the sacrament of penance. In his critique of devotional confession, Ronald Modras noted that "proper understanding of the sacrament of penance demands appreciation of the virtue of penance, which in turn demands an understanding of the nature of sin, to which penance is antithetic."[86] Likewise, a Benedictine who was reexamining the liturgical year commented on the season of Lent: "As for the penitential elements the faithful are to be instructed on both the social consequences of sin and also that essence of the virtue of penance which leads to the detestation of sin as an offense against God."[87] The author notes that the understanding of penance in the past had been too individualistic and hence should be understood as a reentering into union with God and God's people, but he fails to mention the sacrament of confession in relation to this, relying instead on the penitential practices of the season of Lent.

Yet despite this conviction that there were many penitential acts beyond those involved in the sacrament of penance, the new emphases in theology of the sacrament of penance and the pastoral application of this theology simultaneously minimized the benefit of the sacrament while undermining penance as a whole. The new emphases did not fully connect sacramental and nonsacramental penance as both expressions of the virtue of penance, nor did they propose them as mutually supportive and beneficial. Despite the occasional reference to the virtue of penance, those hoping to renew the sacrament of penance did not consider the

85. Ibid., 184.
86. Modras, "Frequent Devotional Confession," 653.
87. Emeric A. Lawrence, OSB, "The Liturgical Year," *HPR* 65, no. 1 (October 1964): 51.

decrease of sacramental penance in tandem with the dramatic decline of nonsacramental penitential practices among American Catholics.

Rather, the emphasis on making the sacrament seem more communal or social, combined with the broadened sacramental understanding beyond the acts of contrition, confession, and satisfaction, took the focus away from the importance of the form and matter of the sacrament. In particular, this reduced the significant role of the penitent's external actions in making reparation for sin; contrition, confession, and satisfaction aimed to remove the person's personal, actual sin. The diminished appreciation of the person's penitential acts of confession and satisfaction corresponded to the change in the conception of sin from something concrete and tangible understood as the individual's personal, actual sin to something more elusive—a general sense of sin and sorrow rather than identifiable sins that were verbally confessed and atoned for when the penitent performed the penance assigned by a confessor.

Though theologians such as Peter Lombard and Thomas Aquinas emphasized contrition as an interior act of the will, both also thought it should be expressed through external acts of the penitent. The push for general absolution without verbal confession of sin circumvented the person's external acts. A verbal confession required an examination of conscience in order to articulate one's sins and hence was more likely to elicit contrition than simply the general sense of being a sinner but not naming any specific sins. General absolution did not necessitate an examination of conscience, verbal confession, or even contrition, for that matter. In this sense, it provided form with no matter. The excitement over communal penance services with general absolution and face-to-face spiritual direction in place of sacramental confession detracted from the benefit of an articulated confession of sin to another person. In fact, a common denominator of the various suggested penitential practices (nonsacramental communal penance services, acts of contrition, the penitential rite at the beginning of Mass) was that they did not require the faithful to articulate their sins. Though an examination of conscience was implied in these practices, the need for a good *examen* was not as crucial as when the person would be verbalizing sins to a priest. In a sense, the omission of this act made penance potentially easier in some sense, but less beneficial in fostering penitence in the faithful.

Outside the Box

One of the criticisms that moral theologians like Bernard Häring had about manual-based moral theology was that it tended to foster a minimalistic morality. The faithful tended to do the bare minimum to fulfill what they saw as their Christian duty and confess what was clearly delineated as a transgression of law. The focus on obligatory practices such as Friday meat abstinence and attendance at Sunday Mass, as well as a preoccupation with sexual sins detracted from a holistic sense of charity that would foster awareness of a more diverse number of sins, including social sins such as racism or buying grapes that were harvested by unjustly paid farm workers. The manual-based morality of the confessional was regarded as minimalistic in the sense that the faithful did not strive to advance beyond what was required of them by the church. It was narrow because it often failed to consider the bigger picture—the many sins that were not detailed in the manuals but could be just as important.

Häring saw his work as moving beyond this minimalistic and narrow morality rooted in the confessional. Häring and those influenced by his work saw themselves as calling the faithful beyond the bare minimum required by the law to something greater—"the law of love"—that truly would lead to sanctity rather than scrupulosity caused by legalism. It is somewhat ironic, therefore, that one of the theological emphases in the wake of Vatican II concerned the question of necessity as regards the sacrament of penance. Theologians adamantly explained that even with the required annual prescription set forth by Lateran IV, the sacrament of penance was only strictly necessary in the case of mortal sin. Though this was not theologically inaccurate, the practical result of downplaying the benefit of the sacrament for venial sins was to promote a minimalism in regard to identification of sin and use of the sacrament of confession. Rather than expanding the typical examination of conscience to consider social sins in addition to those that had been more emphasized in the past, numerous priests instead insisted on the superfluous nature of devotional confession, discouraging penitents from approaching the sacrament frequently. Such an approach, though seeking to address legitimate concerns as regards unreflective routine, could only have contributed to the decline of the sacrament.

O'Toole rightly points to the shifting relationship of the sacrament of penance and that of the Eucharist. The laity were instructed to receive communion more often (even at every Mass attendance) and told that they need not go to confession before doing so, except in the case of mortal sin. Again, while this was theologically correct in fact, it supported a minimalistic practice of the sacrament of penance; priests had long taught that the reception of the Eucharist would be more fruitful if preceded by the sacrament of penance. But if confession was not necessary as a condition for receiving the Eucharist, then why bother?[88] Whereas the two sacraments had previously been viewed as a team, working together, they were increasingly contrasted, with the sacrament of penance appearing outdated and unnecessary while Eucharistic vigor was renewed with the celebration of Mass in the vernacular and regular reception encouraged until it became normative, with little thought as to the benefit of preparing by addressing one's personal, actual sins.

In the case of both discouraging the practice of devotional confession and delaying children's first confession, the faithful were not provided with the opportunity to develop practices of penance as they had had in the past. There was no longer a pressing need for the frequent exercise of self-examination and identification of sin required by recurrent partaking of the sacrament of penance, and without the recognition of their personal and actual sins the faithful were unlikely to understand the need for the sacrament of penance or nonsacramental penitential practices such as the Friday sacrifice. While the regular confession of only venial sins doubtlessly could have its problems, like the tendency toward scrupulosity and a problematic, unreflective routinization, it nonetheless had served an important role by providing the possibility for forming a worthwhile habit of recognizing and naming sins. Beyond just a regular examination of conscience, the practice of devotional confession forced the faithful to articulate their sins. When they sought the sacrament of penance, they actually had to perform the penitential acts of confession and satisfaction. And they did this under the direction of a priest, representing Christ and the church. There was an accountability and a humility inherent in this particular practice that had the potential to strengthen penance in the church, though it often failed in doing so. Such accountability and humility were not present in some newly proposed forms of

---

88. O'Toole, "In the Court of Conscience," 182.

the sacrament, nor were they present in the decision to forego the sacrament based on the theological explanations given by priests.

Perhaps those most affected by the change in the conception of sin and decline of the sacrament of penance were the children raised in the late 1960s and the decades that followed. By delaying the age of first confession until several years after first communion, children lost a few years of working to develop the penitential habit in response to their sins and to see penance as an important preparation for reception of the Eucharist. By discouraging devotional confession among children there was a lost opportunity during a formative time period for strengthening a habit of naming sins and learning to do penance for these personal, actual sins.

There was some theological and historical support in favor of delaying children's first confession despite offering them an early first communion, especially since the communion age had just been lowered by Pius X in 1910. Yet the practice of separating first confession from first communion further served to separate penance from the Eucharist. Children would be in the habit of receiving communion for several years before they could even begin a habit of regular confession.[89] It should not be a surprise that for many of these children, the two sacraments were not even necessarily linked as they had been for their parents, grandparents, and great-grandparents. For even after receiving the sacrament of reconciliation for the first time, they were likely instructed that they need not seek it regularly prior to receiving communion. An early first confession linked with the Eucharist, in contrast, allowed for the possibility of developing a sense of sin, the ability to identify and name sin, and the recognition of the benefit of penitential preparation prior to Eucharistic reception. The postponement of confession did the opposite, effectually postponing the development of penitential sensibility through the acts of contrition, confession, and satisfaction.

It is therefore not surprising that O'Toole reports a generational difference in attitude toward the sacrament of confession, with college-

---

89. Although the Sacred Congregation for the Clergy's "General Catechetical Directory" insisted on first confession prior to first communion, the opposite order apparently continued to be practiced into the 1980s in some places, including my own parish in Iowa. My first communion was in 1986, and my first confession was in 1988.

aged young adults in the 1970s expressing the most dissatisfaction with the traditional practice of confession.[90] It was generally this segment of the Catholic population who was subject to delayed confession accompanied by an emphasis on frequent reception of the Eucharist. The Catholic who was seven and making her first communion (but not first confession) in 1965, for example, would have been in college by 1976. Others who made their first communion and confession in the years preceding the close of Vatican II were no doubt also affected to some degree by the separation of first communion and confession; perhaps they had made their first confession at age seven but were then told in the years after Vatican II that they need not go again until they were much older.

The new theological emphases in American Catholicism that sought to limit the practice of the sacrament to only when strictly necessary might also have been detrimental to nonsacramental penance, even though some theologians promoted nonsacramental acts of penance in place of the sacrament of confession. For if the sacrament were not necessary or even beneficial on a frequent basis, why would weekly nonsacramental penance such as the Friday sacrifice be worthwhile? In minimizing the sacrament of confession, there was a lost opportunity for identifying and naming personal, actual sin and cultivating penance through regular penitential acts such as contrition, confession, and satisfaction. These sacramental acts of penance helped the faithful in the awareness of their own sins and could aid the sensibility for the benefit of regular nonsacramental penance, as well.

Another great cause for the decline of the sacrament of confession was the change in the American Catholic understanding of sin and a reconsideration of specific sins. The growing primacy of conscience and freedom was detrimental to church teaching on what constituted a sin; though penitents had always in some sense been the first judge as to their sin, now the discernment of the faithful became more absolute, even when in contradiction to church teaching. The resulting reduction in the conventional list of sins may have likewise contributed to a diminishment of the sacrament of penance. Less identifiable personal and actual sins meant less contrition, confession, and satisfaction. In partic-

---

90. O'Toole, "In the Court of Conscience," 170.

ular, the position that saw contraception as morally acceptable became paradigmatic as a case of conscience and moral autonomy for the laity struggling with complicated decisions in this area. The sympathetic response to the difficulty of raising a large family caused a reevaluation of sexual sins, suggesting that though the church might maintain the stance against artificial birth control, this position could not be understood in absolute terms as it once had.

The distinction between mortal and venial sin, emphasized in the manualist era, became largely insignificant. Peter Riga observed a change in theological thinking as regards sin when he wrote, "It must be noted ... that theology today is again rethinking the whole concept of 'mortal' and 'venial' sins, which, after all, is not older than the high Middle Ages, at least as judgment as to whether a person should approach the Eucharist or not."[91] Riga also observed that new studies of psychiatry and sociology indicated that people are actually limited in many choices that seem to be free. He added to this a comment on the change to the conventional list of sins:

> Moreover, we have also seen the rather shocking (at least for some of the faithful) changing of what was once considered to be "mortal" sin (meat on Friday, fasting during Advent, and soon doubtless, obligatory Sunday attendance) to being either optional or non-existent. What of all those of the faithful who committed such faults and died before "penance"? Many of the faithful simply do not see that something can be a "mortal sin" today and tomorrow by the decree of a Pope or any other man, is nothing of the sort.[92]

In this Riga seemed rightly to capture the laity's changing notion of sin that included a lack of confidence in Catholic Church teaching and practice, given the emphasis on such actions as sinful prior to the changes. The abrupt changes to nonsacramental penitential practice delegitimized for the faithful the church's authority in determining sin.

Last, from a theological perspective, one might also note that the minimizing of the sacrament diminished not only the penitential acts of the penitent, but disregarded the benefit of receiving absolution from a priest. The Catholic tradition adopted from the language of Thomas

---

91. Riga, "Liturgy Today," 414.
92. Ibid.

Aquinas argued that it was the absolution that perfected the necessary acts of the penitent within confession. Together the acts of penitent and priest combined in the sacrament removed personal, actual sin, and such removal of sin was important for the person's salvation. While penitential acts could be a cause for the forgiveness of sins even outside of the sacrament of penance, the acts of contrition, confession, and satisfaction performed in conjunction with absolution perfected them with grace, bringing greater assurance of the forgiveness of sins and aiding the recovery and strengthening of all the virtues. Thomas had compared the Eucharist to nourishment and the sacrament of penance to medicine.[93] A person without sin could be adequately sustained by the Eucharist, but those with sin would have greater benefit from the medicine of the sacrament of penance to remove sin in combination with the nourishment of the Eucharist. It is difficult to be nourished when sick, and the medicine of penance was beneficial preparation for the Eucharist.

The Sacrament of Penance Is Hard

As Dorothy Day noted in the quotation at the beginning of this chapter, "Going to confession is hard—hard when you have sins to confess, hard when you haven't, and you rack your brain for even the beginnings of sins against charity, chastity, sins of detraction, sloth or gluttony."[94] That which makes the sacrament of confession hard is precisely those acts of the penitent—contrition, confession, and satisfaction—performed in the sacrament of confession. These acts require the identification and naming of sins, as well as sorrow for these sins. These acts are necessary for the reception of the sacrament of penance, but they are the foundation for nonsacramental penance, as well. Though these penitential acts are difficult, without adequate reflection on sin and the identification and naming of sin, the benefit of penance quickly becomes undervalued for the faithful.

The changes to the sacrament during this time period addressed what were often rightly perceived as problems with the practice of the sacra-

---

93. *ST* III, q. 84, a. 6.
94. Day, *Long Loneliness*, 9–10.

Outside the Box

ment of confession. Perhaps because of the use of manuals in the training of confessors, the sacrament had a legalistic tendency, with some of the primary sins confessed being the violations of church ritual laws, such as breaking the Friday meat abstinence or failing to fulfill the Sunday obligation of Mass attendance. Such an emphasis detracted from the more relational nature of sin, and as personalism became popular, theologians worried that this aspect was missing from the common American practice of the confession. So also, it could appear that the sacrament was practiced in a merely external sort of way, lacking in the appropriate interior sentiment of true sorrow and contrition.

Scrupulosity and an overabundance of "Catholic guilt" indicated a problem in conscience and conscience formation. Perhaps the church was simply not realistic about human weaknesses and tendencies toward sin, and perhaps it had erred in making the faithful preoccupied about sin. This was related to the changes in the idea of freedom. Catholic schoolchildren who had long been taken to confession regularly throughout the school year before First Fridays now appeared as victims who had the sacrament forced on them.[95] It could be argued that their freedom was being impinged upon rather than facilitated by formation in a penitential sensibility that would serve them well for the rest of their lives.

With the rising popularity of psychology and counseling services, many worried that the confessional did not adequately address spiritual problems or personal problems and perhaps even exacerbated them by reinforcing shame. Especially as Catholics moved out of close-knit urban Catholic communities, the practice of confession seemed ill-suited to address the concerns of life in the religiously pluralistic suburbs. For the younger generation, this was particularly the case; confession did not make sense or seem an effective way of addressing the problems of life. Moreover, the sacrament seemed individualistic; the communal nature of reconciliation with the church was unclear as each person headed into the box for a couple of minutes alone with a priest. And the focus of sins confessed was of a highly personal nature, again, with emphasis on church law and little attention to pressing social sins.

The alteration in theological emphases and pastoral applications of

---

95. Greeley, "Authority and Freedom," 1002.

these emphases was made with the best of intentions. In the wake of Vatican II, the faithful—both lay and clergy—had the courage to address the failings of this sacramental practice and try to amend them in order to reinvigorate the sacrament of confession to counter perceived problems. However, these criticisms and resultant changes did little more than seemingly contribute to the decline of the sacrament while simultaneously undermining nonsacramental penitential practices that had been abruptly changed in 1966. The repetition, or the habit—whether annual or weekly—of receiving the sacrament of penance was ultimately not the problem. What needed reexamination was whether the external acts of confession and satisfaction were properly motivated by interior contrition and how the faithful might work on making the sacrament not simply routine, but authentically penitential.

The sacrament of penance was seen as falling short of its potential for serving as a structure to develop penitence among American Catholics; nonsacramental penance such as the Friday meat abstinence was also judged wanting. And yet, the 1966 changes to nonsacramental penitential practices further diminished the potential for serving as a structure for penitential development, as did the altered attitudes toward the sacrament of penance. Penance, both nonsacramental and sacramental, was not always practiced as thoughtfully or as well as it might have been, but at least penance *was* practiced by the great majority of American Catholics. Though the church in the United States made significant changes during this time period, it did so with a much reduced penitential sensibility that would be inherited by subsequent generations. The lack of regular penitential practice is perhaps the most distinctive point of contrast between contemporary American Catholicism and the Catholicism that preceded on this continent.

Bibliography

Primary Sources

Aquinas, St. Thomas. *Summa theologiae*. http://www.corpusthomisticum.org/sth4084.html. Latin text accessed on November 25, 2007.

Augustine. *City of God*. Translated by Henry Bettenson. New York: Penguin, 1972.

Baltimore Catechism, Answer to Question 766. http://www.ourladyswarriors.org/faith/bc3–18.htm. Accessed on September 28, 2012.

Beckman, Joseph F. "Frequent Confession: Homily for Low Sunday." *Homiletic and Pastoral Review* [hereafter *HPR*] 63, no. 6 (1963).

———. "To Once-a-Year Catholics: Easter Sunday." *HPR* 63, no. 6 (1963).

Benedict XVI. *Spe salvi*. Encyclical on Saving Hope. 2007. http://www.vatican.va/holy_father/benedict_xvi/encyclicals/documents/hf_ben-xvi_enc_20071130_spe-salvi_en.html. Accessed on December 4, 2012.

———. "Meeting with the Parish Priests and the Clergy of Rome: Address of His Holiness Pope Benedict XVI, February 14, 2013." http://www.vatican.va/holy_father/benedict_xvi/speeches/2013/february/documents/hf_ben-xvi_spe_20130214_clero-roma_en.html. Accessed on April 9, 2013.

Bernard, Ken J. "Let's Teach Christian Morality." *HPR* 69, no. 2 (1968).

Bishops' Committee on the Liturgy, National Conference of Catholic Bishops. *Rite of Penance*. New York: Catholic Book Publishing, 1975.

Burns, Vincent M., SJ. "More than Exhortation." Letters to the Editor. *America* 116, no. 1 (January 7, 1967).

Carr, Aidan M. "Questions Answered: Guidelines for Children's First Reception of Holy Eucharist and Penance from an Unknown Diocese." *HPR* 70, no. 4 (1970).

Cassela, John J. "Prepare!: Second Sunday of Advent." Homilies on the Liturgy of Sundays and Feasts. *HPR* 65, no. 2 (1964).

Champlin, Joseph M. "Father Confessor and Future Sister." *HPR* 63, no. 2 (1962).

Clement VI. *Unigenitus*. In *Documents of the Christian Church*, edited by Henry Bettenson and Chris Maunder. New York: Oxford University Press, 2011.

Codex iuris canonici. Rome: Tipografia Poliglotta Vaticana, 1917.

Connell, Francis J., CSsR. *Father Connell's Confraternity Edition: New Baltimore Catechism No. 3*. Cincinnati: Benziger Brothers, 1955. Originally published in 1949.

——. "A Nourishing Drink on a Fast Day." *American Ecclesiastical Review* 136 (1957): 364.

——. "Some Recent Statements on the Sacrament of Penance." *American Ecclesiastical Review* 155 (1966).

Connell, Francis, with Walter J. Schmitz. "A Problem in Fasting." Answers to Questions. *American Ecclesiastical Review* 136 (1957).

Coogan, John E. "Sacrifice in Hope: First Sunday in Advent." Homilies on the Liturgy of Sundays and Feasts. *HPR* 63, no. 2 (1962).

Corrigan, John E. "The Priest as Confessor and Spiritual Director." *HPR* 67, no. 3 (December 1966).

——. *"Bless Me, Father": A Guide to Confession for Men and Women of Today, with Advice on the Examination of Conscience and Practical Examples*. Chicago: Claretian, 1967.

Cylwicki, Albert W. "Advent Preparation: Second Sunday of Advent." Homilies on the Liturgy of Sundays and Feasts. *HPR* 73, no. 2 (1972).

Danagher, John C., CM. "Journeys and the Law of Fasting." Questions Answered. *HPR* 56, no. 8 (1956).

——. "Notes on Fasting and Abstinence." *HPR* 56, no. 5 (1956).

——. "Journeys and the Law of Fasting." Questions Answered. *HPR* 56, no. 8 (1956).

——. "Was the Penitent Sorry or Not?" *HPR* 56, no. 12 (1956).

Day, Dorothy. *The Long Loneliness*. New York: Harper and Row, 1952.

Didache. http://www.earlychristianwritings.com/text/didache-roberts.html. Accessed on January 27, 2013.

Drouin, Francis, OP. "The Awakening of Moral Conscience in Children." *HPR* 66, no. 1 (1965).

Dukette, Jerome, OFM Conv. "Third Sunday after Pentecost: Unpublished Miracles of the Confessional." *HPR* 56, no. 8 (1956).

"Eighteenth Sunday after Pentecost: The Confessional 'Bogey.'" *HPR* 61, no. 11 (1956).

The English-Latin Sacramentary for the United States of America. New York: Catholic Book Publishing, 1966.

Faherty, William B. "How Best to Prepare for Christmas?: First Sunday of Advent." Homilies on the Liturgy of Sundays and Feasts. *HPR* 60 (1959).

Farren, Paul. *Freedom and Forgiveness: A Fresh Look at the Sacrament of Reconciliation.* Dublin: Columba Press, 2014.

Fisher, John J., CM. "The Confessional Bogey." *HPR* 57, no. 11 (1956).

Flynn, Vinny. *7 Secrets of Confession.* Stockbridge, Mass.: MercySong, 2013.

Ford, John C., SJ, and Gerald Kelly, SJ. *Contemporary Moral Theology: Questions in Fundamental Moral Theology.* Vol. 1. Westminster, Md.: Newman Press, 1960. Originally published in 1958.

Fox, Robert J. "Has the Church Gone Permissive?" *HPR* 73, no. 5 (1973).

"Friday Laws Modified." Current Comment. *America* 115, no. 23 (December 3, 1966).

General Instruction of the Roman Missal. 3rd ed. Washington, D.C.: United States Catholic Conference of Bishops, 2010.

Gomez, David F., CSP. "The Sacrament of Penance Today." *HPR* 70, no. 9 (1970).

Greeley, Andrew M. "Authority and Freedom." *HPR* 65, no. 12 (1965).

Hahn, Scott. *Lord Have Mercy: The Healing Power of Confession.* New York: Doubleday, 2003.

Hanrahan, Thomas S. "Whither Confession?" *HPR* 67, no. 4 (1967).

Häring, Bernard. *The Law of Christ.* Vol. 1, *General Moral Theology.* Translated by Edwin G. Kaiser. Westminster, Md.: Newman Press, 1961.

———. *Confession and Happiness.* Derby, N.Y.: St. Paul, 1966.

———. *Liberty of the Children of God.* Staten Island, N.Y.: Alba House, 1966.

———. *Road to Renewal: Perspectives of Vatican II.* New York: Alba House, 1966.

———. *Bernard Häring Replies: Answers to 50 Moral and Religious Questions.* Staten Island, N.Y.: Alba House, 1967.

———. *Christian Maturity.* Translated by Arlene Swidler. New York: Herder and Herder, 1967.

———. *Shalom: Peace; The Sacrament of Reconciliation*. Garden City, N.Y.: Image, 1969. Originally published in 1967.

———. *Sin in the Secular Age*. Garden City, N.Y.: Doubleday, 1974.

———. *Free and Faithful in Christ*. Vol. 1, *Moral Theology for Clergy and Laity*. New York: Seabury Press, 1978.

———. *My Witness for the Church*. Introduction and translation by Leonard Swidler. Mahwah, N.J.: Paulist Press, 1992. Originally published in German in 1989.

Harris, Thomas. *I'm OK—You're OK*. New York: HarperCollins, 1973. Originally published in 1967.

Herbst, Winifrid, SDS. "The Priest's Confession." *HPR* 61, no. 3 (1960).

Hindery, Roderick. "Penance, Sacrament of Conversion." *HPR* 65, no. 3 (December 1964).

Keller, Paul Jerome. *101 Questions on the Sacraments of Healing: Penance and Anointing of the Sick*. Mahwah, N.J.: Paulist Press, 2010.

Kelly, Gerald. "Notes on Moral Theology." *Theological Studies* 8 (1947): 112–14.

———. "Notes on Moral Theology." *Theological Studies* (December 1963).

Landini, Lawrence, OFM. "Drop-Off in Confession: The Epistles of St. Cyprian of Carthage." *American Ecclesiastical Review* 169, no. 2 (February 1975).

Lawrence, Emeric A., OSB. "The Liturgical Year." *HPR* 65, no. 1 (1964).

Leehan, James, OSC. "Penance and Its Social Dimension." *HPR* 68, no. 6 (1968).

Lefebvre, Gaspar. *Saint Andrew Daily Missal with Vespers for Sundays and Feasts*. St. Paul, Minn.: E. M. Lohmann, 1952.

The Life of Adam and Eve. See http://wesley.nnu.edu/sermons-essays-books/noncanonical-literature/noncanonical-literature-ot-pseudepigrapha/the-books-of-adam-and-eve/. Accessed on January 27, 2013.

Liturgical Press, eds. *Divine Office: The Hours of the Divine Office in English and Latin*. Vol. 1. Prepared by the staff of the Liturgical Press. Collegeville, Minn.: Liturgical Press, 1963.

Lowery, Daniel L., CSsR. "A 'Piety Void'?" *American Ecclesiastic Review* 154, no. 1 (1966).

Luther, Martin. "The Ninety-Five Theses on the Power and Efficacy of Indulgences" [1517]. Translated by Adolph Spaeth, L. D. Reed, and Henry Eyster Jacobs. In *Works of Martin Luther*, vol. 1. Philadelphia: Holman, 1915.

Massa, Mark S., SJ. Chap. 4, "The Charles Curran Affair." In *The American Catholic Revolution: How the Sixties Changed the Church Forever*. New York: Oxford, 2010.

McGuire, Michael A. *Father McGuire's The New Baltimore Catechism and Mass No. 1*. Cincinnati: Benziger Brothers, 1942.

McManus, Frederick R., ed. *Thirty Years of Liturgical Renewal: Statements of the Bishops' Committee on the Liturgy*. Washington, D.C.: United States Catholic Conference, 1987.

"Meat on Friday." Current Comment. *America* 115, no. 20 (November 12, 1966).

"Meatless Fridays in Lent." Current Comment. *America* 115, no. 24 (December 10, 1966).

Milhaven, John G. "Be Like Me! Be Free!" *America* 116, no. 81 (March 18, 1967).

Miller, Charles E. "Advent Has Its Problems." *HPR* 73, no. 2 (1972).

Miller, Oscar J., CM. "Confession: Suggested Rite of Communal Celebration." *HPR* 67, no. 5 (1967).

———. "I'm an Innovator: Fourth Sunday in Advent." *HPR* 70, no. 2 (1969).

Minogue, Gerard P. "First Sunday of Lent: For a More Positive Lent." *HPR* 56, no. 4 (1956).

Modras, Ronald. "Frequent Devotional Confession: How Often a Change in Heart?" *HPR* 66, no. 8 (1966).

National Conference of Catholic Bishops. "Pastoral Statement on Penance and Abstinence: A Statement Issued by the National Conference of Catholic Bishops." November 18, 1966.

O'Loughlin, Frank. *The Future of the Sacrament of Penance*. Mahwah, N.J.: Paulist Press, 2009.

Parres, Cecil L. "In Doubt about Fast and Abstinence." Questions Answered. *HPR* 57, no. 9 (1957).

———. "Quality and Grave Matter in Fasting." Questions Answered. *HPR* 59, no. 4 (1959).

———. "Vitamins and Fasting." Questions Answered. *HPR* 59, no. 7 (1959).

Paul VI. *Paenitemini*, 1966. http://www.vatican.va/holy_father/paul_vi/apost_constitutions/documents/hf_p-vi_apc_19660217_paenitemini_en.html.

Pius XI. *Casti connubii*: Encyclical on Christian Marriage, December 31, 1930; http://www.vatican.va/holy_father/pius_xi/encyclicals/documents/hf_p-xi_enc_31121930_casti-connubii_en.html. Accessed on May 14, 2010.

Pius XII. *Mystici corporis Christi*. June 29, 1943. http://www.vatican.va/holy_father/pius_xii/encyclicals/documents/hf_p-xii_enc_29061943_mystici-corporis-christi_en.html. Accessed on September 24, 2012.

———. *Mediator Dei*. Encyclical on the Sacred Liturgy. November 20, 1947. http://www.vatican.va/holy_father/pius_xii/encyclicals/documents/hf_p-xii_enc_20111947_mediator-dei_en.html. Accessed on November 21, 2012.

———. "Christus Dominus: Concerning the Discipline to Be Observed with Respect to the Eucharistic Fast." January 6, 1953. http://www.ewtn.com/library/papaldoc/p12chdom.htm. Accessed on April 12, 2013.

———. *Sacram communionem: On Laws of Fasting and the Evening Mass. Motu proprio* issued March 19, 1957. http://www.papalencyclicals.net/Pius12/P12FAST.HTM. Accessed on April 12, 2013.

Poschmann, Bernhard. *Penance and the Anointing of the Sick*. Translated by Francis Courtney. New York: Herder, 1964.

"Report: The American Catholic Psychological Association Meeting." *Bulletin of the National Guild of Catholic Psychiatrists* 16 (June 1969).

Resolutions from 1930, the Lambeth Conference. http://www.lambethconference.org/resolutions/1930/1930-15.cfm. Accessed on March 14, 2013.

Riga, Peter J. "Liturgy Today: Penance; A New Orientation." *American Ecclesiastic Review* 163, no. 5 (November 1970).

Ruano, Gerald P. "Imaginative Penances." *HPR* 66, no. 10 (1966).

Rumble, Leslie. "Redemptive Mission of Christ: First Sunday in Advent." Homilies on the Liturgy of Sundays and Feasts. *HPR* 61, no. 1 (1960).

Sacred Congregation for the Clergy. "General Catechetical Directory," 1971. http://www.vatican.va/roman_curia/congregations/cclergy/documents/rc_con_cclergy_doc_11041971_gcat_en.html. Accessed on October 12, 2012.

Schwegler, Very Rev. Msgr. Edward S. "Christmas Parties: Fourth Sunday of Advent." Homilies on the Liturgy of Sundays and Feasts. *HPR* 58, no. 2 (1957).

Shaughnessy, James D. "Spotlight on the Liturgy: First Communion before First Penance." *HPR* 70, no. 4 (1970).

Sheen, Fulton. *Peace of the Soul: A Magnificent Message of Hope and Inspiration for All Men*. Garden City, N.Y.: Doubleday, 1954. Originally published in 1949.

———. "Psychology and Psychiatry." *Life Is Worth Living*. Original broadcast 1957. http://www.youtube.com/watch?v=ChF4P7PIx4I (part 1); http://www.youtube.com/watch?v=V4lAgxidT4w&feature=related (part 2); and http://www.youtube.com/watch?v=uYzYVr8xCTs&feature=related (part 3). Accessed on February 5, 2010.

———. "Psychoanalytic Couch." *The Fulton Sheen Program*. Original broadcast 1966. http://www.youtube.com/watch?v=09c6rX3UQmo. Accessed on February 5, 2010.

Sitzmann, Marion J. "Penance and Joy: Second Sunday of Advent." Homilies on the Liturgy of Sundays and Feasts. *Homiletic and Pastoral Review* 75, no. 1 (1974).

Stedman, Joseph. *My Sunday Missal Explained*. Latin-English ed. Brooklyn: Confraternity of the Precious Blood, 1941. Originally published in 1938.

Stegmann, Basil. "The Opening Scene: Advent." *Worship* 26, no. 1 (December 1951).

Bibliography

Sullivan, John P. "First Sunday of Advent: Just in Time." Homilies on the Liturgy of Sundays and Feasts. *HPR* 57, no. 2 (1956).

Tanner, Norman P., SJ, ed. *Decrees of the Ecumenical Councils.* Vol. 1, *Nicaea I–Lateran V.* Washington, D.C.: Georgetown University Press, 1990.

———, ed. *Decrees of the Ecumenical Councils.* Vol. 2, *Trent–Vatican II.* Washington, D.C.: Georgetown University Press, 1990.

"Twenty-first Sunday after Pentecost: Freedom and True Contrition." *HPR* 56, no. 12 (1956).

Vaughan, Richard P., SJ. "Personal Approach to the Scrupulous." *HPR* 60, no. 7 (1959).

Vitry, Ermin. "Aspirations for Advent." *Worship* 28, no. 1 (1953).

Walsh, Christopher. *The Untapped Power of the Sacrament of Penance: A Priest's View.* Cincinnati, Ohio: St. Anthony Messenger Press, 2005.

Whelan, Lincoln F. "Sorrow for Ourselves—or for Our Sins?" Homily for 12th Sunday after Pentecost. *HPR* 58, no. 10 (1958).

Wiebler, William F. "First Sunday of Lent: Exterior and Interior Worship." *HPR* 57, no. 5 (1957).

———. "Christmas Trees Sprung from Decay: Fourth Sunday of Advent." Homilies on the Liturgy of Sundays and Feasts. *HPR* 59, no. 2 (1958).

Secondary Sources

Anderson, Gary A. *The Genesis of Perfection: Adam and Eve in Jewish and Christian Imagination.* Louisville: Westminster John Knox Press, 2001.

———. "From Israel's Burden to Israel's Debt: Towards a Theology of Sin in Biblical and Early Second Temple Sources." In *Reworking the Bible: Apocryphal and Related Texts at Qumran,* edited by Esther G. Chazon, Devorah Dimant, and Ruth Clements, 1–30. Leiden: Brill, 2005.

———. "Redeem Your Sins by the Giving of Alms: Sin, Debt, and the 'Treasury of Merit' in Early Jewish and Christian Tradition." *Letter and Spirit* 3 (2007): 39–69.

———. *Sin: A History.* New Haven: Yale University Press, 2009.

———. *Charity: The Place of the Poor in the Biblical Tradition.* New Haven: Yale University Press, 2013.

Baltzer, Klaus. "Liberation from Debt Slavery after the Exile in Second Isaiah and Nehemiah." In *Ancient Israelite Religion: Essays in Honor of Frank Moore Cross,* edited by Patrick D. Miller, Jr., Paul D. Hanson, and S. Dean McBride, 477–84. Philadelphia: Fortress Press, 1987.

Bergsma, John Sietze. *The Jubilee from Leviticus to Qumran: A History of Interpretation*. Leiden: Brill, 2007.

Bireley, Robert. *The Refashioning of Catholicism, 1450–1700*. Washington, D.C.: The Catholic University of America Press, 1999.

Blenkinsopp, Joseph. *Isaiah 40–55*. New Haven: Yale University Press, 2000.

Bouscaren, T. Lincoln, SJ, and Adam C. Ellis, SJ. *Canon Law: A Text and Commentary*. Milwaukee: Bruce, 1946.

Boyle, Leonard E. *The Setting of the Summa theologiae of Saint Thomas*. Toronto: Pontifical Institute of Mediaeval Studies, 1982.

Brown, Raymond E., SS. "The Pater Noster as an Eschatological Prayer." *Theological Studies* 22, no. 2 (1961): 175–208.

Bysted, Ane. *The Crusade Indulgence: Spiritual Rewards and the Theology of the Crusades, c. 1095–1216*. Leiden: Brill, 2015.

Cahalan, Kathleen A. *Formed in the Image of Christ: The Sacramental-Moral Theology of Bernard Häring, C.Ss.R.* Collegeville, Minn.: Liturgical Press, 2004.

Carey, Patrick W. *Catholics in America: A History*. New York: Sheed and Ward, 2004. Originally published in 1993.

Carr, David M. *The Formation of the Hebrew Bible: A New Reconstruction*. Oxford: Oxford University Press, 2011.

Cessario, Romanus, OP. *The Godly Image: Christ and Salvation in Catholic Thought from Anselm to Aquinas*. Petersham, Mass.: St. Bede's Publications, 1990.

———. *A Short History of Thomism*. Washington, D.C.: The Catholic University of America Press, 2003.

———. "The Sacraments of the Church." In *Vatican II: Renewal within Tradition*, edited by Matthew L. Lamb and Matthew Levering. Oxford: Oxford University Press, 2008.

———. *The Moral Virtues and Theological Ethics*. 2nd ed. Notre Dame: University of Notre Dame Press, 2009.

Chinnici, Joseph P., OFM. *Living Stones: The History and Structure of Catholic Spiritual Life in the United States*. New York: MacMillan, 1989.

———. "Changing Religious Practice and the End of Christendom in the United States 1965–1986." *U.S. Catholic Historian* 23, no. 4 (Fall 2005): 61–82.

Chinnici, Joseph P., OFM, and Angelyn Dries, eds. *Prayer and Practice in the American Catholic Community: Original Documents from More Than 200 Years of Catholic History*. Maryknoll, N.Y.: Orbis, 2000.

Chirichigno, Gregory C. *Debt-Slavery in Israel and the Ancient Near East*. Sheffield: Journal for the Study of the Old Testament Press, 1993.

Colish, Marcia L. *Peter Lombard*. Vol. 2. Leiden: Brill, 1994.

Connolly, Hugh. *The Irish Penitentials: And Their Significance for Penance Today*. Dublin: Four Courts Press, 1995.

Curran, Charles A. *Counseling in Catholic Life and Education*. New York: MacMillan, 1952.

——. *Religious Values in Counseling and Psychotherapy*. New York: Sheed and Ward, 1969.

Curran, Charles E. *Catholic Moral Theology in the United States: A History*. Washington, D.C.: Georgetown University Press, 2008.

Davidson, James D. *Catholicism in Motion*. Liguori, Mo.: Liguori, 2005.

De Boer, Wieste. *The Conquest of the Soul: Confession, Discipline, and Public Order in Counter-Reformation Milan*. Leiden: Brill, 2001.

Dolan, Jay P. *The American Catholic Experience*. Notre Dame: University of Notre Dame Press, 1985.

Dulles, Avery. "'*Humanae vitae*' and the Crisis of Dissent." *Origins* (April 22, 1993): 774–77.

Ellis, John Tracy. *American Catholicism*. 2nd ed. Chicago: University of Chicago Press, 1969. Originally published in 1956.

Favazza, Joseph A. *The Order of Penitents: Historical Roots and Pastoral Future*. Collegeville, Minn.: Liturgical Press, 1988.

Fishbane, Michael. *Biblical Interpretation in Ancient Israel*. Oxford: Clarendon Press, 1985.

Fitzgerald, Allan D., OSA. "Penance." In *Augustine through the Ages: An Encyclopedia*, edited by Allan D. Fitzgerald. Grand Rapids, Mich.: Eerdmans, 1999.

Gallagher, John A. *Time Past, Time Future: An Historical Study of Catholic Moral Theology*. Eugene, Ore.: Wipf and Stock, 2003. First published in 1990.

Gillespie, C. Kevin, SJ. *Psychology and American Catholicism: From Confession to Therapy?* New York: Crossroad, 2001.

Gleason, Philip. *Contending With Modernity: Catholic Higher Education in the Twentieth Century*. Oxford: Oxford University Press, 1995.

Goizueta, Roberto. "The Symbolic Realism of U.S. Latino/a Popular Catholicism." *Theological Studies* 65 (2004): 225–74.

Grantham, Dewey W. *The United States Since 1945: The Ordeal of Power*. New York: McGraw-Hill, 1976.

Greeley, Andrew M. *The Church and the Suburbs*. New York: Sheed and Ward, 1959.

——. *The Catholic Revolution: New Wine, Old Wineskins, and the Second Vatican Council*. Berkeley: University of California Press, 2004.

Halvorson-Taylor, Martien A. *Enduring Exile: The Metaphorization of Exile in the Hebrew Bible*. Leiden: Brill, 2011.

Horn, Cornelia B. "Penitence in Early Christianity in Its Historical and Theological Setting: Trajectories from Eastern and Western Sources." In *Repentance in Christian Theology*, edited by Mark J. Boda and Gordon T. Smith, 153–88. Collegeville, Minn.: Liturgical Press, 2006.

Inglis, John. "Aquinas's Replication of the Acquired Moral Virtues: Rethinking the Standard Philosophical Interpretation of Moral Virtue in Aquinas." *Journal of Religious Ethics* 27 (1999): 3–27.

Irvin, Dale T., and Scott W. Sunquist. *History of the World Christian Movement*. Vol. 1, *Earliest Christianity to 1453*. Maryknoll, N.Y.: Orbis, 2001.

Jansen, Katherine Ludwig. *The Making of the Magdalen: Preaching and Popular Devotion in the Later Middle Ages*. Princeton: Princeton University Press, 2000.

Jonsen, Albert. *Responsibility in Modern Religious Ethics*. Washington, D.C.: Corpus, 1968.

Keenan, James F. *A History of Catholic Moral Theology in the Twentieth Century: From Confessing Sins to Liberating Consciences*. New York: Continuum, 2010.

Kelly, John Norman Davidson. *Early Christian Doctrines*. San Francisco: Harper and Row, 1978. First published in 1960.

Kerr, Fergus. *After Aquinas: Versions of Thomism*. Malden, Mass., and Oxford: Blackwell, 2002.

Lamb, Matthew L., and Matthew Levering, eds. *Vatican II: Renewal within Tradition*. Oxford: Oxford University Press, 2008.

Marenbon, John, and Giovanni Orlandi, eds. "Introduction." From *Collationes.*, by Peter Abelard. Oxford: Oxford University Press, 2003. Originally published in 2001.

Mattison, William C., III. "Can Christians Possess the Acquired Cardinal Virtues?" *Theological Studies* 72 (2011): 558–85.

McBrien, Richard P., ed. *The HarperCollins Encyclopedia of Catholicism*. New York: HarperCollins, 1995.

McGreevy, John T. *Parish Boundaries: The Catholic Encounter with Race in the Twentieth-Century Urban North*. Chicago: University of Chicago Press, 1996.

———. *Catholicism and American Freedom: A History*. New York: Norton, 2003.

Menninger, Karl. *Whatever Became of Sin?* New York: Hawthorn, 1973.

Mershman, Francis. "Ember Days." In *The Catholic Encyclopedia*. Vol. 5. New York: Robert Appleton, 1909. http://www.newadvent.org/cathen/05399b.htm. Accessed on April 6, 2013.

Milgrom, Jacob. "The Paradox of the Red Cow (Num. XIX)." *Vetus Testamentum* 31 (1981): 62–72.

———. *Leviticus 23–27*. New Haven: Yale University Press, 2000.

———. *Leviticus: A Book of Ritual and Ethics*. Minneapolis: Augsburg Fortress, 2004.

Morgenstern, Julian. "The Book of the Covenant, Part III: The Ḥuqqim." *Hebrew Union College Annual* 8–9 (1931–32): 16–22.
Morrow, Maria C. "The Change in the Conception of Sin among Catholics in the United States, 1955–1975." *American Catholic Studies* 122, no. 1 (2011): 55–76.
Murdoch, Brian. *The Apocryphal Adam and Eve in Medieval Europe: Vernacular Translations and Adaptations of the Vita Adae et Evae*. Oxford: Oxford University Press, 2009.
O'Banion, Patrick. *The Sacrament of Penance and Religious Life in Golden Age Spain*. University Park, Pa.: Pennsylvania State University Press, 2012.
Oberman, Heiko A. *The Dawn of the Reformation: Essays in Late Medieval and Early Reformation Thought*. Grand Rapids, Mich.: Eerdmans, 1986.
——. *The Reformation: Roots and Ramifications*. New York: T. and T. Clark, 1994.
O'Malley, John. *What Happened at Vatican II*. Cambridge, Mass.: Harvard University Press, 2008.
O'Neill, James David. "Abstinence." In *The Catholic Encyclopedia*. Vol. 1. New York: Robert Appleton, 1907.
Orsi, Robert A. *Thank You, St. Jude: Women's Devotion to the Patron Saint of Hopeless Causes*. New Haven: Yale University Press, 1996.
——. *Between Heaven and Earth: The Religious Worlds People Make and the Scholars Who Study Them*. Princeton: Princeton University Press, 2005.
Osiek, Carolyn. *Shepherd of Hermas: A Commentary*. Minneapolis: Fortress Press, 1999.
O'Toole, James M. "In the Court of Conscience: American Catholics and Confession, 1900–1975." In *Habits of Devotion: Catholic Religious Practice in Twentieth Century America*, edited by James M. O'Toole, 131–86. Ithaca: Cornell University Press, 2004.
——. *The Faithful: A History of Catholics in America*. Cambridge, Mass.: Harvard University Press, 2008.
Pace, E. "Quietism." In *The Catholic Encyclopedia*. New York: Robert Appleton, 1911.
Pinckaers, Servais, OP. *The Sources of Christian Ethics*. Translated by Mary Thomas Noble, OP. Washington, D.C.: The Catholic University of America Press, 1995. Originally published in 1985.
Pitre, Brant. "The Lord's Prayer and the New Exodus." *Letter and Spirit* 2 (2006): 69–96.
Portier, William L. "Here Come the Evangelical Catholics." *Communio* 31 (2004): 35–66.
Portier-Young, Anathea E. *Apocalypse against Empire: Theologies of Resistance in Early Judaism*. Grand Rapids, Mich.: Eerdmans, 2011.

Rahner, Karl. *Theological Investigations*. Vol. 15, *Penance in the Early Church*. New York: Crossroad, 1982.

Rittgers, Ronald K. "Embracing the 'True Relic' of Christ: Suffering, Penance, and Private Confession in the Thought of Martin Luther." In *A New History of Penance*, edited by Abigail Firey. Leiden: Brill, 2008.

Root, Michael. "Aquinas, Merit, and Reformation Theology after the Joint Declaration on the Doctrine of Justification." *Modern Theology* 20 (2004): 5–22.

Rosemann, Philipp W. *Peter Lombard*. Oxford: Oxford University Press, 2004.

Schultenover, David G., ed. *Vatican II: Did Anything Happen?* New York: Continuum, 2007.

Schwartz, Baruch J. "The Bearing of Sin in Priestly Literature." In *Pomegranates and Golden Bells: Studies in Biblical, Jewish, and Near Eastern Rituals, Laws, and Literature in Honor of Jacob Milgrom*, edited by David P. Wright, David Noel Freedman, and Avi Hurvitz, 3–21. Winona Lake, Indiana: Eisenbrauns, 1995.

Siker, Jeffrey S. *Scripture and Ethics: Twentieth-Century Portraits*. Oxford: Oxford University Press, 1997.

Steinfels, Peter. *A People Adrift: The Crisis of the Roman Catholic Church in America*. New York: Simon and Schuster, 2003.

Steinmetz, David. *Calvin in Context*. Oxford: Oxford University Press, 1995.

Stone, Michael E. *Adam's Contract with Satan: The Legend of the Cheirograph of Adam*. Bloomington: Indiana University Press, 2002.

Stuhlmueller, Carroll. *Creative Redemption in Deutero-Isaiah*. Rome: Biblical Institute Press, 1970.

Tentler, Leslie Woodcock. *Catholics and Contraception: An American History*. Ithaca, N.Y.: Cornell University Press, 2004.

Tentler, Thomas N. "Response and Retractio." In *The Pursuit of Holiness in Late Medieval and Renaissance Religion*, edited by Charles Edward Trinkaus and Heiko A. Oberman, 131–39. Leiden: Brill, 1974.

———. *Sin and Confession on the Eve of the Reformation*. Princeton: Princeton University Press, 1977.

Torrell, Jean-Pierre. *Saint Thomas Aquinas: The Person and His Work*. Washington, D.C.: The Catholic University of America Press, 2005. Originally published in 1996.

Unterman, Jeremiah. "The Social-Legal Origin for the Image of God as Redeemer גואל of Israel." In *Pomegranates and Golden Bells: Studies in Biblical, Jewish, and Near Eastern Rituals, Laws, and Literature in Honor of Jacob Milgrom*, edited by David P. Wright, David Noel Freedman, and Avi Hurvitz, 399–406. Winona Lake, Ind.: Eisenbrauns, 1995.

Wawrykow, Joseph. "John Calvin and Condign Merit." *Archiv für Reformationsgeschichte* 83 (1992): 73–90.

Webber, Christopher. *Welcome to Sunday: An Introduction to Worship in the Episcopal Church*. Harrisburg, Pa.: Morehouse, 2003.

White, James F. "The Spatial Setting." In *Oxford History of Christian Worship*, edited by Geoffrey Wainright and Karen B. Vesterfield Tucker, 793–816. New York: Oxford University Press, 2006.

Wilken, Robert Louis. *The First Thousand Years: A Global History of Christianity*. New Haven: Yale University Press, 2012.

Woywod, Stanislaus, OFM. *The New Canon Law: A Commentary and Summary of the New Code of Canon Law*. 7th ed. New York: Joseph F. Wagner, 1929.

Index

Abelard, Peter, 80
Academia Alphonsiana, 95
Act of Contrition, 29, 61, 92, 194, 210, 227–29, 236, 239, 242
Aeterni Patris, 82
African American, 93n38
Alexander, Ron, 60n60
Allers, Rudolf, 57
Alphonsian, 103
anamchara, 207
Anderson, Gary A., 15, 16n5–8, 17n9–10, 18–19, 33n60, 35, 251
Andrews, James F., 49, 65, 72–73
Aquinas, Thomas St., xvi, 27, 29–32, 34n62, 45n3, 48, 62, 83, 84n10, 209–10, 228, 236, 241–42, 245
Archdiocese of Washington, D.C., 1
Aristotle, 27, 84n10
Augustine, 22–24, 31, 45n3, 48, 245

Bailard, Marcy, 149–50
Baltzer, Klaus, 16n8, 251

Barrett, E. Boyd, 57
Barth, Karl, 97
Bathsheba, 18
Bergsma, John Sietze, 16n8, 17n10, 252
Bernard, Ken J., 64n69–70, 245
Berne, Eric, 61–62
Bettenson, Henry, 23n30, 37n70, 245–46
Biblical, 15, 30–31, 35, 110, 233
Binz, Archbishop Leo, 123, 125n16, 156n97
Bireley, Robert, 38–39, 252
Blenkinsopp, Joseph, 16n8, 252
Boda, Mark J., 20n18, 254
Bonhoeffer, Dietrich, 97
Boorstein, Michelle, 1n1
Borromeo, Charles, 39, 198
Bouscaren, T. Lincoln, SJ, 126n20, 252
Boyle, Leonard E., 29n52
Brown, Helen Gurley, 68
Brown, Raymond E., SS, 16n5, 19n13, 252
Bruehl, Charles, 57–58
Burns, Vincent M., SJ, 177n29, 179n33, 246
Bysted, Ane, 35n67, 252

259

Callahan, Daniel, 87
Calvin, 45n3
Carey, Pat (Patrick W. Carey), xv, 40, 41n92, 46, 52–53, 54n32, 54n34, 68, 75, 252
Carr, Aidan M., 226n63, 246
Carr, David M., 17n10, 252
Cassela, John J., 135n42, 246
casuist, 87, 94
casuistic, 95
casuistry, 82, 84–85, 88, 113, 155
Cavalca, Domenico, 29
Champlin, Joseph M., 199, 246
Chazon, Esther G., 15n3, 251
Chinnici, Joseph P., OFM, 50–51, 94n41, 151, 252
Chirichigno, Gregory C., 16n8, 252
Christ-like, 36, 222
church: xii–xiv, 1, 4–9, 12–14, 18, 20–23, 25–27, 31n58, 33, 36–38, 41, 44–46, 51–54, 61, 65, 67, 69–78, 80–81, 85, 87–88, 90, 93–95, 97–101, 104–8, 109n83, 111–15, 117, 119–21, 125, 132–33, 135, 140, 144–45, 148–49, 151, 153n92, 156–58, 161–66, 168–70, 173–74, 176–79, 181–82, 184, 186, 188–89, 195, 206–7, 211–13, 220, 222–23, 226–27, 229–30, 234, 237–38, 240–41, 243–44; Catholic Church: 34, 37, 68, 71–73, 75, 100, 106, 108, 110–11, 123, 133, 142n53, 150, 161, 163–64, 172, 174, 177, 181–82, 186, 197, 210, 241 (as in Catholic Church), Eastern or Western Church: 13, 27; parish: 42; Western Church: 13, 27
Clements, Ruth, 15n3, 251
Cody, John, 123
Colish, Marcia L., 28n50–51, 29n51, 252
colonial period, 160
confession, xiv, 1–5, 13n1, 14, 21–22, 24–30, 37–42, 44, 47–50, 59, 61–64, 70, 74–75, 78, 80, 83, 85, 87, 93–95, 104, 106n78, 111–13, 116, 118, 142, 150, 158, 191–99, 206–17, 219–29, 231–40, 242–44
Connell, Francis J., CSsR, 126, 128, 132n28, 148n74, 173n26, 212, 227–28, 246
Connolly, Hugh, 207n18, 253

continent (Europe), 24
Coogan, John E., 134n40, 246
Corrigan, John E., 220–21, 246
countercultural, 141–43, 186
Courtney, Francis, 250
Crowley, Patty, 75–76
Curran, Charles A., 59n57, 222, 253
Curran, Charles E., 8, 59n57, 82n4, 85n13, 253
Cylwicki, Albert W., 141n51, 246
Cyrus, 17

Danagher, John, 127–28, 208, 215n36, 246
David, 18
Davidson, James D., 253
Day, Dorothy, 72, 94n41, 192, 242, 246
De Boer, Wieste, 39n85, 253
debt-slavery, 16
de Caussade, Jean Pierre, 104n74
decision-making, 109, 115
Decius, 21
de Las Casas, Bartolome, 37n75
de Zutter, Albert, 180n37
Diller, Phyllis, 68
Dimant, Devorah, 15n3, 251
Diocletian, 21
Divine Office, 133
Dolan, Jay P., 46, 47n10, 48n13, 50n16, 54, 149, 151–52, 253
Donatists, 21
Doyle, Eugene J., 183n48, 185
Dries, Angelyn, 50, 151, 252
Drouin, Francis, OP, 216n38, 247
Dukette, Jerome, OFM Conv., 197n9, 247
Dulles, Avery, 71n101, 253
Duns Scotus, 29n51

Eastern Church, 13
Ellis, Adam C., SJ, 252
Ellis, John Tracy, 40n91, 41n95, 45, 253
Ember Days, xiii, 3, 119, 126, 145–47, 168, 171
Episcopal Church, 143
Erikson, Erik, 110
Eucharist, 3, 14, 22, 26, 39, 41, 47, 153n94, 212, 215–17, 227–29, 232, 237–42

Eucharistic, 10, 65, 170, 193, 231, 238–39
exomologesis, 22, 24

Faber, Nancy, 61n63
Faherty, William B., 140n46, 247
Fall of Adam and Eve, 30
farm workers, 5, 237
Farren, Paul, 2n2, 247
Favazza, Joseph A., 20n18, 37n72, 224n57, 253
Fishbane, Michael, 17n10, 253
Fisher, John J., CM, 214n35, 247
Fitzgerald, Allan D., OSA, 22n26, 253
Flynn, Vinny, 2n2, 247
Ford, John C., SJ, 8, 67, 69n94, 81, 85–96, 98–99, 101–4, 106n78, 110, 112–16, 175–76, 187, 247
Fox, Robert J., 186n56, 247
Francis, Dale, 181
Freedman, David Noel, 15n3, 16n8, 256
Freud, 55–57, 84
fundamental option, 109–10

Gallagher, John A., 21n21, 24–25, 27, 253
General Instruction of the Roman Missal, 142, 147, 247
Gibbons, Cardinal James, 121–22
Gillespie, C. Kevin, SJ, 57nn40–47, 58–59, 70, 214n33, 222n53, 253
Gleason, Philip, 45, 55, 74, 75n114, 79, 83, 253
Goizueta, Roberto, 40, 253
Gomez, David F., CSP, 222n54, 225, 247
Gospel, 18, 19, 20, 106, 132, 216, 225, 233
Grady, Thomas, 49n14
Grantham, Dewey W., 60n61
Gratian, 25
Greeley, Andrew, xii, 50–52, 68n91, 75, 185–86, 215, 243n95, 247, 253

Hahn, Scott, 2n2, 247
Halvorson-Taylor, Martien A., 16n8, 253
Hanrahan, Thomas S., 227–28, 247
Hanson, Paul D., 17n8, 251
Häring, Bernard, CSsR, 8–9, 59n57, 81, 85, 86n14, 94n41, 95–111, 113–16, 142, 167, 175–77, 187–90, 218n42, 225, 237, 247–48
Harris, Thomas A., 61–63, 76, 105–6, 248
Heaven, 33, 36, 53, 65, 84, 92, 96, 113–14, 143, 165, 179, 181
Hegel, 84
Herbst, Winifrid, SDS, 198, 248
Hermas, 19–20, 225
Hindery, Roderick, 206n16, 248
Horn, Cornelia B., 20n18, 254
Humanae vitae, 3, 6, 45, 67, 68, 70–71, 85, 107–9, 114–15
Hurvitz, Avi, 15n3, 16n8, 256

Indultum quadragesimale, 122
Inglis, John, 254
intellectual apostolate, 27
Irenaeus, 19n16
Irvin, Dale T., 21n20, 254

Jacobs, Henry Eyster, 34n61, 248
Jacobs, William J., 73
Jansen, Katherine Ludwig, 26, 27n47, 29, 32, 254
Johann, Robert, 97
John the Baptist, 19, 33, 134
Johnson, Virginia, 68
Jonsen, Albert, 97, 254

Kant, Immanuel, 84n10, 101n64
Kantian, 81, 101n64
Karch, P., ix, 130
Keenan, James F., 81, 82n4, 85–86, 93, 95n42, 109, 254
Keller, Paul Jerome, 2n2, 94n41, 248
Kelly, Gerald, SJ, 8, 81, 85–96, 98–99, 101–7, 112–16, 175–76, 187, 247–48
Kelly, J. N. D., 22, 23n31, 24n32, 254
Kennedy, John F., 60
Kerr, Fergus, 82n5, 254
Krosnicki, Thomas, SVD, 167n11

Lamb, Matthew L., 53n30, 224n59, 252, 254
Landini, Lawrence, OFM, 228n68, 248
Lateran IV Council, 13–14, 26, 28, 37–38, 211, 237

Lawrence, Emeric A., OSB, 235n87, 248
Leary, Timothy, 61
Leclercq, Jacques, 88
Leehan, James, OSC, 207n18, 223–24, 248
Lefebvre, Gaspar, 145n63, 248
Lennon, John, 61
Levering, Matthew, 53n30, 224n59, 252, 254
Libri quatuor sententiarum, 27
lifecycles, 110
Liguori, Alphonsus, 124
Lombard, Peter, 27–29, 37, 236
Lord's Prayer, 19, 22–23, 233
Lowery, Daniel L., CSsR, 217n41, 220n43, 248
Luther, Martin, 14, 33–34, 36–37, 45n3, 248

Marenbon, John, 80n1, 254
Marx, Karl, 84, 111
Mass, xii, 3, 5, 29, 39, 41, 47, 74, 77, 90, 93n38, 102, 112n94, 113, 123, 132–33, 135, 142, 146, 149, 156–57, 165, 171, 183, 189, 193, 195, 213, 229–32, 236–38, 243
Massa, Mark S., SJ, 8n7, 53n30, 54n34, 68, 75n116, 248
Masters, William, 68
Mattison, William C., III, xv, 254
Maunder, Chris, 36n70, 246
McBride, S. Dean, 17n8, 251
McBrien, Richard P., 48n11, 254
McGreevy, John T., 50–51, 52n23, 66n77, 66n81, 69n94, 86, 89n25, 254
McGuire, Michael A., 48n12, 248
McManus, Frederick R., 120n3, 121n3, 125nn16–17, 144n58–59, 155n96, 156n97, 167n11, 231n76, 249
Menninger, Karl, 44, 45n3, 60–61, 63–64, 66n75, 254
Mershman, Francis, 145n62, 254
Milgrom, Jacob, 15n3, 16n8, 254
Milhaven, John G., 77n122, 144n99, 249
Miller, Charles E., 142n54, 249
Miller, Patrick D. Jr., 17n8, 251
Miller, Oscar J., CM, 142n53, 225n60, 249
minnow-munchers, xii

Minogue, Gerard P., 132n30, 249
Modras, Ronald, 209–10, 223n55, 235, 249
Mooney, Edward Cardinal, 125n16, 156n97
Moore, Thomas Verner, 57
Morgan, Marabel, 68
Morgenstern, Julian, 15n3, 255
Morrow, Maria C., 43n1, 82n4, 167n11, 212n30, 255
Murdoch, Brian 20n19, 255

National Conference of Catholic Bishops, 5, 9, 80, 161, 166, 167n11, 233n80, 246, 249
neo-Scholastic, 8, 58, 81–85, 93
Nominalist, 81, 83, 91
noncanonical, 19, 20n19
nonsacramental, xiii, xvi, 4, 6–7, 9–11, 13–14, 23–24, 28–29, 32, 38, 43, 116–20, 158, 161–62, 167, 188, 191–92, 225–29, 234–36, 238, 240, 241–42, 244
non-schismatic, 21
Novak, Michael, 157–58
Novatianists, 21–22
Niebuhr, H. Richard, 45n3, 97
Nietzsche, 84

O'Banion, Patrick, 13n1, 255
obedience, 5, 8, 69–70, 72–73, 77, 80–81, 84–85, 89–91, 93–100, 101n64, 105, 108, 115–16, 167, 174, 176, 181, 189, 192
Oberman, Heiko A., 26n45, 34n62, 255–56
obligationism, 89
O'Connor, William, 123
O'Loughlin, Frank, 2n2, 249
O'Malley, John, 40n90, 67n87, 98n53, 255
O'Neill, George, 68
O'Neill, James David, 133n33, 255
O'Neill, Nena, 68
Orlandi, Giovanni 80n1, 254
Orsi, Robert A., 52n24, 148–52, 154n95, 255
Osiek, Carolyn, 20n18, 255
Ostendorf, Lloyd, ix, 201
O'Sullivan, Joe, 61n62
O'Toole, James M., 2–3, 41n96, 42n100, 56, 59n55, 60n59, 68n89, 69, 70n98, 74–77, 118n1, 125n19, 193, 195, 208n22, 211n27,

213, 214n33, 222n52, 231–32, 233n79, 234, 237, 238n88, 239, 240n90, 255

Paenitemini, 9, 80, 160–62, 164–66, 168, 173n24, 175–78, 180n34, 187, 249
Parres, Cecil L., 128n25, 128n27, 132n29, 249
Pascal, 45n3
Peale, Norman Vincent, 60–61
Penance, xii–xiii, xvi, 1–15, 17–19, 21–43, 49, 59, 61, 63, 78–84, 89, 95, 112n94, 114–20, 123, 127, 132–35, 140–44, 147–95, 197–99, 201, 206–10, 213, 215–17, 219–20, 222–30, 232–42, 244
penitentials, 24–27
Peraldus, Willelmus, 30
Pinckaers, Servais, OP, 83–86, 255
Pitre, Brant, 16n5, 16n8, 255
Pope Benedict XV, 122
Pope Benedict XVI, 119n2, 122, 230, 245
Pope Clement VI, 36, 246
Pope Gregory VII, 25, 145
Pope Gregory XVI, 121
Pope Honorius III, 29
Pope John XXIII, 67, 125, 144
Pope Leo XIII, 82, 121
Pope Paul VI, 9, 45, 67–68, 70–71, 108, 109n83, 147, 159, 161–66, 173, 249
Pope Pius IX, 121
Pope Pius X, 215, 239
Pope Pius XI, 66, 212, 249
Pope Pius XII, 57, 122, 124, 133, 134n37, 153n92, 197, 231, 232n77, 249–50
Portier, William L., xv, 46, 51n21, 53n29, 255
Portier-Young, Anathea E., 17n10, 255
Poschmann, Bernhard, 250
post-baptismal, 20–21
post-Reformation, 40
post-Vatican II, xiii, 45n4, 59n57, 74, 76, 85, 181, 224
postwar, 51–52, 212
preconciliar, 54, 106, 232
priest-theologians, 79, 84, 195

Quietism, 90, 104

Rahner, Karl, 20n18, 84n10, 109, 256
Rawson, Carter, 121n3
Raymond of Peñafort, 29
Record, Anna Margaret, 148n75, 149n79, 151
Redemptorist priest, 8, 81, 95, 217, 219
Reed, L. D., 34n61, 248
Reedy, John L., CSC, 49, 65, 72–73
re-evangelize, 37
Reformation, 13, 33–34, 38, 40
Regino of Prüm, 35
Reilly, William, 184n49
Riga, Peter J., 229–30, 241, 250
Rittgers, Ronald K., 34, 35n63, 36n71, 37n73, 256
Root, Michael, 34n62, 256
Rosemann, Philip, 27, 29n51, 38n76, 256
Ruano, Gerald P., 220, 250
Rumble, Leslie, 140n47, 250

Sacred Congregation for the Clergy, 217, 239n89, 250
Schillebeeckx, Edward, 225
Scholastic method, 25
schoolchildren, 215, 243
Schwartz, Baruch J., 15nn3–4, 256
Schwegler, Very Rev. Msgr. Edward S., 140n45, 250
scripture, 14–15, 110, 171. *See* Word [of God].
Shaughnessy, James D., 216n39, 250
Sheen, Fulton, 55–56, 60, 63, 250
Siker, Jeffrey S., 110, 256
sin-crimes, 25
Sitzmann, Marion J., 141n52, 250
Skinner, B. F., 111
Smith, Gordon T., 20n18, 254
socioeconomic, 45
Sorrowful Mother Novena, 48, 149
Spaeth, Adolph, 34n61, 248
Spera, Jim (James), xvi, 212n30
Stations of the Cross, 171
Stedman, Joseph, 92n35, 133n36, 250
Stegmann, Basil, 134, 250
Steinfels, Peter, 53, 71–72, 75, 178, 256
Steinmetz, David, 34n62, 256

St. Ignatius of Loyola, 37n75, 42, 198
Stone, Michael E., 16n5, 256
Stuhlmueller, Carroll, 17n8, 256
Sullivan, John P., 135n41, 251
Summae confessorum, 26–27
Summa de casibus, 29
Summa theologiae, 27, 29, 30n56, 31nn57–58, 32, 209n23, 242n93, 245
Summa virtutum, 30
Summa vitiorum, 30
Sunquist, Scott W., 21n20, 254
Suprenant, Leon, 143n56
Swidler, Arlene, 96n43, 96n46, 247–48

Tanner, Norman P., SJ, 26n45, 38nn77–78, 38n80, 251
Te Deum, 133
Telos, 176
Tentler, Leslie Woodcock, 66–67, 69, 70n98, 71, 211–12, 256
Tentler, Thomas N., 24n32, 25–26, 29n51, 35n64, 37, 256
Tertullian, 19n16
Torrell, Jean-Pierre, 29nn53–54, 256
Transcendental Thomism, 84
Tridentine Latin Mass, xii, 230
Trinkaus, Charles Edward, 26n45, 256
Tucker, Karen B. Vesterfield, 39n84, 257

Unterman, Jeremiah, 16n8, 256

Vatican Council II, xii, 45, 53–54, 58–59, 67, 75–76, 84, 87, 97, 100, 118–19, 153, 162–63, 165, 190
Vaughan, Richard P., SJ, 214n34, 251
Vigil Fasts, xiii, 3, 125, 144–45, 155n96, 171–72
Vitry, Ermin, 141, 251

Wainright, Geoffrey, 39n84, 257
Walsh, Christopher, 2n2, 251
Wawrykow, Joseph, 34n62, 257
Webber, Christopher, 143n57, 257
Whelan, Lincoln F., 197, 198n10, 251
White, James F., 39n84, 257
Wiebler, William F., 132n31, 140n48, 251
Wilken, Robert Louis, 21n20, 257
William of Ockham, 83
Willpower, 168, 186, 189
Word [of God], 37, 225. *See* scripture
Woywod, Stanislaus, OFM, 126n20, 133n33, 257
Wright, David P., 15n3, 16n8, 256

Yocum, Sandra A., xv, 63n67

Zalba, Marcelino, 76
Zirkel, Don, 182–83

❖

Sin in the Sixties: Catholics and Confession, 1955–1975 was designed in Filosofia with Swiss Extra Compressed and Oz Handicraft display type and composed by Kachergis Book Design of Pittsboro, North Carolina. It was printed on 60-pound Natures Book Natural and bound by Thomson-Shore of Dexter, Michigan.

www.ingramcontent.com/pod-product-compliance
Lightning Source LLC
Chambersburg PA
CBHW020856020526
44107CB00076B/1877